Canning

by Sue & Bill Deeming

Sue Deeming received her bachelor's degree in Food Science at Iowa State University and her doctorate in Biochemistry and Nutrition at the University of Arizona. Since that time, she has worked continually to broaden her food skills. She feels that food quality and nutrition depend greatly on how the food is prepared and served at home. Through books and other projects, Sue shares the results of her food research by providing todays's cook with recipes that are flavorful and fun to prepare.

Sue and her husband, Bill, are the authors of the HPBook, *Bean Cookery*. They are also founders of The Authors' Kitchen. Located in Portland, Oregon, this company provides educational and promotional materials on food, recipe development and nutritional consultation for businesses interested in promoting good health. What began as the Deemings' shared interest in food for their own entertainment has grown into the shared excitement of a prospering family business.

On previous pages: Canning equipment including standard canning jars, canner rack, jar tongs, timer, measuring cups, pressure canner, measuring spoons, colander and wide-mouth funnel. Produce includes peaches, tomatoes, okra, apples and beans.

Canning

by Sue & Bill Deeming

ANOTHER BESTSELLING VOLUME FROM HPBOOKS

Publishers: Bill and Helen Fisher; Executive Editor: Rick Bailey; Editorial Director: Helen Fisher; Editor: Carroll Latham; Art Director: Don Burton; Book Design: Dana Martin; Technical Reader: June Gibbs, Extension Specialist in Foods & Nutrition; Food Stylists: Mable Hoffman, Sue Deeming; Photography: George de Gennaro Studios

The authors wish to thank the following: Dr. Milton Baldauf, Extension Service U.S.D.A.; Dr. Gerald Sapers, U.S.D.A.; Ball Corp.; Kerr Glass Mfg. Corp.; National Presto Industries, Inc.; Mirro Corp.; Leasure Tech. Inc. (Producers of Earth Grown Utensils).

Published by HPBooks
P.O. Box 5367, Tucson, AZ 85703   602/888-2150
ISBN 0-89586-185-2
Library of Congress Catalog Card Number: 82-82855
©1983 Fisher Publishing Inc. Printed in U.S.A.

Canning — Yesterday & Today

At the end of the 18th century, Nicolas Appert, a French baker, developed canning as a food-preservation method. In response to Napoleon's request for ways to preserve food for his army and navy, Appert experimented with food preservation for 15 years. Appert filled wide-mouth glass bottles, closed them with cork stoppers and heated them in boiling water five or more hours! He did not know that microorganisms cause food spoilage. However, he learned by trial and error that some foods did not spoil for several years after his processing.

When scientists learned what causes food spoilage, they made improvements in equipment and methods. By designing equipment to heat foods quickly to high temperatures, processing times were reduced. Today, home-canning methods are continually being refined so foods can be safely preserved with retention of maximum color, flavor and nutrients.

There has been a renewed interest in home canning in recent years. But modern home canners should not rely on Grandma's undependable methods. Always use standard canning jars and lids, the right water-bath and pressure-canning equipment and recipes that follow up-to-date canning methods and procedures. Before you use Grandma's old-fashioned recipe for green-tomato chutney, adapt it to today's safe procedures. Or find a similar modern recipe that follows accepted safe methods.

All canning jars and lids form airtight seals in essentially the same way. During processing, food and jars reach 212F (100C) in a boiling-water bath and 240F (115C) in a pressure canner. Air remaining in the food and in the space at the top of the jar is forced out between the jar and lid. As jars with self-sealing lids cool, they automatically form a tight seal without additional tightening. As food cools, it contracts, creating a vacuum. The lid is sucked down tight, preventing air from passing in or out of the jar. Lids with rubber rings must be tightened as they are taken from the canner. An airtight seal prevents invasion by microorganisms. With proper storage, the seal will remain tight.

There are only two accepted, safe methods for home canning: boiling-water bath and pressure canning. The choice is determined solely by the food to be canned. It is not a question of which method is most convenient or what equipment is available.

Not long ago, jams, jellies, pickles and relishes were canned using the *open-kettle method.* Boiling-hot food was ladled into scalded jars, then the lids were put on the jars. Food was hot enough to cause a seal to form as it cooled, but there was no further processing.

Today, open-kettle canning is recommended only for jellies. The high sugar content and short storage make canning by this method safe up to six months.

This method is not safe for any other food because microorganisms can be introduced into the food as jars are filled and closed. Because there is no further processing, microorganisms are not destroyed.

Steam canners use steam from boiling water for

processing. A steam canner cannot be used as a substitute for a pressure canner or boiling-water bath. There is no pressure and the temperature reaches only 212F (100C), not high enough to destroy bacterial spores. The circulation of steam and distribution of heat around the jars is inadequate to destroy active bacteria. **Do not use steam canners to can food.**

Oven canning uses the oven heat to process. As with steam canning, heat distribution is a problem. Food throughout the jar may not reach the required canning temperature. **Do not use conventional ovens for canning.**

A *microwave oven* is an efficient, time-saving appliance, but not for canning. Microwave canning will not distribute heat evenly throughout the jar. It leaves some food underprocessed. **Do not use microwave ovens for canning.**

There are no canning shortcuts! Adding aspirin, vinegar or ascorbic acid to jars of food to cut down processing time is not safe. Follow procedures and recipes in this book for safe, appealing, home-canned foods.

This book has something for everyone. It has complete instructions for the first-time canner and new recipes and the latest techniques for the experienced home canner. It is divided into three sections: *Basic Canning, Canning with Flair* and *Using Canned Foods.*

Basic Canning gives detailed steps for canning fruits, vegetables, jams and jellies, and meats, poultry and fish. It also gives specific recipes for each food. You'll learn the best produce varieties for canning, and characteristics to look for in foods to be canned. To make full use of this section, read the material at the beginning of each chapter. Then look in the index of the book for the specific fruit, vegetable or meat you want to can.

Canning with Flair contains recipes for specially prepared foods, from Pink-Champagne Jelly to Calcutta-Style Chutney and Texas Spiced Okra. These small-batch recipes generally make six to eight pints. The section includes specialty canning of fruits, vegetables, pickles and relishes, sweet spreads, and sauces and condiments.

Using Canned Foods suggests ways to use canned foods in a variety of pleasing dishes. You'll find ideas for snack treats, light meals, side-dish salads and vegetables, main dishes, breads and desserts.

Modern canning offers the same benefits today that it did in Grandma's time—and more! These benefits include year-round availability, nutrition, economy, special-diet foods and convenience.

Availability—Canning vegetables and fruits from the garden or orchard makes them available all year. Beans and tomatoes enjoyed fresh off the vine in summer can be simmered in a hearty vegetable stew during winter months. Long after fresh peaches have disappeared from the supermarkets, the home canner can fill the kitchen with the spicy aroma of a peach cobbler.

Nutrition—Fresh fruits and vegetables available during winter months are shipped long distances and often wilt and lose considerable nutritive value before they are eaten. If processed properly, nutritional quality of home-canned foods is often better than that of out-of-season fresh produce. Fruits and vegetables can be picked at the peak of flavor and nutrient value, and processed within hours. Once canned, there is little nutrient loss under proper storage conditions.

Economy—Canning is an economical way to preserve the bounty of a summer garden and an inexpensive alternative to out-of-season fresh fruits and vegetables. The only costly piece of canning equipment is the pressure canner which will last many years. It is essential for canning most vegetables and meats. It can also be used to process fruits.

Storage of canned goods requires no energy or special equipment. Most homes have a cool, dark, dry closet or corner that would be ideal for storage.

Specially Prepared Foods—Small batches of Plum Barbecue Sauce, page 130, Sweet Midgets, page 109, or exotic Kiwi Preserves, page 126, give a unique personal touch to meals. These *extras* liven family meals, delight dinner guests or make heart-warming gifts.

As a home canner, you know only the freshest, most flavorful foods have gone into the jars. You can prepare food to meet special dietary needs. Put little or no sugar in fruits for those who must restrict their sugar intake. Prepare meats and vegetables with no added salt. Add sugar or salt substitutes when foods are served.

Convenience—Having jars of fruits, vegetables, meats, sauces, pickles and sweet spreads makes meal preparation fast and easy. Combinations for casseroles, such as Spanish Chicken & Rice, page 163, are almost endless. Tasty side dishes—or complete meals—can be ready in minutes.

Canning Equipment

Modern canning equipment makes canning easy, convenient and safe. It gives you confidence in the safety and quality of home-canned food.

Some canning equipment is essential. Specialized tools save time and make canning safe. Jar tongs or lifters prevent accidental scalding as jars are removed from the canner. Other aids are useful to have and make canning simpler, but common kitchen utensils may be substituted.

Most hardware stores or cookware shops have everything you require for canning. Before buying any canning supplies, determine what you need. Will you do quantity canning or only small-batch, specialty canning? Will you can only fruits, pickles and jams that can be water-bath processed? Or do you want to can meats and vegetables that require a pressure canner? Make sure you have all the necessary basic equipment and it is in working order. Then choose canning aids and specialized tools from the lists that follow.

Some communities have canning kitchens where canning equipment is used cooperatively. They are usually staffed by a trained specialist or volunteer who can answer questions about canning directions and use of the equipment. These are often sponsored by local colleges, cooperative extension services or churches. Check newspaper advertisements or call your county extension agent to determine whether there are any in your locality.

ESSENTIAL CANNING EQUIPMENT

Jars—Canning jars are made of tempered glass to withstand high temperatures and changes in temperature as jars are removed from canners. *We recommend you do not use the one-trip, commercial jars that mayonnaise, peanut butter and other foods come in.* Canning lids may fit these jars, but the glass is thinner than standard canning jars and may crack. If you decide to use one-trip jars, use only in water-bath canning or for jellies. Expect about 10% breakage if you use these jars.

Canning jars are made with a *regular mouth* or *wide mouth.* Food left in larger pieces looks more attractive and is easier to put into and remove from wide-mouth jars. However, they are slightly more expensive than regular-mouth jars.

Handle jars carefully to prevent nicks and cracks and they will last year after year. Do not use scouring pads, steel wool or wire brushes that may damage jars.

Recommended jar sizes include 1/2-pint or 8-ounce, pint, 1-1/2-pint and quart. Other jars are specially designed for jellies that are sealed with paraffin. Use jar sizes that are appropriate for your family. Pints generally are best for a family of two or three. Quarts or 1-1/2-pints are best for a family of four or more. Two-quart canning jars are manufactured, but are not recommended for pressure canning. Few canners are built to handle jars this large and it requires a long time for heat to penetrate to the food at the center of the jar.

Lids—Several types of lids are available. *Plastic lids are not recommended for water-bath or pressure canning.*

Standard canning jars come in a variety of sizes and shapes.

Self-sealing lids are the most dependable canning lids. They consist of a flat metal disk and a metal screwband. The disks are not reusable. Discard them after the jar is opened. Screwbands may be used again if they are not bent or rusted. Disks are flanged around the edge to fit over the jar rim. The underside is coated with enamel where food may come in contact with it, and the edge is covered with a rubber sealing compound. The sealing compound must fit exactly over the jar rim for a seal to form.

Several manufacturers make these lids. If possible, use lids and jars by the same manufacturer. Lids are readily available in most supermarkets. For this reason, recipe directions are written for using this type of lid. If you use another type of lid, follow the manufacturer's directions for closing and sealing jars.

Zinc-porcelain caps or lids are difficult to find new. Rubber rings for use with them are readily available. These caps fit modern canning jars. The lid and screwband are one piece and are made of zinc. Because zinc can be a dangerous contaminant in foods, the lid is lined with porcelain. *If the porcelain is chipped, do not use the lid for canning or food storage.*

To seal a jar with this type of lid, place a rubber ring over the threads so the ring rests on the ledge below the threads. The seal is completed by tightening the lid when the jar is removed from the canner. Follow the directions that come with the rubber rings. Rubber rings cannot be reused. Discard them after opening jars.

Three-piece glass lids are still manufactured, though they are not common. Similar in appearance to a self-sealing vacuum lid, they consist of a glass lid and metal screwband. A rubber ring sits on the rim of the jar and forms the seal. The lid and screwband are tightened as the jar is removed from the canner. Follow the manufacturer's directions *exactly* when using three-piece glass lids. Rubber rings cannot be reused.

Jars with wire bails and dome glass lids, although old-fashioned, are still manufactured and are available in gift stores. They have become collector's items. A rubber ring sits on the rim of the jar. The dome lid rests on the ring. The longer loop of the bail holds the lid in place. After processing, the seal must be completed by snapping down the shorter bail wire. *These jars are not recommended for canning.* If the jars are old, they are likely to be chipped or have rough rims. The wire bails may be rusted and too weak to hold a tight seal. Many of the newer jars are made for decorative purposes only and will not withstand high temperatures.

Tin cans, most commonly used for commercial canning, are not readily available to the home canner. They are actually made of steel and are plated with tin or enameled on the inside where there is contact with food. The can and lid are separate pieces requiring a special can sealer. *Do not use procedures or processing times in this book when using metal cans.*

Canners—The type of canner needed depends on the foods to be processed. For high-acid fruits and tomatoes, use a water-bath canner. All types of meat, poultry and fish, most vegetables and mixed dishes must be processed in a pressure canner.

Water-bath canners are specially designed for canning fruits, pickles, relishes, sweet spreads and condiments. They are usually made from lightweight aluminum or enameled metal, but you can use other large, flat-bottom pots. Lightweight pots are easier and safer to handle than heavier pots, especially when filled with hot water.

A *rack* must hold jars off the bottom so water circulates freely around the jars during processing.

Place filled jars in rack. Water must be deep enough to cover jars with 1 to 2 inches of water.

The rack should have dividers to keep jars from touching as they are moved by the boiling water. Canning racks are available separate from the canner, but must fit your pot.

A water-bath canner should be at least 4 inches taller than the canning jars. It must be deep enough so jars in the rack are covered by 1 to 2 inches of water and have about 2 more inches above the water for boiling room. If the pot is deep enough to process a quart jar, you can also use it for smaller jars. There must be a *lid* to control evaporation.

Take care of your water-bath canner and it will last for years. To prevent water deposits on metal and enameled pots, put several tablespoons of distilled white vinegar in the water before you start processing. If water appears clean and clear, it can be used to process other batches. When you're finished canning, immediately remove and dry the rack so it won't rust. For safer handling, let the water cool at least 1 hour before emptying the pot. Dry and store the canner out of the way so it will not get chipped, dented or bent.

A water-bath canner can *only* be used to process high-acid foods that require a temperature of 212F (100C). Recipe directions throughout the book specify when a water-bath canner may be used. Also consult *Acidity of Fruits, Vegetables & Meats,* page 13.

Pressure canners are made of heavy-gauge metal, usually aluminum. A *rack* keeps jars off the bottom and allows free circulation of steam. The *lid* locks into place and has a *rubber gasket* that forms an airtight seal during processing. The lid also has a *vent or petcock, a weighted pressure regulator and a pressure safety valve.* Some canners also have a *dial pressure gauge.*

Always check the vent for blockage before the canner is used. Simply hold the lid up to a light and look through the vent. If it is not clear, push a small wire or a pipe cleaner through the vent. After you place filled jars in the canner and attach the lid, heat the canner until a steady column of steam comes from the vent. This requires about 10 minutes. Place the weight or pressure regulator over the vent. If your users' manual directs, place weight or pressure regulator over the vent immediately after the lid is placed on the canner.

The pressure regulator controls the escape of steam so a constant pressure is maintained. The periodic release of steam through the vent causes the regulator to rock or jiggle gently. Most regulators are weighted for 10 pounds of pressure, though 15-pound and multiple-weight—5-, 10- and 15-pound—regulators are available. One regulator comes in three pieces. The basic piece will give you 5 pounds pressure. Add the second and third weight rings to get 10 and 15 pounds

Each pressure-canner lid has a vent or petcock, a weighted regulator and pressure safety valve. Weighted regulator on canner to left rocks or jiggles to indicate when pressure is reached. Canner to right has a dial pressure gauge that indicates pressure in canner.

pressure. Canners with weighted regulators do not have to be checked for accuracy. However, a weighted regulator does not indicate pressure as accurately as a dial gauge.

Canners with dial gauges also have weighted regulators that rock and release steam during processing. But it is the dial gauge that accurately displays the pressure inside the canner. An advantage of canners with dial gauges is that pressure is indicated in 1-pound graduations. This is especially helpful when canning at higher altitudes.

The safety pressure valve is a small metal or rubber plug in the lid. If excessive pressure builds up in the canner, this plug blows out, releasing steam. Replacement valves are available in hardware or cookware stores.

Several manufacturers make pressure canners. Each canner differs slightly in physical structure and operating procedures, but all are designed to process foods safely and efficiently. Read and carefully follow the manufacturer's directions for operation. Always keep the users' manual available for quick reference.

Pressure canners range in size from 4-quart to 22-quart capacities. The most commonly used sizes are 8 to 16 quarts. A 4-quart canner will process only 1/2-pint jars. A 12-quart canner will process thirteen 1/2-pint jars, 8 pint jars or 7 quart jars at a time. **Pressure cookers** should not be used as canners unless they are designed for it. Check the users' manual. Pint jars can be processed in 4- and 6-quart cookers if the bottom rack is turned upside down. *In pressure cookers, canning time must be increased by 20 minutes.* If time in a pressure canner is 25 minutes, the time in a pressure cooker is 45 minutes plus any adjustments for altitude.

Wash the pressure canner in hot soapy water after each use. Remove the rubber gasket from the lid. Wash the gasket and the groove in which it fits. Rinse and dry all pieces thoroughly. Replace the rack and rubber gasket. Store the canner with the lid inverted over the pot. Lay paper towels between the rim and the lid to prevent scratches. Do not store with the lid locked on the canner.

Before each use, check the vent to be sure it is open. Examine the rubber ring for wear. And have the dial pressure gauge checked for accuracy. See *Organize for Canning*, pages 14-15. As with the water-bath canner, add a tablespoon of vinegar to the water before processing food. This will prevent water rings.

REQUIRED CANNING AIDS

The following small pieces of equipment are essential to successful canning:

Food brushes are necessary to clean firm fruits and vegetables thoroughly.

Knives should be made of good-quality steel that will not discolor fruits and vegetables. Use a paring knife for peeling, coring and slicing. A chef's knife is best for chopping and excellent for slicing. Keep knives clean and sharp.

Measuring cups and spoons are essential. You'll need a 1-cup and a 4-cup glass or clear plastic liquid-measuring cup.

Large kitchen pots and pans should hold the food to be precooked and allow boiling room. Stainless-steel, unchipped enamel or aluminum pots that hold 6 to 8 quarts of food are best for canning.

Long-handled spoons let you stir boiling mixtures without the risk of burning yourself. Use slotted spoons to lift foods from boiling water, antioxidant solutions or cooking liquid.

Colanders or sieves are helpful in washing and draining fruits and vegetables. Use them to strain juices for syrups and jellies. Force cooked fruits or vegetables through a sieve to make butters and sauces.

Ladles make it easy to pour hot sauces, syrups or cooking liquid into canning jars. Special canning ladles are available with extended, flattened edges that make pouring easier with fewer spills and drips.

Wide-mouth canning funnels help prevent spills and keep jar rims clean. They are designed to fit inside the mouth of regular and wide-mouth canning jars.

Clean towels are used to wipe rims of filled jars before putting on lids. Also use towels under and around hot jars while filling them and while cooling them after processing. Paper towels may also be used.

Jar tongs or lifters fit snugly around the necks of jars. Regular food tongs slip off.

A 1-minute-interval timer keeps an accurate account of processing times. Underprocessing means inadequate heating and may cause spoilage. Overprocessing results in unnecessary loss of flavor, texture and color. An oven timer, 3-minute timer or a watch with a second hand may be used.

Hot pads must be kept dry and within easy reach. Wet pads conduct heat and cause burns.

Canning labels may be self-adhesive or gum-type. Plain white labels of either type can be purchased at office-supply stores. Fancy labels are available in gift stores or card shops.

SPECIALIZED TOOLS

Cherry pitters push seeds from cherries, leaving the fruit nearly intact. Hand pitters are inexpensive and are sold in hardware stores or cookware shops. A more expensive table model pits cherries more quickly. You can use a knife to cut the cherries in half and remove the pits, but the cherries will not be as attractive.

Saw-tooth corn cutter fits around the ear of corn and removes kernels as you twist and turn it around the cob, page 49.

Apple corer and peeler removes the core while cutting away the peel. It is helpful when doing a large amount of apples or when making apple rings.

Vegetable peelers make light work of peeling fruits and vegetables. Or use a sharp paring knife.

Melon baller or pear corer cuts balls of fruit or vegetables, or removes cores from pear halves, page 77. A rounded 1/2-teaspoon measuring spoon works almost as well.

Jelly bag and stand consists of a fine-mesh nylon bag suspended from a stand so that juice drips into a bowl, page 58. A colander or sieve lined with cheesecloth serves the same purpose.

A thermometer must measure temperatures to 220F (105C). Temperature indicates doneness of jams or jellies that have no added pectin. Candy or deep-frying thermometers, marked in 1- or 2-degree graduations, may be used.

Crocks are needed to make pickles and for brining vegetables. Food-grade plastic pails may also be used, page 110.

Cabbage shredder shreds cabbage for sauerkraut. You can also use a chef's knife.

Jelmeter measures the potential jelling strength of a juice for jelly making. It is helpful when making jelly without adding pectin.

French-bean slicer cuts beans lengthwise for French-style green beans.

Corn holder can be made by hammering a stainless-steel nail through a piece of wood or a bread board. To use, remove the husk and silk from the corn, rinse it, then push stem-end down onto the nail. The nail holds the ear of corn and makes it easy to cut off the kernels.

Onion holder is made in the same way as a corn holder, but has 2 nails in it, 1 to 2 inches apart. It holds an onion steady, while slicing.

OTHER AIDS

The following items will make canning easier and more pleasant, but are not necessary for successful canning.

Lid lifter is a useful tool for removing lids from hot water, page 29.

Small scale should weigh amounts up to 5 pounds in 1-ounce graduations. To weigh foods over 5 pounds, use a bathroom scale. Produce purchased in a market can be weighed there.

Long narrow food tongs are specially designed for canning. They make it easy to arrange fruit or vegetables in jars, page 37.

Bubble freer is a long, flat plastic tool used to release trapped air in jars. The flat handle of a plastic or wooden spoon may be used. Do not use a knife. It may crack or chip the jar.

Food mill is a hand-operated utensil for pureeing and separating pulp and liquid, page 135. Use it to make sauces and fruit butters.

Electric blender or food processor makes chopping easier and faster, and is excellent for making smooth-textured sauces and spreads.

Cooling racks allow quick, even cooling of hot jars. Or use several layers of towels or newspaper.

The Canning Process

Fruits and vegetables begin to deteriorate as soon as they are picked. For many, juiciness and flavor decline drastically within 24 hours. Canning interrupts deterioration. During canning, heat inactivates plant enzymes, kills microorganisms and forms an airtight seal between the jar and lid so new microorganisms cannot get into the food.

Canning destroys plant enzymes that control the development of color in a ripe tomato, the crispness of a firm, juicy apple and the softness and brown color of an overripe banana. If storage conditions are adequate, last year's canned peaches will be as colorful and firm as the day they were canned.

Safety—Microorganisms are everywhere—in the air, on all surfaces, even on your hands. Yeasts, molds and bacteria are microorganisms that live in and on foods. Some toxins they produce make food inedible and may cause illness. Canning kills microorganisms with a combination of heat, acidity and processing time.

Yeasts and molds are destroyed at temperatures of 140F to 190F (60C to 88C) or in a boiling-water bath. Active bacteria are destroyed in boiling water, but bacterial spores must be heated to 240F (115C) in a pressure canner.

Clostridium botulinum produces a toxin that causes botulism food poisoning, which can be fatal. Other bacteria, including *Staphylococcus aureus* and *Salmonella,* can cause food poisoning, but the resulting illness is not as serious as botulism.

Clostridium botulinum is common in most soils. It may be present on any fruit or vegetable in an *active* state or as a *spore.* Spores become active in *low-acid, oxygen-free conditions.* If canning heat is insufficient, spores may become active and begin producing the toxin that causes botulism.

Usually, *acidity* is thought of as the sour taste of lemon juice or tartness of a firm, red plum. Because acidity of food determines whether it is to be canned in a boiling-water bath or in a pressure canner, you must have more specific information.

The scientific measure of acidity is called *pH.* For canning, foods with a pH of 4.5 or lower are considered high-acid foods. See *Acidity of Fruits, Vegetables & Meats,* below. These include fruits, berries and pickles. With a pH of 4.5 or lower, conditions are unfavorable for spores to become active and produce toxin. Therefore, a processing temperature of 212F (100C), or boiling water, is safe.

Jar size also affects processing time. It requires more time for food in a quart jar to reach the desired temperature than the same food in a pint or 1/2-pint jar. *Cold-packed* food that has not been precooked or heated requires more time to process than *hot-packed* or precooked food.

Processing time starts when the required temperature is reached in the canner. In a boiling-water bath, that means when the water comes to a boil. In a pressure canner at sea level, 240F (115C) is reached when 10 pounds pressure is indicated by the pressure gauge or regulator. To assure safely canned food, the temperature must be maintained throughout the processing time. *If the boil or pressure is lost during processing, it must be reestablished and the processing time started again from the beginning.*

Acidity of Fruits, Vegetables & Meats

Acidity	pH	Food	Canning Method Water Bath	Pressure Canner
High-Acid Foods	2	lemons, limes	X	
	2.5	cranberries, pickles, relishes	X	
	3	plums, gooseberries, apples, grapefruit, blackberries, apricots, strawberries, rhubarb	X	
	3.5	sour cherries, pineapple, peaches, raspberries, sweet cherries, sauerkraut, pears	X	
	4	tomatoes	X	X
	4.5	(Neutral)		
Low-Acid Foods	5	figs (add lemon juice)	X	
	5	okra, carrots, turnips, beets, green beans, asparagus, lima beans		X
	6	potatoes, peas, corn		X
	7	beef, chicken, fish, shellfish		X

Most vegetables and meats have a pH above 4.5 and are considered low acid. Therefore, they must be processed in a pressure canner with at least 10 pounds pressure.

Food throughout canning jars must reach the correct processing temperature and heat must be maintained long enough to kill any micro-organisms. Processing times vary with the type of food canned, from as little as 10 minutes for highly acidic pickles, to as much as 100 minutes for tuna fish.

Processing time also depends upon how quickly heat penetrates to food in the center of the jar. The more dense or compact the food being canned, the slower heat penetrates. Starchy solid foods, such as corn, meat or beans, require long processing times. Heat quickly penetrates to the center of porous food such as apples, pears and green beans.

ALTITUDE VARIATIONS

Altitude affects both water-bath canning and pressure canning. When processing in a boiling-water bath, increase processing time 1 or 2 minutes for each 1000 feet above sea level. See *Altitude Adjustments for Water-Bath Canning,* page 20. Your Chamber of Commerce can tell you the local altitude.

When using a pressure canner at altitudes above 2000 feet, time does not change, but pressure must be increased. If your canner has a dial pressure gauge, increase pressure 1 pound for each additional 2000 feet altitude. Canners with weighted regulators can be operated only at 10 or 15 pounds of pressure. If using a weighted regulator at altitudes of 2000 feet or higher, process at 15 pounds pressure. This will slightly overprocess. **When adjusting for altitude, do not shorten the processing time.** See *Altitude Adjustments for Pressure Canning,* page 21.

HOW TO CAN: START TO FINISH

Canning all of the produce from a home garden or a tree weighted down with fruit seems like an overwhelming task. Planning and organization are the keys to making the task a rewarding effort. Divide canning into the following steps to make it easier to understand and follow:
- Organize for Canning
- Choose, Wash and Prepare Food
- Pack and Close Jars
- Process
- Store and Use Canned Foods

Organize for Canning: Before the beginning of canning season, determine which fruits and vegetables will be available at a price that makes canning worthwhile. This will include produce from your own garden and from other sources. Choose foods your family enjoys. If the pantry shelves are still lined with last year's beets, you probably canned too many. Look for different ways to season beets or recipes for making beet relish.

Second, determine how much to can. When you have a tree laden with sweet, purple plums, it is easy to become overzealous. Plan to can only the number of jars the family will use before next season. This will be difficult to estimate the first year, but from then on, base the estimate on the number of jars of last year's crop that have been used. Sell or give away the rest of the plums.

Third, check canning equipment *before* the season begins. Make sure all required equipment is available and in working order. If your pressure-canner manual is lost, write to the manufacturer for another. Carefully examine the pressure canner. Check the rubber gasket for wear. Read your users' manual as you test the canner with only water in it. Check for leakage.

Examine empty canning jars by running your finger around the jar rim. Discard any with cracks or chips.

If the canner has a dial pressure gauge, have the gauge checked for accuracy at a hardware store or ask your county extension agent for the name of an individual who checks gauges. If testing shows the gauge to be inaccurate, make adjustments. If the gauge reads 10 pounds pressure but testing shows the true pressure is 12 pounds, adjust the heat until the gauge reads 8 pounds. If the gauge reads 10 pounds but the true pressure is 8 pounds, adjust the heat until the gauge reads 12 pounds.

Fourth, examine empty canning jars and screwbands. Discard any jars that are cracked or chipped. Screwbands may be reused if they are not bent or rusty. Discard all used self-seal lids. Make an early purchase of the number and size of jars and lids you will need. Supplies are often short during the peak of the canning season. Check new jars for cracks and chips.

Fifth, review boiling-water bath and pressure canning, pages 20 and 21. Read the recipes you plan to use. Some recipes call for salting or brining overnight or for several days. Plan this into your schedule. Have all the recipe ingredients on hand.

Set aside uninterrupted time for canning. When you are hurried or interrupted with other demands, mistakes or accidents can occur.

When canning day arrives, make a clear work area. Arrange the work area so you can sit during some of the steps. Scrub the sink and all surfaces. Wash and rinse all canning equipment and canning aids.

Wash canning jars in hot soapy water, then rinse in hot water. Place clean jars in a large pot of very hot—but not boiling—water until they are needed. Jars may also be washed in a dishwasher. Leave them in the dishwasher with the door closed after the cycle is finished. They will stay hot about 30 minutes. Follow the manufacturer's directions for preparing lids.

Zinc caps must be sterilized by boiling in water 15 minutes. Remove the pot of boiling water from the heat. Leave the caps in the hot water until needed. Wash rubber rings and keep them wet until they are used.

Choose, Wash and Prepare Food: Canning preserves, but does not improve flavor. Choose just-picked, vine- or tree-ripened produce, if possible. Meats, poultry and fish *must* be fresh.

Fruits and vegetables should be of uniform size and ripeness. They will cook more evenly. Do not can overripe, decaying or badly bruised produce, especially tomatoes. Overripe tomatoes may not be acidic enough to process in a boiling-water bath. Use the best fruits and vegetables for canning whole or sliced. Slightly bruised fruits and vegetables can be used in jams or relishes. Cut out and discard small bruises or damaged areas.

Wash fruits and vegetables in cool water to cover. Lift them out of the water to a clean container. They can also be washed under cool running water. *Wash only the amount that can be processed in one batch.*

Preparation is usually the most time-consuming step of canning. Each food in *Basic Canning,* pages 24 to 73, has instructions for peeling, coring, cutting, brining or precooking. Save time and energy by using special kitchen utensils, such as a corn cutter, apple peeler or cherry pitter, page 12. Sharpen knives ahead of time. Work quickly when cutting fruits and vegetables to avoid long exposure to air or water and loss of nutrients. Treat light-colored fruits with an antioxidant to prevent browning, page 25.

Pack and Close Jars: Following the directions for each food, pack food in jars raw or precooked. Some delicate foods, such as raspberries, must be packed cold to keep their shape. Others, such as

Wash fruits and vegetables in cool water. Lift them out of the water. Scrub firm produce under running water.

beets, potatoes and peppers, must be packed hot for safe canning.

To *cold pack,* pack the raw food tightly in hot jars. The food will shrink during processing. Pour boiling syrup, broth or water over the food until it is covered.

To *hot pack,* heat the food as specified, then pack it in hot jars. Pack the jars carefully because food is more fragile after cooking. Pour boiling cooking liquid, syrup or broth over the food until it is covered.

Hot pack is recommended when there is a choice. Precooking releases air from the food, resulting in less air in the canning jar. The food shrinks, so more can be packed in each jar. With less air in the jar, fruit is less likely to float to the top.

Pack tightly or loosely, according to recipe directions. Some foods shrink, but others, such as starchy vegetables, expand. Use a jar funnel when filling jars, to prevent spills and keep the jar rim clean.

Headspace is the space that *must* be left at the top of a jar between the food or liquid and the lid. This space allows for expansion and boiling during processing, without forcing liquid out of the jar. Liquid should cover food in jars. Food left

uncovered does not spoil during storage, but it may darken. Too much or too little headspace may prevent an airtight seal from forming. Unless specified otherwise in recipes, follow this guideline for headspace:

1/8 inch	jellies and fruit syrups
1/4 inch	jams, preserves, pickles, relishes, sauces, syrups and juices
1/2 inch	most fruits and vegetables
1 inch	low-acid and starchy vegetables that are pressure canned, such as corn, beets, peas, potatoes and dry beans; meats, poultry and fish

Release air trapped in canning jars. Insert a thin, flat plastic or wooden utensil at the side of the jar. Air bubbles will rise to the top. Do not use a sharp knife or metal utensil.

Wipe jar rims before putting on lids. Food and droplets of syrup or liquid left on the jar rim will prevent an airtight seal. Use a clean dry cloth or paper towel to wipe away fatty droplets when canning meats. A damp cloth works best for sticky syrups used for canning fruits.

Fill and close one jar at a time. This decreases the possibility of introducing microorganisms into filled jars waiting to be closed.

1/Cold pack or hot pack foods leaving recommended headspace. These beans are being cold packed.

2/Release trapped air by inserting a thin flat utensil at the side of the jar.

Wipe jar rims before putting on lids. Use a wet cloth for syrupy mixtures and a dry cloth for those containing fat droplets.

Closing canning jars is simple with self-sealing vacuum lids. Place a hot lid on top of a filled jar with the rubber sealing compound against the rim of the jar. Making sure it is on straight, screw the metal band down firmly *by hand.* Do not use a jar wrench to tighten bands. Lids must be loose enough to let air escape during processing. If the lids buckle or bend, you attached the screwband too tightly. Follow the manufacturer's directions for closing jars with zinc-porcelain or glass tops.

Pour hot water into the water-bath canner until half full and into the pressure canner until 2 to 3 inches deep. Keep the water hot. As each jar is filled and closed, place it on the rack in the canner. This will keep jars of hot food hot and begin heating cold raw food.

Process: Each recipe specifies whether to use a boiling-water bath or a pressure canner. Do not substitute other methods, shorten processing times or use lower pressure. Safety and quality will be sacrificed.

Use a **boiling-water bath** to process fruits, tomatoes, sweet spreads, pickles, relishes, sauces and condiments. The canner must be deep enough for the closed jars to be covered with boiling water.

To protect your hands, use a jar lifter to place filled and closed jars in the rack, leaving enough room between the jars for water to circulate. When all jars are in place, pour hot water around the jars until there is 1 to 2 inches of water above the jars. Do not use boiling water or pour water directly on the jars. Cover the canner and bring the water to a full boil.

Begin counting processing time. Reduce the heat until the water boils gently. Follow the processing time exactly as given in the recipe or as adjusted for altitudes of 1000 feet or higher, page 20. If the processing time is more than 30 minutes, have some boiling water ready to add to the canner to keep the jars covered with water.

Place a cooling rack or several layers of towels or newspapers in a place free from drafts. When processing time is finished, use a jar lifter to remove jars from the boiling water. Place the jars on the rack or towels. Do not set jars directly on a cool counter top or in a draft. It may cause them to crack. If using self-sealing lids, do not tighten bands or touch lids. Water on lids will evaporate. Follow manufacturer's directions for other lids. Let the jars cool undisturbed for 10 to 12 hours.

Always use a **pressure canner** when canning low-acid foods. This includes most vegetables and all meats, poultry and fish. Review the pressure-canner manual before you begin. Correct operation of the canner is critical for a safe and appealing product. Don't trust your memory.

Fill the pressure canner with the amount of hot water recommended in the users' manual —usually 2 to 3 inches. Place filled and closed jars on the rack in the canner. Close the canner and fasten the lid securely.

If your canner has a dial pressure gauge, leave the vent open about 10 minutes after steam begins escaping, or until a steady column of steam flows from the vent. The air must be removed before the heat can be raised to 240F (115C) needed to can low-acid foods safely. There is also danger of blowing the safety plug from the canner. Close the vent by setting the weighted regulator on it. Build pressure until the dial reads 10 pounds or the adjusted pressure for altitudes over 2000 feet, page 21.

If your canner has a weighted pressure regulator, follow the directions in your users' manual. There are two possible methods for expelling air. In one, air is exhausted from the canner with the vent open, as with the dial pressure gauge. In the other, the weighted pressure regulator is put on the vent from the beginning. Air is exhausted around the regulator. After 10 minutes, it will begin to jiggle.

When the canner reaches 10 pounds pressure, or 15 pounds pressure at altitudes of 2000 feet or higher, reduce the heat to maintain a constant pressure. Pressure is indicated by the dial gauge or the weighted pressure regulator rocking gently or jiggling.

Start counting processing time when the desired pressure is reached in the canner. A steady, even pressure must be maintained throughout the processing time. *If pressure is lost, bring the pressure back to what it should be. Process again for the full canning time.*

When processing time is completed, carefully remove the canner from the heat. Let it cool, undisturbed, until the pressure gauge reads zero or steam no longer comes from the vent when the regulator is nudged. This may require 30 to 60 minutes, depending on the size of the canner. *Do not quick-cool the canner by running water over it or releasing pressure through the vent.* Rapid cooling may cause jars to break or the contents to boil out of the jars.

Open the canner carefully by releasing the lid and sliding it toward you so any remaining steam will escape from the far side. Set the lid loosely on the canner for at least 2 minutes to cool. Remove the lid. Let the jars cool in the canner 10 minutes. The contents of the jars will still be boiling vigorously when the canner is opened.

Use jar lifters to remove jars from the canner. Cool the jars on a cooling rack or several layers of towels or newspapers in a place free from drafts. Do not tighten bands on self-sealing lids. Complete the seal of jars with rubber rings according to manufacturer's directions.

Store and Use Canned Foods: Before placing newly canned foods on the pantry shelf, several small tasks remain. Check the seal on each thoroughly cooled jar. Self-sealing vacuum lids sometimes make a loud *ping* as the seal forms. This usually happens within the first 20 minutes of cooling. After 12 hours, sealed metal vacuum lids are concave and cannot be pressed down.

Lids that are not concave and spring back when pressed in the center are not sealed. If the lid is not concave, but remains down when pushed in the center, the seal is questionable.

Remove screwbands from all jars. Tip any questionable jars to the side. If there is leakage, the jar did not seal. Also lift the jar about an inch off the counter by holding the edge of the lid with several fingers of one hand. If the lid stays on the jar, it is

sealed. If liquid has been lost from the jars during processing, do not open them to replace the liquid. *Store all jars without the screwbands.*

Check jars with rubber rings by tipping and looking for leakage. Do not loosen or tighten lids once the jars have cooled. If any leakage occurs, the jar is not sealed.

Refrigerate unsealed jars and use the food within 7 days. The food can be reprocessed, but must be put in clean hot jars and processed for the full time.

Before labeling, wipe the sealed jars with a damp cloth. For easy reading, place gummed or adhesive labels on lids if jars will be stored in boxes. Place labels on the side of jars that will be stored on shelves. On the label, write the name of the food, the date, batch number if appropriate, recipe used and variety of fruit or vegetable. Other helpful information includes whether hot packed or cold packed and the type of syrup used. All information will be helpful in evaluating and planning next year's canning.

Storage conditions determine how long canned

Remove screwbands from cooled jars. Tip jars to the side to check for leakage.

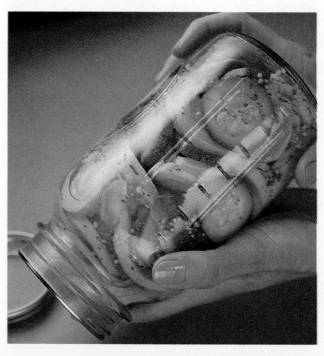

food will remain safe and keep its nutritive value, color and flavor. Storage areas should be cool, clean, dry and dark. Too much moisture will cause metal lids to rust and lose their seal. Light causes food color to fade quickly.

Temperature is probably the most important factor. The ideal temperature is between 40F and 50F (4C and 10C). Canned foods deteriorate more quickly above 50F (10C). Never store canned foods at temperatures above 80F (27C). Use storage areas away from the furnace, water heater and hot-water pipes. Keep a thermometer in the area so you always know the temperature. Lower shelves in storage areas will be cooler than upper shelves. Do not place jars directly on the floor. Place boards 2 or 3 inches apart on the floor, then place the jars or boxes of jars on the boards. In hot climates where there is no cool place to store canned foods, store in a dark place. Check the jars periodically for spoilage and deterioration.

If canned foods freeze, it will not cause the foods to spoil, but may damage the seal or break the jar.

Keep an inventory list of canned foods by the storage area or in another convenient place. List the amount of each type of canned food by the size and number of jars. An inventory is a great help in planning menus.

Use canned foods in a wide variety of ways. Don't be tied to opening, heating and serving green beans. See *Using Canned Foods,* pages 138 to 186.

When using canned foods, include broth, syrup or canning liquid whenever possible. They contain valuable nutrients. When syrups can't be used with the fruit, serve them as a juice drink alone or combined with other juices. Or freeze the syrup in ice-cube trays and use to cool drinks.

Before using any home-canned food, check for spoilage. *Never taste food as a test for spoilage.* Depend on your eyes and nose. Examine the jar before opening. A bulging lid or leaking seal is a sure indication of spoilage. Other indicators are bubbles inside the jar, changes in color and a cloudy liquid or sediment in the jar. Any of these *may* be caused by spoilage. As you open jars, listen for the *pop* as the airtight seal is broken. If liquid spurts from the jar or the contents smell yeasty, sour or putrid, it is spoiled. Mushy or slimy food is not safe. A film or cotton-like growth on the surface of the food also indicates spoilage.

Do not taste, cook or serve food that has spoiled.

In the past, mold was not considered particularly harmful. Mold on jams or jellies was scraped off and the remaining spread used. Today, it is recognized that molds produce toxins that may be harmful. When there are signs of mold or other spoilage, destroy the food.

When in doubt, throw it out—but not in the garbage. Any toxins that are present must first be destroyed by boiling. Empty the contents of the jar into a saucepan. Bring it to a boil, then boil 20 minutes. Wash your hands and any other surfaces exposed to the food with a chlorine-bleach solution, using 2 tablespoons of chlorine bleach to 1 quart of water. Dispose of the boiled food in a garbage disposal or toilet. Also, boil the jar and lid 15 minutes in soapy water.

Even though a canned food shows no signs of spoilage, it may not be safe. To destroy toxins that may be present, *most vegetables should be boiled 15 minutes before serving. Meats, poultry, fish, corn, potatoes and vegetable greens should be boiled 20 minutes.* Vegetables and meats you want to serve cold should be boiled, then chilled in the refrigerator.

Label jars before storing in a cool, clean, dry, dark place.

Sources of Produce for Canning

Home gardens or fruit trees are the least expensive sources of fruits and vegetables.

Local farms often supply produce through *roadside stands, farmers' markets* in the city or *U-pick*. Purchased this way, food is comparatively inexpensive. At a U-pick, customers go into the field or orchard to pick and pack the produce. You can choose the best quality.

Supermarkets generally have the most expensive fresh produce, but may be a good source for small-batch specialty canning. Exotic fruits or those not grown locally may be available in supermarkets. It is not economical to can large amounts of fruits and vegetables purchased in a supermarket unless the food is specially priced.

Tailgate sales of excess produce flourish in many parts of the world. Foods from the family garden or from farms off the main thoroughfare are sold from the back of a truck or car.

Cooperatives may order produce in quantity and pass the savings on to members.

Water-Bath Canning At A Glance

Read pages 6 through 19 and 43-44 before using this information.
1. Prepare and pack food in canning jars as directed in recipe.
2. Fill water-bath canner about half full with hot water.
3. Lower filled and closed jars into canner. Add hot water until 1 to 2 inches above jars.
4. Cover canner. Bring water to a full boil. Adjust heat to maintain boil.
5. Begin counting processing time indicated in recipe or as adjusted for altitudes of 1000 feet or higher.
6. Set timer or look at time on clock. Be sure water continues to boil and jars are covered with water.
7. When processing time is completed, remove jars.
8. Cool jars 10 to 12 hours on a cooling rack or several layers of towels or newspapers, away from drafts.
9. If water in canner appears clean and clear, it can be used to process other batches.

Altitude Adjustments for Water-Bath Canning

Altitude in Feet	Processing time 20 minutes or less	Processing time more than 20 minutes
under 1000	time called for in recipe	time called for in recipe
1000	time called for plus 1 min.	time called for plus 2 min.
2000	time called for plus 2 min.	time called for plus 4 min.
3000	time called for plus 3 min.	time called for plus 6 min.
4000	time called for plus 4 min.	time called for plus 8 min.
5000	time called for plus 5 min.	time called for plus 10 min.
6000	time called for plus 6 min.	time called for plus 12 min.
7000	time called for plus 7 min.	time called for plus 14 min.
8000	time called for plus 8 min.	time called for plus 16 min.
9000	time called for plus 9 min	time called for plus 18 min.
10,000 or more	time called for plus 10 min.	time called for plus 20 min.

Pressure Canning At A Glance

Read pages 6 through 19 before using this information.
1. Prepare and pack food in canning jars as directed in recipe.
2. Fill pressure canner with recommended amount of water—usually 2 to 3 inches.
3. Arrange filled and closed jars in canner so steam can circulate around them.
4. Close canner; fasten lid securely.
5. If users' manual directs, exhaust air from canner until a steady column of steam comes from vent.
6. Bring canner up to pressure following manufacturer's directions. Adjust heat to maintain pressure.
7. Begin counting processing time when canner reaches 10 pounds pressure or pressure adjusted for altitudes of 2000 feet or higher.
8. Set timer or look at time on clock. Be sure pressure is maintained throughout processing time.
9. When processing time is completed, carefully remove canner from heat.
10. Let canner cool, undisturbed, until pressure registers zero or steam does not hiss when regulator is nudged.
11. Release lid. Slide lid toward you, letting steam escape from far side of canner. Set lid loosely on top. Let stand 2 minutes.
12. Remove lid. Let jars cool another 10 minutes in canner.
13. Remove jars to a cooling rack or several layers of towels or newspapers, away from drafts. Cool 10 to 12 hours.

Altitude Adjustments for Pressure Canning

Altitude in Feet	Processing Pressure with Dial Gauge	Processing Pressure with Weighted Regulator
below 2000	10 pounds	10 pounds
2000	11 pounds	15 pounds
3000	11.5 pounds	15 pounds
4000	12 pounds	15 pounds
5000	12.5 pounds	15 pounds
6000	13 pounds	15 pounds
7000	13.5 pounds	15 pounds
8000	14 pounds	15 pounds
9000	14.5 pounds	15 pounds
10,000 or more	15 pounds	15 pounds

 Tip
_____

Measure the space between the top of the food and lid carefully to allow proper venting of air during processing. This will assure a good seal.

If There's a Question

GENERAL CANNING

Problem	Cause	Solution
Liquid lost from jars during processing.	Jars too full; pressure or heat not constant.	Leave adequate space, page 16.
Jars seal, then lose seal during storage. **Food is spoiled; destroy it.**	Underprocessed. Poor lids or not properly heated.	Follow processing times exactly.
	Food particles left on jar rim.	Wipe rims before putting on lids.
	Cracked or nicked jars.	Check jars for cracks and nicks.
Food is dark at top of jar.	Liquid did not cover food.	Make sure food is covered with liquid before closing jars.
	Underprocessed.	Follow processing times exactly. Begin counting processing time as pressure is reached or water boils. Maintain pressure or boil throughout processing time.
Cloudy liquid or sediment on bottom of sealed jars.	May indicate spoilage. Look for other signs, pages 18-19.	Follow recipe directions exactly.
	Minerals in canning water.	Use softened or bottled water.
	Starch from foods, especially vegetables, may settle to bottom.	No way to prevent this harmless sediment.
Jars not sealed after processing.	Variety of causes.	Check jars before canning. Carefully follow directions. Do not reuse self-sealing lids.
Lids buckled.	Screw band too tight.	Tighten screw band only until firm.

JAMS & JELLIES

Problem	Cause	Solution
Sugar crystals in jelly.	Too much sugar.	Read recipe; follow exactly.
	Jelly cooked too long.	Boil jelly to gel point.
	Tartaric acid in grape jelly.	Refrigerate juice; strain before making jelly.
Soft jelly.	Incorrect ratio of juice to sugar or doubling recipe.	Read recipe; follow exactly.
Stiff jelly or jam.	Overcooking.	Test for doneness more often.
	Too much pectin in fruit or too much added pectin.	When adding pectin, use fully ripe fruit.
Cloudy jelly.	Fruit too green.	Use 1/3 underripe fruit and 2/3 ripe fruit when no pectin is added. Use fully ripe fruit when pectin is added.
Floating fruit in jam.	Fruit not fully ripe or crushed.	Use fully ripe fruit for jam.
	Jam not cooled slightly before put in jars.	Stir and skim jam 5 minutes before ladling into jars.
Fading or darkening of jam or jelly.	Stored at too high temperature or too long, especially red fruits.	Store jams & jellies below 80F (25C), no longer than 4 to 6 months.
Mold on jams or jellies. **Spread is spoiled; discard it.**	Inadequate processing or jars not sealed.	Process jams in a boiling water bath. Sterilize jars for jelly by boiling 15 minutes.

MEATS, POULTRY & FISH

Problem	Cause	Solution
Canning liquid lost from jar during processing.	Jars packed too full.	Leave 1-1/2 inches headspace.
	Pressure in canner not constant during processing.	Adjust heat to maintain steady pressure.
	Canner cooled too quickly.	Remove canner from heat when processing time is up. Let pressure drop, undisturbed.
Underside of self-sealing lid has black or brown deposit. **If jar is not sealed, food is spoiled. Destroy it!**	Compounds in food corroded metal lid.	Harmless deposit; cannot be avoided.

FRUITS

Problem	Cause	Solution
Fruits darken after removed from jar.	Underprocessed.	Process as directed. Begin counting time when water comes to a boil.
Pink, red, blue or purple color on canned apples, pears or peaches.	Natural change that sometimes occurs as fruit is cooked.	No way to prevent this harmless discoloration.
Fruit floats to top of jar.	Fruit not packed tightly in jar or fruit too ripe.	Pack jars tightly with ripe fruit.
	Syrup too sweet.	Use a lighter sugar syrup.

VEGETABLES

Problem	Cause	Solution
Green vegetables turn brown.	Overcooked or overprocessed.	Time cooking and processing carefully.
White crystals in canned spinach.	Calcium and oxalic acid in spinach form calcium-oxalate crystals.	No way to prevent this harmless deposit.
Corn turns brown.	Variety of corn or corn too mature.	Use freshly picked canning varieties at peak of maturity.
	Processing temperature too high.	Keep pressure in canner constant. Check gauge for accuracy.

PICKLES & SAUERKRAUT

Problem	Cause	Solution
Soft, slippery pickles. **Indicates spoilage; destroy pickles!**	Brine too weak.	Follow recipe. Use canning salt and vinegar of 4% to 6% acidity.
	Blossom not removed.	Remove cucumber blossoms.
	Cucumbers not covered with brine.	Use a weighted plate to hold cucumbers below surface of brine.
	Scum from surface stirred into brine during fermentation.	Carefully remove scum from surface.
	Temperature too high during fermentation.	Ferment pickles at 75F to 80F (20C to 25C).
	Pickles not processed long enough.	Process pickles in a boiling-water bath for required time.
Hollow pickles.	Cucumbers not freshly picked.	Pickle immediately after picking.
	Cucumbers fermented too quickly. Room too warm.	Keep temperature between 75F and 80F (20C and 25C) during fermentation.
Shriveled, tough pickles.	Too much salt, vinegar or sugar added at one time.	With very sweet or very sour pickles, add sugar, vinegar or salt gradually over several days' time.
Darkened pickles.	Minerals in brine water.	Use softened or bottled water.
	Spices left in jars or ground spices used.	Remove spices before processing.
White sediment in bottom of sealed jars. **If pickles are soft and slippery, they are spoiled; destroy them!**	Harmless yeast has settled to bottom.	A small amount of sediment is normal.
Soft, dark or pink sauerkraut; rotting odor. **Sauerkraut is spoiled; destroy it!**	Not enough salt or not evenly distributed.	Be sure salt is thoroughly mixed with shredded cabbage before packing in jars.
	Temperature too high during fermentation.	Keep room temperature at 70F to 80F (20C to 25C).
	Cabbage not covered with brine during fermentation.	When fermenting in a crock, keep entire surface covered with plastic bag.
	Cabbage not washed and trimmed before shredding.	Wash and trim cabbage before shredding.

Basic Canning:
Fruits

Fruits are high-acid foods and simple to process in a boiling-water bath. Even first-time canners are successful. Imagine the reward of displaying colorful jars of fruit you have canned. In addition, the whole family enjoys home-canned fruits sweetened to taste.

Can fruits whole, halved or in slices. Processing time in a water bath is relatively short, so you are soon lifting jars of colorful fruit from the water-bath canner.

Fruits may be pressure canned if the canner is removed from the heat as soon as 15 pounds pressure is reached. See the box on page 26.

Tomatoes are considered a vegetable and are treated in that section even though they contain enough acid to be canned in a boiling-water bath.

Before you begin to can, read *How to Can: Start to Finish,* pages 14-19. It tells you how to organize to make canning easier. Also refer to *Water-Bath Canning at a Glance,* page 20.

Know the variety of fruit you want to can and its characteristics. Use firm-textured fruit when it is important to retain shapes. Freestone varieties make more attractive canned fruit because the pit separates easily from the flesh.

The cooperative extension or agricultural agents in your area will know which locally grown fruit varieties will give the best results when canned. Also talk with local growers and grocers where you buy fruit. If information about canning results is not available, experiment by processing several quarts of a variety, then evaluate the canned fruit. If the results are satisfactory, continue with your canning. If the fruit is too soft after canning, use that variety in a fruit butter or sauce. Look for another variety to can whole or sliced.

Generally, tree-ripened fruit has a better flavor than fruit that is picked green. An exception is pears, whose flavor and sweetness develop after being picked. When fruit is ready to can, the flesh should be firm or just beginning to soften. Do not can soft, overripe or hard, underripe fruit. Avoid fruit that is badly bruised or has a broken skin. Cut out small bruises and blemishes when the fruit is to be canned in chunks. Avoid fruit with dry, shriveled skin. This means the fruit is old and will lack flavor and juiciness.

Whole fruit or large pieces will require more jars than small pieces. Hot-packed fruit packs tighter, using fewer jars than cold-packed.

HOW TO CAN FRUIT

At the peak of freshness and flavor, fruit is fragile, bruises easily and deteriorates quickly. Handle it gently. Avoid stacking ripe fruit more than two layers deep. Process it as soon as possible after it is picked. Refrigerate it no more than two days.

Cover Fruits with Liquid: Fruit must be covered with liquid to prevent darkening. This may be water, fruit juice or syrup.

Sugar is not essential for safe preservation of fruit. The combination of fruit acidity and processing heat makes canning without sugar safe. However, sugar does help fruit keep brighter color, better shape and better texture.

Water may be used in place of sugar syrup for individuals on diets. Flavor and texture are generally inferior to fruits canned with some sweetening. Exceptions are blueberries and sour cherries that will be used in pies and other baked goods. Fruit to be used in baking may be canned in water or light syrup.

Vary the sweetness of *sugar syrup,* page 26, depending on tartness of the fruit being canned or individual preference. Generally, medium syrup best preserves the color and flavor of home-canned fruits and therefore is most often recommended. For very tart fruit, a heavy syrup may be preferable. A light syrup may always be used when calories or sugar are a dietary concern.

Juice may be made by lightly sprinkling very juicy fruit with sugar and then slowly heating the mixture. Use the juice that forms to cover the fruit. Or mash some of the fruit and heat it with little or no added sugar to make juice, stirring to prevent scorching. Strain the juice through 2 layers of cheesecloth or a jelly bag, page 58.

Unsweetened pineapple, white grape, apple, cranapple, and in some cases, orange juice may be used as liquid. They provide sugar naturally present in juice and add a unique flavor. Cranapple and apple juices will darken light-color fruits. Unsweetened pineapple juice strained through cheesecloth is excellent with pears.

Honey contributes a flavor of its own that may interfere with natural fruit flavor. However, a mild-flavored honey may be substituted for up to half the amount of sugar in syrup. *Do not use honey to sweeten foods that will be given to infants.* It may contain bacteria that infant digestive systems cannot tolerate.

Light corn syrup may be substituted for half the sugar in syrup. Do not use other syrups such as *molasses* or *sorghum.* Their flavors are too strong and they will discolor the fruit.

Brown sugar also has a distinctive flavor and will darken light-color fruit. However, it may be used to impart an intriguing flavor when color is not affected, as in Regal Plums, page 77.

Artificial sweeteners should not be used in canning fruits. Some sweeteners give fruit a bitter taste. Can the fruit with water, then add artificial sweetener after opening the jar.

Wash all fruit in generous amounts of cold water before it is cut, even if it is to be peeled.

Gently agitate fragile berries, then lift them from the water. While in the water, use your hands to gently rub sturdier fruits, such as pears, peaches, plums, apricots and apples. Scrub thick-skinned fruit, such as pineapple or grapefruit, with a soft brush. Lift the fruit from the water.

Peel apples with a vegetable peeler. Apricots, nectarines, plums, peaches and pears have skins that come off easily after blanching 30 seconds in very hot water. Gently lift the peel from the stem-end of the blanched fruit, then with gentle pressure of your hands, push or *slip* the skin off. If the skin doesn't slip easily, use a paring knife to lift and pull the skin away from the fruit.

How canned fruit is to be used will determine whether pitting, slicing or cubing is desirable. You may want to leave the seeds in small fruit, such as cherries, apricots and plums. Cherries especially maintain better shape if they are not pitted. For salads, shape is important. If the fruit is to be used in baking, pitting may be a convenience that far outweighs any loss in shape. Sliced or cut pieces are more attractive when uniform in size and shape. Pack the prepared fruit in hot jars according to directions.

Antioxidant Treatment: Some light-color fruits turn brown when exposed to air. To prevent browning, work quickly with only as much fruit as can be processed in one canner load. Treat the fruit with an *antioxidant* as soon as it is peeled or cut. Use one of the solutions listed below.

Salt-vinegar solution: Add 2 tablespoons salt and 2 tablespoons distilled white vinegar to 1 gallon water. Immerse cut fruit in the solution. Work quickly so it doesn't remain in the solution more than 20 minutes. Nutrients will leach out with longer exposure. When all the fruit is peeled or sliced, lift it out of the solution. Rinse the fruit in clear water and pack it in jars.

Ascorbic-acid solution: Ascorbic-acid or vitamin-C crystals may be purchased in any drug store, supermarket or health-food store. Usual concentration of crystalline vitamin C is 3000 to 4000 milligrams per teaspoon. Dissolve four teaspoons crystals in 1 gallon water. Immerse fruit in this solution as it is peeled and cut.

Commercial antioxidant: Readily available in supermarkets, commercial antioxidants are a mixture of ascorbic and citric acids or just citric acid with sugar added. Follow label directions for treating cut fruit.

Canning Fruit in a Pressure Canner

Prepare fruit as directed in each recipe. Fill and close jars. Arrange jars in pressure canner, leaving room between jars for steam to circulate, page 17. Place lid on canner. Bring pressure to 15 pounds as directed by manufacturer. *Immediately* remove canner from heat. Let cool undisturbed until all pressure is gone. Remove canner lid. Let jars stand 10 minutes in canner. Lift jars from canner. Cool to room temperature in a place free from drafts. Check seals. Label and store in a cool dark place.

Sugar Syrups

Use any of these syrups or the variations below when canning fruits.

	Light	**Medium**	**Heavy**
Sugar	2 cups	3 cups	4-3/4 cups
Water	4 cups	4 cups	4 cups

Combine sugar and water in a large saucepan. Gently stir over medium heat until sugar dissolves. Bring to a boil. Remove from heat. Cover; keep hot until needed. Bring back to a boil before adding to jars of fruit. Makes 5 to 6-1/2 cups.

Variations

Honey Syrup: Substitute mild-flavored honey for half the sugar in the medium, light or heavy syrup above. Heat as above.

Corn Syrup: Substitute light corn syrup for half the sugar in the medium, light or heavy syrup above. Heat as above.

Fruits: A to Z

Apples, Sliced

Varieties Best for Canning: Golden Delicious, Granny Smith, Jonathan, Newtown Pippin, Rome Beauty or other firm-textured, tart varieties, especially early fall apples.

Selection: Choose apples firm to the touch, with good color for variety and of uniform size. Skins should be smooth, have no bruises and no decaying spots. Golden Delicious, Newtown Pippin and Granny Smith should be yellow-green to green. Rome Beauty and Jonathan should be bright red.

Yield: 2 to 3 pounds (6 to 9 medium apples) = 1 quart; 1 bushel (48 pounds) = 16 to 20 quarts.

Canning Method: *Hot pack* in light or medium syrup. Process in a boiling-water bath.

Preparation: Wash pint, 1-1/2-pint or quart jars in hot soapy water; rinse. Keep hot until needed. Prepare lids as manufacturer directs. Prepare enough light or medium syrup, above, for all apples to be canned. Wash apples. Core, peel and slice uniformly. Treat with an antioxidant to prevent darkening, page 25. Prepare only as many apples as can be processed at one time. Lift slices out of solution; rinse. In a large pot, barely cover apple slices with syrup. Bring to a boil; boil 5 minutes. Pack hot apple slices into 1 hot jar at a time, leaving 1/2 inch headspace. Add boiling syrup to cover. Release trapped air. Wipe rim of jar with a clean damp cloth. Attach lid. Place in canner. Fill and close remaining jars.

Process in a boiling-water bath, page 17.
  Pints: 15 minutes
  Quarts: 20 minutes
Adjust times for altitude, page 20.

How to Use: Enjoy canned apples in pies, fillings for crepes or cakes, in breads and in desserts, such as apple crisp. When sweetened with sugar, puree and use for baby food.

Applesauce

Varieties Best for Applesauce: Beacon, Cortland, Gravenstein, Lodi or Wealthy. Use varieties with a soft to semifirm texture that are juicy and relatively sweet. Hard tart apples do not make good applesauce.

Selection: Do not use green, immature apples or early apples. Use fully mature apples, semifirm, not overripe. Cut away bruised areas. Avoid fruit with shriveled skins.

Yield: 2 to 3 pounds (6 to 9 medium apples) = 1 quart; 1 bushel (48 pounds) = 15 to 18 quarts.

Canning Method: *Hot pack* with or without sweetening. Process in a boiling-water bath.

Preparation: Wash pint, 1-1/2-pint or quart jars in hot soapy water; rinse. Keep hot until needed. Prepare lids as manufacturer directs. Wash and peel apples for a light-yellow applesauce or leave skins on for a deeper color. Cut apples into quarters; remove cores. Treat with an antioxidant to prevent darkening, page 25. Drain and rinse apples. Pour 1/4 to 1/2 cup water into a 4-quart or larger pot. Fill pot with apples to within 2 inches of top; cover. Stirring occasionally, cook over medium heat until apples are tender, 15 to 20 minutes. Stir to break up peeled apples to make chunky applesauce. Press unpeeled or peeled apples through a food mill for coarse applesauce. Or make a smooth applesauce by pureeing peeled apples in a blender or food processor. Sweeten to taste with sugar or honey, starting with 1 tablespoon per pound of apples. Add cinnamon to taste, if desired. Stirring constantly, bring just to a boil. Ladle hot applesauce into 1 hot jar at a time, leaving 1/4 inch headspace. Release trapped air. Wipe rim of jar with a clean damp cloth. Attach lid. Place in canner. Fill and close remaining jars.

Process in a boiling-water bath, page 17.

Pints, 1-1/2-pints or quarts: 20 minutes
Adjust time for altitude, page 20.

How to Use: Serve hot or cold. When sweetened with sugar, serve as baby food or flavoring for baby's cereal, page 25. Flavor cakes or breads as in Apple-Yogurt Wheat Loaf, page 170.

Apricots

Varieties Best for Canning: Autumn Royal, Earligold, Gold Kist, Goldcot, Golden Amber, Rival, Royal (Blenheim).

Selection: Should be tree-ripened, firm, plump and yellow to golden-orange. Avoid green, soft or shriveled apricots.

Yield: 2 pounds (about 20 apricots) = 1 quart; 1 lug (22 pounds) = 10 to 12 quarts.

Canning Method: Test apricots by dropping 3 or 4 in boiling water for 1 minute. *Hot pack* those that hold their shape. *Cold pack* more fragile varieties. Use a light or medium syrup. Process in a boiling-water bath.

Preparation: Wash pint, 1-1/2-pint or quart jars in hot soapy water; rinse. Keep hot until needed. Prepare lids as manufacturer directs. Prepare enough light or medium syrup, page 26, for all apricots to be canned. Wash apricots. If desired, drop in boiling water 30 seconds. Plunge into cold water; slip off skins, page 25. Leave whole or cut in half and remove pit. Treat with an antioxidant to prevent darkening, page 25. Lift apricots out of solution; rinse.

Cold Pack: Pack apricots into 1 hot jar at a time, cut-side down, overlapping halves. Or tightly pack whole apricots, leaving 1/2 inch headspace. Add boiling syrup to cover. Release trapped air. Wipe rim of jar with a clean damp cloth. Attach lid. Place in canner. Fill and close remaining jars.

Hot Pack: In a large pot, heat a single layer of apricots at a time in syrup until just heated

Place pared fruit in an antioxidant solution, page 25, to prevent darkening.

through. Pack hot apricots into 1 hot jar at a time, leaving 1/2 inch headspace. Add boiling syrup to cover. While another layer of fruit heats, release trapped air. Wipe rim of jar with a clean damp cloth. Attach lid. Place in canner. Fill and close remaining jars.

Process in a boiling-water bath, page 17.

> *Cold pack:*
> > Pints: 25 minutes
> > 1-1/2-pints or quarts: 30 minutes
> *Hot pack:*
> > Pints: 20 minutes
> > 1-1/2-pints or quarts: 25 minutes

Adjust times for altitude, page 20.

How to Use: Add to salads for color and flavor. Use in upside-down cake, fruit cakes, dumplings or meat dishes.

Bananas

Bananas are a soft-textured fruit that lose shape and darken with heating. Not generallly recommended for canning, but excellent in Spiced Bananas, page 79.

Berries

Varieties Best for Canning: *Soft berries:* blackberries, boysenberries, dewberries, loganberries, raspberries and youngberries. *Firm berries:* blueberries, currants, elderberries, gooseberries and huckleberries. Blueberries, opposite, and Gooseberries, page 32, require specific procedures to maintain whole, plump berries. Also see Cranberries, page 30. Strawberries do not can well by themselves.

Selection: Choose firm, plump, mature and full-colored berries. Avoid soft and mushy or hard and light-colored berries.

Yield: 5 to 8 (1/2-pint) baskets or 2 quarts (about 3 pounds) = 1 quart; 24-quart crate (36 pounds) = 12 to 18 quarts.

Canning Method: *Cold pack* soft berries; *hot pack* firm berries. Use a light or medium syrup. Process in a boiling-water bath.

Preparation: Wash pint, 1-1/2-pint or quart jars in hot soapy water; rinse. Keep hot until needed. Prepare lids as manufacturer directs. Wash 2 quarts (3 pounds) berries at a time in enough cold water for berries to float. Gently lift berries from water; remove stems.

Cold Pack: Prepare enough light or medium syrup, page 26, for all berries to be canned. Pack berries into 1 hot jar at a time, leaving 1/2 inch headspace, shaking to pack tightly. Add boiling syrup to cover. Release trapped air. Wipe rim of jar with a clean damp cloth. Attach lid. Place in canner. Fill and close remaining jars.

Hot Pack: In a large pot, combine 2 quarts washed berries and 1/2 to 1 cup sugar depending on sweetness desired. Let stand 1 hour until juice forms. Place over low to medium-low heat. Shaking pot to prevent scorching, heat slowly until mixture comes to a boil. *Do not stir.* Pack hot berries into 1 hot jar at a time, leaving 1/2 inch headspace. Add boiling juice to cover. If there is not enough juice, add boiling water to cover. Release trapped air. Wipe rim of jar with a clean damp cloth. Attach lid. Place in canner. Fill and close remaining jars.

Process in a boiling-water bath, page 17.

> *Cold pack:*
> > Pints: 15 minutes
> > 1-1/2-pints or quarts: 20 minutes
> *Hot pack:*
> > Pints: 10 minutes
> > 1-1/2-pints or quarts: 15 minutes

Adjust times for altitude, page 20.

How to Use: Add canned berries to winter salads, fruit compotes and gelatin molds. Thicken juice with cornstarch to make a syrup or sauce. Serve berries in syrup over ice cream, pudding or pound cake.

Blackberries

See Berries, opposite.

Blueberries

Selection: Choose large, plump, fully ripe blueberries that are deep blue-black. Large berries have a sweeter flavor than small berries. Avoid shriveled berries.

Yield: 5 to 8 (1/2-pint) baskets (about 3 pounds) = 1 quart; 24-quart crate (36 pounds) = 12 to 18 quarts.

Canning Method: Can as other firm berries, opposite. Or, blanch as directed and pack in light syrup. Process in a boiling-water bath.

Preparation: Wash pint, 1-1/2-pint or quart jars in hot soapy water; rinse. Keep hot until needed. Prepare lids as manufacturer directs. Can as other firm berries, to left, or blanch and can in light syrup. To blanch, wash 2 quarts blueberries in enough cold water for berries to float. Gently lift berries out of water; remove stems. Place on a large square of cheesecloth. Pull corners of cheesecloth together over berries. Or place berries in a metal colander or sieve. Prepare enough light syrup, page 26, for all blueberries to be canned. Bring syrup to a boil. Lower berries into boiling syrup, 15 seconds. Remove from boiling syrup; drain briefly over pan. Pack blanched berries into 1 hot jar at a time, leaving 1/2 inch headspace, shaking jar to pack tightly. Add blanching syrup to cover. Wipe rim of jar with a clean damp cloth. Attach lid. Place in canner. Fill and close remaining jars.

Process in a boiling-water bath, page 17.

  Pints: 15 minutes
  1-1/2-pints or quarts: 20 minutes
Adjust times for altitiude, page 20.

How to Use: Add canned whole blueberries to fresh fruit salads or serve on hot oatmeal. Fold into muffins, drop biscuits or fruit breads.

Boysenberries

See Berries, opposite.

Cherries, Sour

Varieties Best for Canning: Early Richmond and English Morello are very sour and considered only good for canning. Montmorency may be eaten fresh or canned. Varieties range from bright, medium red to dark red.

Selection: Choose large, firm, well-colored, blemish-free cherries.

Yield: 2 to 2-1/2 pounds = 1 quart; 1 bushel (56 pounds) = 22 to 32 quarts.

Canning Method: *Cold pack* in water or light syrup, or *hot pack* in their own juice. Light syrup helps color stay bright and gives a good flavor. Process in a boiling-water bath.

Preparation: Wash pint, 1-1/2-pint or quart jars in hot soapy water; rinse. Keep hot until needed. Prepare lids as manufacturer directs. Sterilize cherry pitter by boiling in water 15 minutes. Wash cherries in cold water to cover. Handle gently. Discard cherries that float; they may be wormy. Remove stems and pits.

Cold Pack: Bring 2 quarts water to a boil, or prepare enough light syrup, page 26, for all cherries to be canned. Pack cherries into 1 hot jar at a time, leaving 1/2 inch headspace, shaking to pack tightly. Add boiling water or syrup to cover.

A useful tool for removing lids from hot water is a lid lifter with a magnet on the end. See pages 11 and 12 for other canning aids.

Release trapped air. Wipe rim of jar with a clean damp cloth. Attach lid. Place in canner. Fill and close remaining jars.

Hot Pack: In a large pot, combine 2 quarts washed, pitted cherries, 1 cup sugar and 1/2 cup water. Place over medium-low heat. Shaking pot to prevent scorching, heat slowly over medium-low heat until mixture comes to a boil and juice forms. Pack hot cherries into 1 hot jar at a time, leaving 1/2 inch headspace. Add boiling juice to cover. If there is not enough juice, add boiling water to cover. Release trapped air. Wipe rim of jar with a clean damp cloth. Attach lid. Place in canner. Fill and close remaining jars.

Process in a boiling-water bath, page 17.

  Cold pack:
    Pints: 20 minutes
    1-1/2-pints or quarts: 25 minutes
  Hot pack:
    Pints: 10 minutes
    1-1/2-pints or quarts: 15 minutes
Adjust times for altitude, page 20.

How to Use: Bake in a cherry pie or cherry crisp. If packed in syrup or their own juice, thicken and serve as a sauce for ice cream, cake or crepes.

Cherries, Sweet **Photo on cover.**

Varieties Best for Canning: Bing, Golden Bing, Lambert, Royal Ann, Schmidt and Windsor. Schmidt and Windsor are firm and meaty. Bing and Lambert are usually eaten fresh, but can well. Royal Ann and Golden Bing are almost white, delicate and easily bruised. They are not often shipped fresh, but they can well.

Selection: Choose firm, well-colored, ripe cherries. Discard fruit that is soft, bruised or damaged, shriveled or that floats. Floating cherries may be wormy.

Yield: 2 to 2-1/2 pounds = 1 quart; 1 bushel (56 pounds) = 22 to 32 quarts.

Canning Method: *Cold pack* in light or medium syrup or *hot pack* in their own juice. Process in a boiling-water bath.

Preparation: Wash pint, 1-1/2-pint or quart jars in hot soapy water; rinse. Keep hot until needed. Prepare lids as manufacturer directs. Sterilize cherry pitter by boiling in water 15 minutes. Wash cherries, discarding those that float. Handle gently to prevent bruising. Lift from water; remove stems. Remove pits, if desired. Sweet cherries hold their shape better if they are not pitted. If cherries are not pitted, prick with a sterilized needle to keep skins from splitting.

Cold Pack: Prepare enough light or medium syrup, page 26, for all cherries to be canned. Pack cherries into 1 hot jar at a time, leaving 1/2 inch headspace, shaking to pack tightly. Add boiling syrup to cover. Release trapped air. Wipe rim of jar with a clean damp cloth. Attach lid. Place in canner. Fill and close remaining jars.

Hot Pack: In a large pot, combine 2 quarts washed cherries, 1-1/2 cups sugar and 1/2 cup water. Place over medium heat. Shaking pot to prevent sticking, heat slowly until mixture comes to a boil and juice forms. Pack hot cherries into 1 hot jar at a time, leaving 1/2 inch headspace. Add boiling juice to cover. If there is not enough juice, add boiling water to cover. Release trapped air. Wipe rim of jar with a clean damp cloth. Attach lid. Place in canner. Fill and close remaining jars.

Process in a boiling-water bath, page 17.

> *Cold pack:*
> Pints: 20 minutes
> 1-1/2-pints or quarts: 25 minutes
> *Hot pack:*
> Pints: 10 minutes
> 1-1/2-pints or quarts: 15 minutes

Adjust times for altitude, page 20.

How to Use: Serve alone or add to fruit compotes and molded gelatin salads. Toss with other fruits; top with chopped nuts. Thicken juice; serve cherries in thickened juice as a sauce for baked ham or waffles. Or use cherries in elegant Cherry-Chocolate Meringue Cups, page 176.

Crab Apples

This firm, very tart fruit looks like a small apple, but is not related to the apple. Crab apples make excellent jelly, page 64, or Spiced Crab Apples, page 86, but are not usually canned as a fruit.

Cranberries

Selection: Choose plump, firm berries with a glossy, deep-red skin. Discard any with soft spots or that are shriveled.

Yield: 12 ounces (about 3 cups) = four 1/2-pints whole-berry sauce or three 1/2-pints jellied sauce.

Canning Method: Can as other firm berries, page 28, or as directed below. *Hot pack only.* Process in a boiling-water bath.

Preparation: Use wide-mouth jars with straight sides for jellied sauce so it retains shape when removed from jars. Wash 1/2-pint or pint jars in hot soapy water; rinse. Keep hot until needed. Wash cranberries in enough cold water for berries to float. Lift from water; remove stems.

Whole-Berry Sauce: In a 4-quart pot, combine 4 cups sugar and 4 cups water. Bring to a boil over medium-high heat, stirring until sugar dissolves. Cover pot; boil 1 minute. Add 2 pounds or 8 cups washed cranberries. Cover pot. Reduce heat to medium-low. Cook until skins burst, about 5 minutes. Ladle berry mixture into 1 hot jar at a time, leaving 1/2 inch headspace. Release trapped air. Wipe rim of jar with a clean damp cloth. Attach lid. Place in canner. Fill and close remaining jars.

Jellied-Berry Sauce: In a 4-quart pot, combine 2 pounds or 8 cups washed cranberries and 4 cups water. Cover pot. Bring to a boil over medium heat. Cook until skins stop popping, 7 to 10 minutes. Force mixture through a food mill or fine sieve. Discard skins. Return sauce to pot. Stir in 4 cups sugar. Bring to a boil over medium heat. Place a candy thermometer into boiling mixture. Note temperature on thermometer. Continue to boil until temperature rises 8F (5C) or is done according to plate test as follows: Place 1 tablespoonful of sauce on a chilled plate. Refrigerate 1 to 2 minutes. If sauce does not run when plate is tipped and top wrinkles when lightly pressed with your fingers, sauce will gel when cooled. Ladle hot mixture into 1 hot jar at a time to within 1/8 inch of rim. Release trapped air. Wipe rim of jar with a clean damp cloth. Attach lid. Place in canner. Fill and close remaining jars.

Process in a boiling-water bath, page 17.

Whole-Berry Sauce:
    1/2-pints or pints: 10 minutes
Jellied-Berry Sauce:
    1/2-pints or pints: 10 minutes
Adjust times for altitude, page 20.

How to Use: Cranberry sauce with holiday turkey is a traditional combination. Also spread sauce on bread in meat sandwiches. Add Whole-Berry Sauce to molded salads. Melt Jellied-Berry Sauce; thin with fruit juice or wine to use as a glaze for pork chops, ribs or chicken.

Currants

Fresh currants are not common in fruit markets. Fresh currants are firm and are processed like other firm berries, page 28. Currants also make excellent jelly, page 64.

Elderberries

Small, firm, black elderberries are most often used in jelly or winemaking. Process them as you would other firm berries, page 28.

Figs

Varieties Best for Canning: Sweet Celeste figs are small and pear-shaped, with firm white flesh and ribbed violet over yellow-green skins. Kadota are larger than Celeste, pear-shaped and have yellow-green skins. Black Mission and Brown Turkey figs are also excellent for canning.

Selection: Figs deteriorate very quickly after picking. Process them immediately. Tree-ripened figs are sweeter than those picked green for shipping. Choose firm figs that are not hard, with color appropriate for variety. Avoid overripe figs with a sour or fermented odor and soft flesh.

Yield: 2 to 2-1/2 pounds = 1 quart.

Canning Method: *Hot pack* in light or medium syrup. Add lemon juice. Process in a boiling-water bath.

Preparation: Wash pint, 1-1/2-pint or quart jars in hot soapy water; rinse. Keep hot until needed. Prepare lids as manufacturer directs. Prepare enough light or medium syrup, page 26, for all figs to be canned; keep hot. Wash figs; do not peel or cut off stems. In a large pot, cover figs with hot water. Bring to a boil over medium-high heat. Remove from heat; let stand 3 minutes. Drain; discard liquid. Pack hot figs into 1 hot jar at a time, leaving 1/2 inch headspace. Add lemon juice, using 2 teaspoons in pints, 1 tablespoon in 1-1/2-pints and 1 tablespoon plus 1 teaspoon in quarts. Add boiling syrup to cover. Release trapped air. Wipe rim of jar with a clean damp cloth. Attach lid. Place in canner. Fill and close remaining jars.

Process in a boiling-water bath, page 17.
    Pints: 85 minutes
    1-1/2-pints or quarts: 90 minutes
Adjust times for altitude, page 20.

How to Use: Add figs, whole, halved or cut in chunks, to fruit salads. Use as a garnish for cheese and cold meat platters. Serve warmed in their own juice or over hot oatmeal for breakfast.

Fruit Purees

Fruits Best for Canning: Apples, apricots, peaches, pears or combinations of these fruits.

Selection: Use fruit that is ripe and colorful for its variety. Do not use overripe, bruised or blemished fruit.

Yield: 2 to 2-1/2 pounds = four 1/2-pint jars.

Canning Method: *Hot pack* with or without sweetening. Do not use honey if puree will be served to infants, page 25. Process in a boiling-water bath.

Preparation: Wash 1/2-pint, pint, 1-1/2-pint or quart jars in hot soapy water; rinse. Keep hot until needed. Prepare lids as manufacturer directs. Wash fruit; cut in half. Remove core or pit; cut in large pieces. Peeling is not necessary. Treat with an antioxidant to prevent darkening, page 25. Lift pieces out of solution; rinse. Put a single layer of fruit in a large pot. Crush with a potato masher to make juice. Stir in 1/4 to 1/2 cup water; add remaining fruit. Cover pot; simmer over medium-low heat until fruit is tender, 15 to 30 minutes. Stir occasionally, adding more water as needed to prevent sticking. Force fruit through a sieve or food mill. For a smoother puree, process pulp in a blender or food processor. Sweeten to taste, if desired. Return puree to pot. Over medium heat, bring just to a simmer. Ladle hot puree into 1 hot jar at a time, leaving 1/4 inch headspace. Release trapped air. Wipe rim of jar with a clean damp cloth. Attach lid. Place in canner. Fill and close remaining jars.

Process in a boiling-water bath, page 17.
   1/2-pints or pints: 15 minutes
   1-1/2-pints or quarts: 20 minutes
Adjust times for altitude, page 20.

How to Use: Spread on biscuits or toast for a low-calorie spread. Use as a filling for crepes; swirl through pudding; fold into a soft meringue to make fruit whip.

Gooseberries

Selection: Choose berries that are plump and light amber in color. Green underripe berries are very tart. Large berries are sweeter and more flavorful than small berries.

Yield: 5 to 8 (1/2-pint) baskets (about 3 pounds) = 1 quart.

Canning Method: *Hot pack.* Blanch and pack in medium syrup. If berries are small and green, use a heavy syrup. Process in a boiling-water bath.

Preparation: Wash pint, 1-1/2-pint or quart jars in hot soapy water; rinse. Keep hot until needed. Prepare lids as manufacturer directs. Prepare enough medium or heavy syrup, page 26, for all gooseberries to be canned. Wash gooseberries in enough cold water for berries to float. Gently lift berries out of water. Remove stems and tails. Put 4 cups berries in a metal sieve or colander or on a large square of cheesecloth. Pull corners of cheesecloth together over berries. Bring syrup to a boil. Lower berries into boiling syrup, 30 seconds. Drain briefly over pan. Pour blanched berries into a large pot; keep hot. Repeat until all gooseberries are blanched. Pack blanched berries into 1 hot jar at a time, leaving 1/2 inch headspace, shaking jar to pack tightly. Add boiling blanching syrup to cover. Release trapped air. Wipe rim of jar with a clean damp cloth. Attach lid. Place in canner. Fill and close remaining jars.

Process in a boiling-water bath, page 17.
   Pints: 15 minutes
   1-1/2-pints or quarts: 20 minutes
Adjust times for altitude, page 20.

How to Use: Use in pies, tarts, fruit salads and compotes. Thicken syrup, then heat berries in hot syrup. Use as a fruit filling or drop spoonfuls of dumpling batter in thickened fruit and syrup. Cover and cook over medium-low heat, 20 to 25 minutes.

Grapefruit & Oranges

Varieties Best for Canning: White grapefruit: Duncan or Marsh. Pink grapefruit: Ruby Red, Foster Pink or Marsh Pink. Use navel oranges for sections.

Selection: Choose heavy, firm, smooth-textured, tree-ripened fruit. Minor surface blemishes do not affect fruit quality. Avoid badly bruised or very lightweight fruit. Grapefruit range from pale yellow to russet or bronze. Color may not indicate ripeness. Most oranges have a vegetable dye added to outer skin to make them bright orange.

Yield: 5 pounds grapefruit (6 to 8 medium) = 1 quart. 5 pounds oranges (10 to 12 medium) = 1 quart.

Canning Method: *Cold pack.* Use a light syrup. Process in a boiling-water bath.

Preparation: Wash pint, 1-1/2-pint or quart jars in hot soapy water; rinse. Keep hot until needed. Prepare lids as manufacturer directs. Prepare enough light syrup, page 26, for all fruit to be canned. Wash grapefruit or oranges. Cut a slice from 1 end of fruit with a sharp knife. Work over a large bowl to catch juice. Starting from cut end, cut around fruit, removing peel and all white pith. Cut on both sides of membranes separating sections. Carefully lift out sections, page 121; discard seeds. Add juice in bowl to light syrup. Pack sections into 1 hot jar at a time, shaking to pack tightly. Leave 1/2 inch headspace. Add boiling syrup mixture to cover. Release trapped air. Wipe rim of jar with a clean damp cloth. Attach lid. Place in canner. Fill and close remaining jars.

Process in a boiling-water bath, page 17.
   Pints, 1-1/2-pints or quarts: 10 minutes
Adjust time for altitude, page 20.

How to Use: Arrange sections in decorative patterns in molded salads or add to fruit salad. Add sections to shrimp, crab or tuna salads.

Grapes

Varieties Best for Canning: Thompson seedless are small, olive-shaped and sweet. Process before color turns amber. Other varieties have skins that are not tender enough to can whole.

Selection: Choose small, green grapes with tender skins and no seeds. Bite a grape to test tenderness.

Yield: 4 pounds = 1 quart; 1 lug (28 pounds) = 7 to 8 quarts.

Mint Jelly, pages 64-65; Plum Jam and Strawberry Jam, pages 62-63

Canning Method: *Cold pack or hot pack* in medium syrup. Process in a boiling-water bath.

Preparation: Wash pint, 1-1/2-pint or quart jars in hot soapy water; rinse. Keep hot until needed. Prepare lids as manufacturer directs. Prepare enough medium syrup, page 26, for all grapes to be canned. Wash grapes under running water or in enough cold water for grapes to float. Lift from water; remove stems.

Cold Pack: Pack washed grapes into 1 hot jar at a time, leaving 1/2 inch headspace. Add boiling syrup to cover. Release trapped air. Wipe rim of jar with a clean damp cloth. Attach lid. Place in canner. Fill and close remaining jars.

Hot Pack: Add grapes to boiling syrup in a large pot. Return to a boil. Ladle hot grapes into 1 hot jar at a time, leaving 1/2 inch headspace. Add boiling syrup to cover. Release trapped air. Wipe rim of jar with a clean damp cloth. Attach lid. Place in canner. Fill and close remaining jars.

Process in a boiling-water bath, page 17.
  Cold pack:
    Pints: 20 minutes
    1-1/2-pints or quarts: 25 minutes
  Hot pack:
    Pints: 15 minutes
    1-1/2-pints or quarts: 20 minutes
Adjust times for altitude, page 20.

How to Use: Use canned grapes alone or with other fruits in fruit cocktail. Apples and grapes combined make excellent pies. Add to fruit salads and gelatin molds.

Guava

Selection: Choose firm fruit that are just beginning to soften, with no blemishes. Size varies from that of a walnut to an apple. Medium fruit yield the most pulp for weight. Skin is thin; flesh is red or yellow.

Yield: 2 to 2-1/2 pounds (12 to 15 guava) = 1 quart.

Canning Method: Let stand in light syrup 30 minutes. Process in a boiling-water bath.

Preparation: Wash pint, 1-1/2-pint or quart jars in hot soapy water; rinse. Keep hot until needed. Prepare lids as manufacturer directs. Prepare enough light syrup, page 26, for all guava to be canned. Wash guava; remove stem and peel. Cut in half; scoop out and discard seeds. In several large saucepans or bowls, arrange guava no more than 2 layers deep. Cover fruit with boiling syrup. Cover tightly; let stand 30 minutes. Pack fruit in overlapping layers in 1 hot jar at a time, leaving 1/2 inch headspace. Bring syrup to a boil again. Pour boiling syrup over guava to cover. Release trapped air. Wipe rim of jar with a clean damp cloth. Attach lid. Place in canner. Fill and close remaining jars.

Process in a boiling-water bath, page 17.
  Pints: 15 minutes
  1-1/2-pints or quarts: 20 minutes
Adjust times for altitude, page 20.

How to Use: Toss diced guava with orange sections, pineapple chunks and grated coconut for a light dessert. Fill guava halves with cream-cheese cubes and seafood for a light lunch.

Huckleberries

Often confused with blueberries because of their blue-black color, huckleberries are more acidic and each contains 10 small hard seeds. Can huckleberries like blueberries, page 28.

Kiwifruit or Berries

Originally from China, these fuzzy, brown-skinned fruit are now grown in New Zealand, Australia and California. In New Zealand and Australia, they are called *Chinese gooseberries*. The flesh is bright green with tender, edible black seeds. The fruit is sweet and juicy with a very subtle flavor. Not recommended for canning, they make an attractive preserve, page 126.

Kumquats

Selection: A member of the citrus family, kumquats have a thick, orange rind and are about the size of pecans. Use firm fruit that are heavy for their size. Rind should be uniformly orange, firm and wrinkle-free.

Yield: 1-1/2 to 2 pounds (about 6 cups) = four 1/2-pint jars.

Canning Method: *Hot pack* in medium syrup. Process in a boiling-water bath.

Preparation: Wash kumquats; remove stems. Prick each with a sharp fork to prevent bursting. Drop into boiling water in a large pot; return water to a boil. Reduce heat; cover pot. Simmer over medium-low heat until tender, 10 minutes. Drain; discard water. Prepare enough medium syrup, page 26, for all kumquats to be canned. Boil kumquats in syrup until glossy, 10 minutes. Remove from heat. Let kumquats stand in syrup

24 hours to plump. Wash 1/2-pint jars in hot soapy water; rinse. Keep hot until needed. Prepare lids as manufacturer directs. Remove kumquats from syrup; set syrup aside. Cut kumquats down 1 side; remove and discard seeds. Return seedless fruit to syrup. Bring to a boil; boil 3 minutes. Pack hot kumquats into 1 hot jar at a time, leaving 1/2 inch headspace. Add boiling syrup to cover. Release trapped air. Wipe rim of jar with a clean damp cloth. Attach lid. Place in canner. Fill and close remaining jars.

Process in a boiling-water bath, page 17.

1/2-pints: 15 minutes

Adjust time for altitude, page 20.

How to Use: Add sliced kumquats to fruit salads and compotes. Garnish beef, pork and poultry dishes with whole or sliced kumquats. Stuff kumquats with softened cream cheese and chopped almonds or pecans for an appetizer tray.

Loquats

Selection: Choose tree-ripened, well-colored yellow-orange fruit, free of blemishes and bruises. Flesh should be firm, but not hard. Loquats are similar to kumquats in size, shape and color, but have a thin, downy skin instead of a thick rind. These lightly sweet-tart fruit have tender skins like apricots. They are easily peeled. Loquats are usually available only where grown.

Yield: 1-1/2 to 2 pounds (about 6 cups) = 1 quart.

Canning Method: *Hot pack* in light syrup. Process in a boiling-water bath.

Preparation: Wash pint, 1-1/2-pint or quart jars in hot soapy water; rinse. Keep hot until needed. Prepare lids as manufacturer directs. Prepare enough light syrup, page 26, for all loquats to be canned. Wash loquats; remove stems and blossom fragments. If desired, peel fruit by immersing in boiling water, 30 seconds. Plunge in cold water; slip off skins, page 25. Cut fruit in half; discard seeds. Drop loquat halves in hot syrup; bring to a boil. Cook 3 minutes. Pack hot loquats into 1 hot jar at a time, leaving 1/2 inch headspace. Add boiling syrup to cover. Release trapped air. Wipe rim of jar with a clean damp cloth. Attach lid. Place in canner. Fill and close remaining jars.

Process in a boiling-water bath, page 17.

Pints: 15 minutes

1-1/2-pints or quarts: 20 minutes

Adjust times for altitude, page 20.

How to Use: Use like peaches or apricots in salads, breads, cakes, pies and other desserts.

Mangoes

Selection: Choose ripe, slightly firm mangoes with yellow-orange skins with patches of red. Avoid hard, green or dried, shriveled fruit.

Yield: 2 to 2-1/2 pounds = 1 quart.

Canning Method: *Cold pack* in light syrup. Process in a boiling-water bath.

Preparation: Wash pint, 1-1/2-pint or quart jars in hot soapy water; rinse. Keep hot until needed. Prepare lids as manufacturer directs. Prepare enough light syrup, page 26, for all mangoes to be canned. Wash, peel and slice mangoes. Pack mango slices into 1 hot jar at a time, leaving 1/2 inch headspace. Add boiling syrup to cover. Release trapped air. Wipe rim of jar with a clean damp cloth. Attach lid. Place in canner. Fill and close remaining jars.

Process in a boiling-water bath, page 17.

Pints: 15 minutes

1-1/2-pints or quarts: 20 minutes

Adjust times for altitude, page 20.

How to Use: Heat mango slices and syrup. Stir in 1 teaspoon vanilla and a dash of ground cinnamon. Serve warm with a dollop of pineapple- or lemon-flavored yogurt. Include mango slices in salads and gelatins.

Melon

Melons are not acidic enough to can in a water bath and too delicate to withstand pressure canning. Melon balls may be canned with pineapple as in Honey-Melon Balls, page 80.

Nectarines

Selection: Choose plump, firm fruit that are yellow-orange with patches of red. Do not use hard or shriveled fruit or those with bruised or broken skins.

Yield: 2 to 2-1/2 pounds (6 to 8 medium) = 1 quart; 1 lug (20 pounds) = 7 to 10 quarts.

Canning Method: *Cold pack or hot pack* in light or medium syrup. Process in a boiling-water bath.

Preparation: Wash pint, 1-1/2-pint or quart jars in hot soapy water; rinse. Keep hot until needed. Prepare lids as manufacturer directs. Prepare enough light or medium syrup, page 26, for all nectarines to be canned. If fruit is fully ripe and very juicy, do not peel. To peel less-ripe fruit, drop into boiling water, 30 seconds. Lift out fruit; plunge in cold water. Slip off skins, page 25. Cut nectarines in half; remove pits. Leave in halves or slice. Treat with an antioxidant to prevent darkening, page 25. Lift fruit out of solution; rinse.

Cold Pack: Pack nectarine halves or slices into 1 hot jar at a time, leaving 1/2 inch headspace. Add boiling syrup to cover. Release trapped air. Wipe rim of jar with a clean damp cloth. Attach lid. Place in canner. Fill and close remaining jars.

Hot Pack: In a large saucepan, heat a single layer of fruit in syrup until just heated through. Pack hot nectarine halves or slices into 1 hot jar at a time, leaving 1/2 inch headspace. Add boiling syrup to cover. While another layer of fruit heats, release trapped air. Wipe rim of jar with a clean damp cloth. Attach lid. Place in canner. Fill and close remaining jars.

Process in a boiling-water bath, page 17.
> *Cold pack:*
>> Pints: 25 minutes
>> 1-1/2-pints or quarts: 30 minutes
> *Hot pack:*
>> Pints: 20 minutes
>> 1-1/2-pints or quarts: 25 minutes

Adjust times for altitude, page 20.

How to Use: Use nectarines for a different flavor in dumplings, pies, cobblers, breads and muffins.

Orange Sections

See Grapefruits & Oranges, page 32.

Papaya

Not recommended for canning by itself. This tropical fruit has limited availability because it does not ship well. Papaya is best enjoyed fresh in salads or broiled to accompany meats. Also try it in Tropical Fruit Cocktail, page 80.

Peaches   Photo on cover.

Varieties Best for Canning: Cling: any that are ripe. Freestone: Elberta, Golden Jubilee, Jerseyland, Keystone, Red Top, Sentinel, Suncrest and many others.

Selection: Use fairly firm, tree-ripened peaches. Skin should be yellow or creamy yellow with some red blush. Avoid very firm or hard peaches with a greenish skin. These are immature and will

not ripen. Do not use soft overripe fruit. Peaches that are very tender and juicy do not hold their shape when canned. They are best eaten fresh.

Yield: 2 to 2-1/2 pounds (6 to 8 medium) = 1 quart; 20-pound lug = 7 to 10 quarts.

Canning Method: *Cold pack or hot pack* in light or medium syrup or in their own juice. Process in a boiling-water bath.

Preparation: Wash pint, 1-1/2-pint or quart jars in hot soapy water; rinse. Keep hot until needed. Prepare lids as manufacturer directs. Prepare enough syrup, page 26, for all peaches to be canned. Wash peaches. Drop 4 or 5 peaches at a time in gently boiling water, 30 seconds. Plunge into cold water; slip off skins, page 25. Cut peaches in half; remove stones. Use a spoon to scrape reddish flesh from cavity of peach; stone residue darkens with canning. Slice peach halves, if desired. Treat with an antioxidant to prevent darkening, page 25. Lift fruit out of solution; rinse.

Cold Pack: Pack peach halves, cut-side down, in overlapping layers or, pack slices into 1 hot jar at a time, leaving 1/2 inch headspace. Pour boiling syrup over peaches to cover. Release trapped air. Wipe rim of jar with a clean damp cloth. Attach lid. Place in canner. Fill and close remaining jars.

Hot Pack: Heat peach halves or slices in a single layer in syrup until heated through, about 3 minutes. Pack hot peach halves, cut-side down, in loose overlapping layers into 1 hot jar at a time, leaving 1/2 inch headspace. Add boiling syrup to cover. Release trapped air. Wipe rim of jar with a clean damp cloth. Attach lid. Place in canner. Fill and close remaining jars.

Hot Pack in Own Juice: Combine 4 quarts peach halves or slices, 1-1/2 cups sugar and 1/4 cup water in a large pot. Place over low heat. Shake pot occasionally until all peaches are heated through and juice forms. Stir gently, if necessary. Pack hot fruit into 1 hot jar at a time, leaving 1/2 inch headspace. Add boiling juice from pan to cover. Release trapped air. Wipe rim of jar with a clean damp cloth. Attach lid. Place in canner. Fill and close remaining jars.

Process in a boiling-water bath, page 17.
> *Cold pack:*
>> Pints: 25 minutes
>> 1-1/2-pints or quarts: 30 minutes
> *Hot pack:*
>> Pints: 20 minutes
>> 1-1/2-pints or quarts: 25 minutes

Adjust times for altitude, page 20.

How to Use: Use canned peaches in fruit salads, puddings, muffins and baked desserts. Or, serve as an accompaniment to meats or main dishes.

Pears

Varieties Best for Canning: Bartlett, D'Anjou and Winter Nelis are considered best. Bosc are soft, but may be canned. Keiffer and Seckel are more firm and make excellent spiced or pickled pears. These firm pears may be canned when thoroughly ripe if they are simmered in water until tender before being packed in syrup.

Selection: Pears are one of the few fruit to ripen off the tree. Pears are picked mature, but hard and green and allowed to ripen. Select plump, bell-shaped pears with stems attached. Flesh should be firm but yield to slight pressure at the stem end. Pears may have a faint greenish tinge to an otherwise clear yellow or russet skin.

Yield: 2 to 2-1/2 pounds (6 to 8 medium) = 1 quart; 1 bushel (50 pounds) = 20 to 25 quarts.

Canning Method: *Hot pack* in light or medium syrup. Process in a boiling-water bath.

Preparation: Wash pint, 1-1/2-pint or quart jars in hot soapy water; rinse. Keep hot until needed. Prepare lids as manufacturer directs. Prepare enough syrup, page 26, for all pears to be canned. Wash pears. Peel and cut in halves. Core, using a melon baller or round measuring spoon and paring knife. Treat with an antioxidant to prevent darkening, page 25. Lift pears out of solution; rinse. In a large saucepan, heat pears in a single layer in syrup until heated through, about 3 minutes. Pack hot pear halves into 1 hot jar at a time, leaving 1/2 inch headspace. Add boiling syrup to cover. While another layer of fruit heats, release trapped air. Wipe rim of jar with a clean damp cloth. Attach lid. Place in canner. Fill and close remaining jars.

Process in a boiling-water bath, page 17.
　　Pints: 20 minutes
　　1-1/2-pints or quarts: 25 minutes
Adjust times for altitude, page 20.

How to Use: Use canned pears in fruit compotes, fruit salads, meat or fish salads, pies, tarts or frozen desserts.

Persimmons

Ripe persimmons are very soft and not suitable for canning.

Using long narrow food tongs, arrange peaches, pears and other large fruit in overlapping layers.

Pineapples

Selection: Pineapples are picked at the peak of ripeness and do not ripen once harvested. Select large fruit with a sweet, fresh fragrance and fresh-looking, green crown leaves. Plump fruit will have the greatest proportion of edible fruit. Avoid bruised fruit or fruit with soft spots.

Yield: 3 pounds (1 medium) = 1 quart.

Canning Method: *Hot pack* in a light or medium syrup. Process in a boiling-water bath.

Preparation: Wash pint, 1-1/2-pint or quart jars in hot soapy water; rinse. Use wide mouth jars for pineapple rings. Keep hot until needed. Prepare lids as manufacturer directs. Prepare enough syrup, page 26, for all pineapple to be canned. Scrub pineapple with a brush. Using a long knife, cut a slice off top and bottom of pineapple. Stand pineapple top-side up. Slicing from top to bottom, cut off shell. Remove *eyes* with a paring knife, below. For spears, cut trimmed pineapple from top to bottom in wedges. Cut off about 3/4 inch from wedge point to remove core. Cut each long wedge in half, if desired. To make rings or chunks, lay shelled pineapple, with eyes removed, on its side. Cut in even 1/4 inch slices. Use the center of a doughnut cutter or a knife to remove core from center of each slice. Trim edges to make round slices, if desired. Cut each slice in even pieces to make chunks. Chop trimmings and slices to make crushed pineapple. Bring syrup to a boil in a large pot. Add pineapple; simmer until tender, about 5 minutes. Pack hot pineapple into 1 hot jar at a time, leaving 1/2 inch headspace. Add boiling syrup to cover. Release trapped air. Wipe rim of jar with a clean damp cloth. Attach lid. Place in canner. Fill and close remaining jars.

Process in a boiling-water bath, page 17.

Pints: 15 minutes

1-1/2-pints or quarts: 20 minutes

Adjust times for altitude, page 20.

How to Use: Serve pineapple with cheese and other fruit as appetizers; include in fruit and gelatin salads; cook with meats for a sweet-and-sour main dish. Use pineapple in a wide array of desserts.

Plums & Prune Plums

Varieties Best for Canning: Firm, meaty varieties can better than those that are very juicy. Brooks and Italian or Milton are prune plums especially suited to canning because they hold their

1/Cut a slice off top and bottom of pineapple. Slicing from top to bottom, cut off shell.

2/Use a paring knife to cut diagonal wedges or grooves to remove eyes. Lift out wedge containing eyes.

shape well and the pit separates easily.

Yield: 2 to 2-1/2 pounds (8 to 20 plums) = 1 quart; 20-pound crate = 8 to 13 quarts.

Canning Method: *Cold pack or hot pack* in light, medium or heavy syrup. Process in a boiling-water bath.

Preparation: Wash pint, 1-1/2-pint or quart jars in hot soapy water; rinse. Keep hot until needed. Prepare lids as manufacturer directs. Prepare enough syrup, page 26, for all plums to be canned. Wash plums. If canning whole, prick skins with a scalded needle to keep fruit from bursting. Italian prune plums may be cut in half and pits removed.

Cold Pack: Pack plums tightly into 1 hot jar at a time, leaving 1/2 inch headspace. Add boiling syrup to cover. Release trapped air. Wipe rim of jar with a clean damp cloth. Attach lid. Place in canner. Fill and close remaining jars.

Hot Pack: Add plums to boiling syrup; heat 2 minutes. Pack hot plum halves into 1 hot jar at a time, leaving 1/2 inch headspace. If plums are whole, remove from heat; cover pot. Set aside 30 minutes. Pack whole plums into 1 hot jar at a time, leaving 1/2 inch headspace. Bring syrup to a boil; pour over plums to cover. Release trapped air. Wipe rim of jar with a clean damp cloth.

Attach lid. Place in canner. Fill and close remaining jars.

Process in a boiling-water bath, page 17.

   Cold pack or hot pack:
     Pints: 20 minutes
      1-1/2-pints or quarts: 25 minutes

Adjust times for altitude, page 20.

How to Use: Canned plums are delicious served warm and spiced with cinnamon. Also use them in plum pudding, cobblers and deep-dish pies.

Pomegranates

Leathery skinned pomegranates are not suited to canning by themselves, but are excellent in Grenadine Syrup, page 88.

Raspberries

Can this most fragile of soft berries as directed on page 28. Also use them in jam or jelly, pages 62-65; Berry Syrup, page 89; Cherry-Berry Preserves, page 125; and Peach-Melba Conserve, page 121.

3/For spears, cut trimmed pineapple from top to bottom in wedges. Cut off wedge point to remove core.

4/To make rings, cut pineapple in 1/4-inch slices. Trim edges; cut out center with center of a doughnut cutter.

Rhubarb

Varieties Best for Canning: All varieties can well. Forced or hot-house rhubarb is light pink with slender stalks.

Selection: Choose firm, crisp and bright-red garden stalks or pink hot-house stalks. Pull garden stalks from the ground—do not cut. Avoid wilted, oversized or very thin stalks. Rhubarb leaves contain poisonous oxalic acid. *Discard leaves immediately after picking.*

Yield: 1-1/2 to 2 pounds = 1 quart; 15 pounds = 7 to 10 quarts.

Canning Method: *Hot pack* in syrup made from their own juice. Process in a boiling-water bath.

Preparation: Wash rhubarb stalks; cut in 1/2 inch slices. Measure yield. In a large pot, combine rhubarb and 1/2 cup sugar for each 4 cups rhubarb slices. Stir gently; set aside until juices begin to form, about 2 hours. Wash pint, 1-1/2-pint or quart jars in hot soapy water; rinse. Keep hot until needed. Prepare lids as manufacturer directs. Over medium-low heat, stir gently until rhubarb mixture comes to a boil. Ladle hot rhubarb mixture into 1 hot jar at a time, leaving 1/2 inch headspace. Release trapped air. Wipe rim of jar with a clean damp cloth. Attach lid. Place in canner. Fill and close remaining jars.

Process in a boiling-water bath, page 17.

Pints, 1-1/2-pints or quarts: 10 minutes

Adjust time for altitude, page 20.

How to Use: Serve rhubarb sauce hot or cold to accompany meals or as dessert. Combine with an equal amount of applesauce for a tangy treat. Use to make rhubarb crisp or cobbler. Especially good combined with strawberries in pies.

Strawberries

Canning is not recommended. Strawberries tend to fade in color, float and lose flavor. Use them in jam or jelly, pages 62-65, Berry Juice, below, or May-Day Jam, page 118.

Fruit Juices

Apricot, Pear or Peach Nectar

Selection: Use fully ripe, soft but not overripe fruit. Overripe fruit has a flat flavor. If fruit is very firm or has tinges of green, wait several days for fruit to ripen. Do not use badly bruised or decaying fruit for nectar.

Yield: About 5 pounds = 4 pints or 2 quarts.

Canning Method: *Hot pack.* Process in a boiling-water bath.

Preparation: Wash pint, 1-1/2-pint or quart jars in hot soapy water; rinse. Keep hot until needed. Prepare lids as manufacturer directs. Wash fruit; do not peel. Cut fruit in half; core or pit, then slice. Measure 10 cups sliced fruit into a 4-quart pot. Add 1/2 cup water and 1 tablespoon lemon juice. Cover and cook over low heat until fruit is very soft, about 30 minutes. *Do not boil.* Force mixture through a food mill or fine sieve. Discard peels. Puree sieved mixture in a blender for a smoother nectar. Return nectar to pot. Add syrup and juice as follows: *apricot nectar:* 2 cups light syrup, page 26, and 1/2 cup pineapple juice; *pear nectar:* 2 cups light syrup and 1/2 cup orange-pineapple juice; *peach nectar:* 2 cups light honey syrup, page 26, and 1/2 cup orange juice. Over medium heat, bring just to a simmer, 200F (93C). Pour hot nectar mixture into 1 hot jar at a time, leaving 1/4 inch headspace. Wipe rim of jar with a clean damp cloth. Attach lid. Place in canner. Fill and close remaining jars.

Process in a boiling-water bath, page 17.

Pints, 1-1/2-pints or quarts: 15 minutes

Adjust time for altitude, page 20.

How to Use: Fruit nectars are filling drinks. Serve in small amounts. Use as liquid in gelatin salads.

Berry Juice

Selection: Choose plump sweet blackberries, blueberries, boysenberries, raspberries or strawberries that are full colored. Do not use soft, mushy berries or firm, light-colored or green berries.

Yield: 4 quarts berries = 6 pints or 3 quarts.

Canning Method: *Hot pack* extracted juice. Process in a boiling-water bath.

Preparation: Wash pint, 1-1/2-pint or quart jars in hot soapy water; rinse. Keep hot until needed. Prepare lids as manufacturer directs. Prepare 3 to 4 cups medium syrup, page 26, for each 4 quarts of berries. Wash berries in enough cold water for berries to float. Lift berries from water; remove stems. In a 6-quart pot, crush berries with a potato masher. Cover and cook over low heat to 185F (88C). *Do not boil.* Pour into a damp jelly bag or cheesecloth-lined sieve placed over a bowl. Squeeze to remove as much juice as possible, then strain again into pot. Add syrup to taste. Tart berries will need about 4 cups syrup. Over medium heat, bring just to a simmer, 200F (93C). Pour juice into 1 hot jar at a time, leaving 1/4 inch headspace. Wipe rim of jar with a clean damp cloth. Attach lid. Place in canner. Fill and close remaining jars.

Process in a boiling-water bath, page 17.

Pints, 1-1/2-pints or quarts: 15 minutes
Adjust time for altitude, page 20.

How to Use: Combine berry juices with a thawed 6-ounce can of lemonade concentrate. Puree in a blender with enough ice to fill container. Or combine berry juice with sparkling water. Pour over ice in a tall drinking glass.

Citrus Juices

Selection: Choose firm, heavy grapefruit or oranges. Do not use overripe or shriveled fruit.

Yield: 6 pounds (8 to 10 medium) = about 2 pints or 1 quart.

Canning Method: *Hot pack.* Process in a boiling-water bath.

Preparation: Wash pint, 1-1/2-pint or quart jars in hot soapy water; rinse. Keep hot until needed. Prepare lids as manufacturer directs. Room-temperature fruit release more juice than cold fruit. Scrub fruit under running water. Cut in half. Ream or squeeze out juice. Strain through a cheesecloth-lined sieve or jelly bag. In a 4-quart pot, heat juice to 185F (85C). *Do not boil.* Pour hot juice into 1 hot jar at a time, leaving 1/4 inch headspace. Wipe rim of jar with a clean damp cloth. Attach lid. Place in canner. Fill and close remaining jars.

Process in a boiling-water bath, page 17.

Pints, 1-1/2-pints or quarts: 15 minutes
Adjust time for altitude, page 20.

How to Use: Serve chilled juice as a refreshing breakfast or afternoon drink. Also use grapefruit juice as a cocktail mixer or in punch with orange juice, tea and orange sherbet.

Cranapple Juice

Selection: Choose plump, firm cranberries with deep-red skins. Use freshly pressed or commercial apple juice, sweetened or unsweetened.

Yield: 1 pound cranberries (about 4 cups) plus 6 cups apple juice = 5 pints.

Canning Method: *Hot pack.* Process in a boiling-water bath.

Preparation: Wash pint, 1-1/2-pint or quart jars in hot soapy water; rinse. Keep hot until needed. Prepare lids as manufacturer directs. Prepare cranberry juice without adding sugar, below. Measure juice. For every 4 cups cranberry juice, add 6 cups apple juice. Combine juices in a large pot. Add sugar to taste, about 3/4 cup per quart of juice. Over medium-low heat, bring just to a simmer. Pour juice into 1 hot jar at a time, leaving 1/4 inch headspace. Wipe rim of jar with a clean damp cloth. Attach lid. Place in canner. Fill and close remaining jars.

Process in a boiling-water bath, page 17.

Pints, 1-1/2-pints or quarts: 15 minutes.
Adjust time for altitude, page 20.

How To Use: Use as liquid with unflavored gelatin in molded strawberry or apple-walnut salads. Serve over ice, or serve hot with a cinnamon-candy stick as a swizzle stick.

Cranberry Juice

Selection: Choose plump, firm berries with glossy, deep-red skins. Discard any with soft spots or that are shriveled.

Yield: 1 pound (about 4 cups) = 1 quart.

Canning Method: *Hot pack* extracted juice. Process in a boiling-water bath.

Preparation: Wash pint, 1-1/2-pint or quart jars in hot soapy water; rinse. Keep hot until needed. Prepare lids as manufacturer directs. Wash cranberries; measure. In a large pot, combine cranberries and an equal amount of water. Bring to a boil over medium heat. Cover pot. Reduce heat to medium-low. Cook until skins burst, about 5 minutes. Strain cranberries through a cheesecloth-lined sieve or jelly bag. Squeeze to remove as much juice as possible. Strain again. Return juice to pot. Add sugar to taste, about 1-1/2 cups per quart of juice. Over medium-low heat, bring just to a simmer, 200F (93C). Pour juice into 1 hot jar at a time, leaving 1/4 inch headspace. Wipe rim of jar with a clean damp cloth. Attach lid. Place in canner. Fill and close remaining jars.

Process in a boiling-water bath, page 17.
    Pints, 1-1/2-pints or quarts: 15 minutes
Adjust time for altitude, page 20.

How To Use: Pour chilled juice into a tall drinking glass; top with a scoop of lemon sherbet. Or heat with mulling spices to serve steaming hot.

Grape Juice

Varieties Best for Juice: Use any variety of red or green grape. Concord grapes make an especially full-flavored juice.

Selection: Choose large plump grapes with full color for their variety.

Yield: 4 quarts grapes = 4 quarts grapes in their own juice; 4 quarts grapes = 5 pints extracted juice.

Canning Method: *Cold pack* whole grapes in boiling water; *hot pack* extracted juice. Process in a boiling-water bath.

Preparation: For cold pack, wash pint, 1-1/2-pint or quart jars in hot soapy water; rinse. Keep hot until needed. Prepare lids according to manufacturer's directions. Wash grapes for either pack under running water or in enough cold water for grapes to float. Remove stems.

Cold Pack: Tightly pack washed grapes into 1 hot jar at a time, leaving 1/2 inch headspace. Pour boiling water over grapes to cover. Release trapped air. Wipe rim of jar with a clean damp cloth. Attach lid. Place in canner. Fill and close remaining jars.

Extracted juice: Measure whole grapes as they are put into a large pot; crush grapes. Add 1 cup water for each 4 quarts of whole grapes. Cook over low heat until very soft, about 10 minutes. *Do not boil.* Strain juice through a jelly bag or cheesecloth-lined sieve. Squeeze bag or cheesecloth to remove as much juice as possible. Refrigerate juice 24 hours; strain again to remove tartaric acid crystals that form. Heat juice to 185F (85C). Wash pint, 1-1/2-pint or quart jars in hot soapy water; rinse. Keep hot until needed. Prepare lids according to manufacturer's directions. Pour hot juice into 1 hot jar at a time, leaving 1/4 inch headspace. Wipe rim of jar with a clean damp cloth. Attach lid. Place in canner. Fill and close remaining jars.

Process in a boiling-water bath, page 17.
    Cold pack:
        Pints: 20 minutes
        1-1/2-pints or quarts: 25 minutes
    Extracted juice:
        Pints, 1-1/2-pints or quarts: 15 minutes
Adjust times for altitude, page 20.

How to Use: Use as a delightful cold drink. Grape juice can be used to make jelly, pages 64-65.

Peach Nectar

See page 40.

Pear Nectar

See page 40.

Plum Juice

Varieties: Burbank, Laroda or Santa Rosa make the best juice. Plump, ripe prune plums may also be used for juice.

Selection: Choose plump, tender plums that yield to the touch. They should not be firm, hard or overly soft.

Yield: 6 pounds = 6 pints or 3 quarts.

Canning Method: *Hot pack* extracted juice. Process in a boiling-water bath.

Preparation: Wash pint, 1-1/2-pint or quart jars in hot soapy water; rinse. Keep hot until needed. Prepare lids as manufacturer directs. Wash plums; cut in pieces discarding pits. In a 6-quart pot, combine 14 cups cut plums (6 pounds whole plums) and 10 cups water. Cover and cook over low heat until plums are very soft, about 30 minutes. *Do not boil.* Strain plums through a cheesecloth-lined sieve or jelly bag. Squeeze to remove as much juice as possible. Return juice to pot. Add 2 to 2-1/2 cups sugar or to taste. Over medium heat, bring just to a simmer, 200F (93C). Pour juice into 1 hot jar at a time, leaving 1/4 inch headspace. Wipe rim of jar with a clean damp cloth. Attach lid. Place in canner. Fill and close remaining jars.

Process in a boiling-water bath, page 17.
    Pints, 1-1/2-pints or quarts: 15 minutes
Adjust time for altitude, page 20.

How to Use: Serve chilled with club soda or flavor hot plum juice to taste with cinnamon, nutmeg and cloves.

Basic Canning:
Vegetables

Vegetables, except tomatoes, are low-acid and must be canned with a pressure canner. If you don't have a pressure canner, *do not use any other method!* No other method is safe. Read *How to Can—Start to Finish,* page 14, and *Pressure Canning At A Glance,* page 21.

Some varieties of vegetables withstand high processing temperatures for relatively long periods of time. Others do not. To ensure tender, flavorful vegetables, use varieties we suggest. Talk with your county cooperative extension or agricultural personnel about varieties grown locally. Seed packets and seed catalogs often tell which varieties can best. Without a pressure canner, you may still preserve garden-fresh vegetables by pickling or freezing. Pickled vegetables have a crisp, fresh, tart flavor. See *Canning with Flair—Vegetables,* page 90.

Some vegetables are not recommended for canning for safety reasons or because results are not worth the effort. Though results for some are disappointing, directions have been included for those who may still want to can them. If directions are not given or referred to, do not use the directions for another vegetable. *Follow directions exactly for the specific vegetable you are canning.*

The number of jars you get from a bushel or given weight of a vegetable will vary. Yield depends on quality, size and shape of pieces of the vegetable and whether you use hot or cold pack. With high-quality vegetables, little trimming is necessary and yields are high. It requires fewer jars to can small, uniformly shaped pieces. Heat causes vegetables to shrink, so hot-packed vegetables give a smaller yield than cold-packed.

Salt adds flavor to canned vegetables, but is not needed for safe preservation. You may omit the salt or add less than is suggested. *Do not use salt substitutes in canning.* Some create a disagreeable aftertaste. Process the vegetable without salt, then add a salt substitute before it is served.
Caution—It is possible for canned vegetables to contain food-poisoning toxins without any signs of spoilage, pages 18 and 19. Before serving, bring canned vegetables to a full rolling boil. Cover and boil 15 to 20 minutes. If they are baked in a combination dish, bake at least 30 minutes at 350F (175C). If the vegetable is to be used cold in a salad, boil it as directed above, then chill in the refrigerator before adding to the salad.

Follow directions for packing each vegetable. Starchy vegetables, such as corn, peas, lima beans and dry beans, absorb water during processing and should be loosely packed. Vegetables that are packed raw, such as green beans, should be tightly packed.

Raw- or *cold-packed* food requires more time to process than *hot-packed* food. Some vegetables, such as greens, potatoes, beets and peppers, *must* be hot packed. When both methods may be used, hot-pack usually is recommended. However, whole green beans or asparagus packed raw in jars, are more attractive because they keep their shape and color better than when hot packed in hot canning jars.

Fill and close 1 hot canning jar at a time. Add *boiling liquid* to cover the vegetable. The *headspace* for most vegetables is 1 inch after the liquid is added. When hot packing vegetables, cover them with the water used for heating. This helps retain water-soluble nutrients. Use fresh boiling water when cold packing.

Attach the lid before filling the next jar to minimize the introduction of airborne organisms. Prepare only enough vegetables to make 1 canner load of jars.

Vegetables: A to Z

Artichoke Hearts

Varieties Best for Canning: Globe artichokes are unopened flowers of a thistle-like plant. Can center or heart of the bud. Jerusalem artichoke or sunchoke is a tuber not suitable for canning.
Selection: Choose small, plump and heavy artichokes about 3 inches long with tight-fitting olive-green leaves. Avoid soft brown artichokes.
Yield: 20 to 30 artichokes = 1 quart.
Canning Method: Precook in a vinegar solution. *Hot pack* in a light brine. Process in a pressure canner.
Preparation: Wash pint, 1-1/2-pint or quart jars in hot soapy water; rinse. Keep hot until needed. Prepare lids as manufacturer directs. In a large pot, prepare a canning brine of 3/4 cup white vinegar, 3 tablespoons salt and 1 gallon water. Bring to a boil over high heat; keep hot. Cut stems off artichokes at base. Pull off tough outer leaves down to tender inner leaves. Use pulp from outer leaves in artichoke soup. Cut off top of artichoke bud, leaving choke. In another large pot, combine 3/4 cup white vinegar and 1 gallon water. Bring to a boil. Add trimmed artichokes. Return to a boil; simmer 5 minutes. Drain artichokes on paper towels; discard cooking liquid. Pack hot artichoke hearts into 1 hot jar at a time, leaving 1 inch headspace. Add hot canning brine to cover. Release trapped air. Wipe rim of jar. Attach lid. Place in canner. Fill and close remaining jars.

Process in a pressure canner at 10 pounds pressure, page 17.
Pints, 1-1/2-pints or quarts: 25 minutes
Adjust pressure for altitude, page 21.
How to Use: Remove choke from canned artichokes. Add hearts to tossed vegetable salads or split and use as a base for seafood salads. Add chopped hearts to creamed chicken or seafood dishes. Heat and toss with Italian dressing.

Asparagus

Varieties Best for Canning: Green asparagus varieties are most commonly used for canning. Commercially canned white asparagus is actually green asparagus harvested while the stalk is still below the ground. Asparagus loses its crispness and delicate flavor with canning.
Selection: Can straight, firm stalks with tight, small buds. Avoid wilted stalks with loose buds. Thick stalks with only 1 inch of tough base will be more tender than thin stalks.
Yield: 3 to 4 pounds = 1 quart; 1 bushel (45 pounds) = 11 quarts.
Canning Method: *Cold pack or hot pack.* Process in a pressure canner.
Preparation: Wash pint, 1-1/2-pint or quart jars in hot soapy water; rinse. Keep hot until needed. Prepare lids as manufacturer directs. Wash asparagus; break off tough ends of stalks where they snap easily. Wash again under running water. If

canning spears, sort for uniform size. Trim 1 inch shorter than jars. Or, cut stalks in 1-inch pieces. In a large pot, bring 1 gallon water to a boil.

Cold Pack: Tightly pack asparagus into 1 hot jar at a time, leaving 1 inch headspace. Pack spears stem-end down. Add salt, if desired, using 1/2 teaspoon in pints, 3/4 teaspoon in 1-1/2-pints and 1 teaspoon in quarts. Add boiling water to cover. Release trapped air. Wipe rim of jar. Attach lid. Place in canner. Fill and close remaining jars.

Hot Pack: Place asparagus in a metal basket or sieve or on a large piece of cheesecloth. Tie edges of cheesecloth over asparagus. Blanch by submerging asparagus in boiling water, 2 minutes; lift from water. Pack hot asparagus into 1 hot jar at a time, leaving 1 inch headspace. Pack spears stem-end down. Add salt as in cold pack, if desired. Add boiling blanching water to cover. Release trapped air. Wipe rim of jar. Attach lid. Place in canner. Fill and close remaining jars.

Process in a pressure canner at 10 pounds pressure, page 17.

Cold pack or hot pack:
    Pints: 25 minutes
    1-1/2-pints or quarts: 30 minutes
Adjust pressure for altitude, page 21.

How to Use: For brunch, serve hot asparagus spears topped with poached eggs and a mustard-cream sauce. Toss hot asparagus pieces with seasoned croutons and grated Parmesan cheese.

Beans, Dried

Varieties Best For Canning: Most dried beans can well.

Selection: Choose fully dry, unbroken shelled beans that are uniform in color and size. Discard broken or discolored beans or those with holes.

Yield: 1-1/2 cups dried beans = 1 quart.

Canning Method: *Hot pack after soaking and precooking.* Process in a pressure canner.

Preparation: Rinse dried beans under running water. Place in a large pot. Add water until 3 inches above beans. Bring to a boil; boil 2 minutes. Set aside 1 hour. Drain beans, discarding water. Return beans to pot; cover with water again. Bring to a boil; reduce heat to low. Cover pot; simmer beans 30 minutes. While beans simmer, wash pint, 1-1/2-pint or quart jars in hot soapy water; rinse. Keep hot until needed. Prepare lids as manufacturer directs. Pack hot beans into 1 hot jar at a time, leaving 1 inch headspace. Do not pack tightly or shake down. Pour cooking liquid over beans to cover. Add salt, using 1/2

teaspoon in pints, 3/4 teaspoon in 1-1/2-pints and 1 teaspoon in quarts, if desired. Release trapped air. Wipe rim of jar. Attach lid. Place in canner. Fill and close remaining jars.

Process in a pressure canner at 10 pounds pressure, page 17.

    Pints: 75 minutes
    1-1/2-pints or quarts: 90 minutes
Adjust pressure for altitude, page 21.

How to Use: Add canned beans to soups and stews. Use to stretch meats and add protein to casseroles and main dishes.

Beans, Green & Yellow

Varieties Best for Canning: Beans are of two types: pole and bush. There are many varieties in each type. Blue Lake, Kentucky Wonder and Romano are the best-known varieties.

Selection: Choose bright-green, greenish-white or yellow, fully mature beans with firm bumpy pods. Pods should snap when bent end to end. Canned beans hold their shape better if they are slightly more mature than desirable for eating fresh. Pole beans hold their shape better than bush beans. Avoid soft or rust-spotted pods.

Yield: 1-1/2 to 2-1/2 pounds = 1 quart; 1 bushel (30 pounds) = 15 to 20 quarts.

Canning Method: *Cold pack or hot pack.* Process in a pressure canner.

Preparation: Wash pint, 1-1/2-pint or quart jars in hot soapy water; rinse. Keep hot until needed. Prepare lids as manufacturer directs. Wash beans in cold water. Lift beans out of water. Snap or cut off ends and pull off strings, if necessary. For cut beans, cut or snap into 1-1/2-inch pieces. Use a special cutter to cut beans lengthwise for French-cut. To can whole beans, choose straight beans 1-1/2 inches shorter than jars, or cut to fit. In a large pot, bring about 1 gallon water to a boil over medium heat.

Cold Pack: Pack raw beans tightly into 1 hot jar at a time, leaving 1 inch headspace. Add salt, if desired, using 1/2 teaspoon in pints, 3/4 teaspoon in 1-1/2-pints and 1 teaspoon in quarts. Add boiling water to cover. Release trapped air. Wipe rim of jar. Attach lid. Place in canner. Fill and close remaining jars.

Hot Pack: Place beans in a metal basket or sieve or on a large piece of cheesecloth. Tie edges of cheesecloth over beans. Blanch by submerging in boiling water 5 minutes. Remove beans. Pack hot beans loosely into 1 hot jar at a time, leaving 1 inch headspace. Add salt as in cold pack, if desired. Add blanching liquid to cover. Release trapped air. Wipe rim of jar. Attach lid. Place in canner. Fill and close remaining jars.

Process in a pressure canner at 10 pounds pressure, page 17.

Cold pack or hot pack:
Pints: 20 minutes
1-1/2-pints or quarts: 25 minutes

Adjust pressure for altitude, page 21.

How to Use: Make quick side dishes by sprinkling canned beans with toasted almonds, filberts, sunflower seeds, sesame seeds or crumbled blue cheese. Use in soups, stews and salads. Serve in casseroles with creamed soups and cheese.

Beans, Fresh Lima

Selection: Small limas are known as *butter beans* because of their rich flavor. Whole larger beans are called *potato limas* for their bland, starchy flavor. Purchase lima beans only in firm, dark-green, well-filled pods. Beans inside pods should be plump with a tender, light-green skin. Avoid soft, spotted pods.

Yield: 3 to 5 pounds = 1 quart; 1 bushel (32 pounds) = 6 to 8 quarts.

Canning Method: *Cold pack or hot pack.* Process in a pressure canner.

Preparation: Wash pint, 1-1/2-pint or quart jars in hot soapy water; rinse. Keep hot until needed. Prepare lids as manufacturer directs. Wash beans in pods in cold water. Lift beans from water; shell. Wash beans again. In a large pot, bring about 1 gallon water to a boil over medium heat.

Cold Pack: Loosely pack washed beans into 1 hot jar at a time, leaving 1 inch headspace. Do not pack or shake down beans. Beans will swell during processing. Add salt, if desired, using 1/2 teaspoon in pints, 3/4 teaspoon in 1-1/2-pints and 1 teaspoon in quarts. Add boiling water to cover. Release trapped air. Wipe rim of jar. Attach lid. Place in canner. Fill and close remaining jars.

Hot Pack: Place beans in a metal basket or sieve or on a large piece of cheesecloth. Tie edges of cheesecloth over beans. Submerge in boiling water, 3 minutes. Lift beans from water. Loosely pack hot beans into 1 hot jar at a time, leaving 1 inch headspace. Add salt as in cold pack, if desired. Release trapped air. Wipe rim of jar. Attach lid. Place in canner. Fill and close remaining jars.

Process in a pressure canner at 10 pounds pressure, page 17.

Cold pack or hot pack:
Pints: 40 minutes
1-1/2-pints or quarts: 50 minutes

Adjust pressure for altitude, page 21.

How to Use: Serve lima beans as a vegetable side dish. Toss hot beans with sautéed onion and green pepper; add cubes of cream cheese.

Beets   **Photo on cover.**

Selection: Choose medium, round, deep-red beets. Large beets may be tough and woody. Flesh should be firm and smooth. Beet greens deteriorate rapidly and may look wilted without affecting beet quality. Small beets of uniform size may be canned whole. Others should be sliced or diced. To can beet greens, see Greens, page 50.

Yield: 2-1/2 to 3 pounds = 2 pints; 1 bushel (52 pounds) = 34 to 40 pints.

Canning Method: *Hot pack.* Process in a pressure canner.

Preparation: Wash pint, 1-1/2-pint or quart jars in hot soapy water; rinse. Keep hot until needed. Prepare lids as manufacturer directs. Cut off beet tops 1 to 2 inches above beet. Sort beets by size. Those under 1-1/4 inches in diameter may be canned whole. Wash beets in cold water; do not remove skins, tops or roots. In a large pot, cover beets with hot water. Bring to a boil. Boil 15 to 20 minutes. Drain beets; plunge into cold water. Slip off skins, stem and root ends. Beets will remain hot. For sliced beets, cut large beets in half, top to bottom; slice each half. Or, cut in 1/2-inch cubes. Pour about 1 gallon water into a large pot. Bring to a boil. Pack hot beets into 1 hot jar at a time, leaving 1 inch headspace. Add salt, if desired, using 1/2 teaspoon in pints, 3/4 teaspoon in 1-1/2-pints and 1 teaspoon in quarts. Add boiling water to cover. Release trapped air. Wipe rim of jar. Attach lid. Place in canner. Fill and close remaining jars.

Process in a pressure canner at 10 pounds pressure, page 17.

Pints: 30 minutes
1-1/2-pints or quarts: 35 minutes

Adjust pressure for altitude, page 21.

How to Use: Harvard beets, the most popular sweet-and-sour beet recipe, is quick and easy to prepare with canned beets. Also use in borscht or marinate in a vinegar-and-spice mixture, then add to salads.

Blackeyed Peas

See page 51.

Broccoli

Broccoli flowerets are too delicate to withstand pressure canning. Canning is not recommended.

Brussels Sprouts

Brussels sprouts become grey-green and their strong flavor intensifies with canning. For pickling, see page 93.

Cabbage

Canning is not recommended. Use cabbage to make Sauerkraut, page 101.

Carrots

Selection: Use only young, tender carrots that are firm, smooth and bright colored. Avoid large, woody or soft carrots and those with large green areas at the top.

Yield: 2 to 3 pounds = 1 quart.

Canning Method: *Cold pack or hot pack.* Process in a pressure canner.

Preparation: Wash pint, 1-1/2-pint or quart jars in hot soapy water; rinse. Keep hot until needed. Prepare lids as manufacturer directs. Under running water, scrub carrots with a brush. Peel or scrape large carrots. Leave tiny carrots unpeeled. Can whole, if desired. Sort carrots by size; slice or dice larger carrots. In a large pot, bring about 1 gallon water to a boil over high heat; keep hot.

Cold Pack: Pack carrots into 1 hot jar at a time, leaving 1 inch headspace. Shake jar to pack firmly. Add salt, if desired, using 1/2 teaspoon in pints, 3/4 teaspoon in 1-1/2-pints and 1 teaspoon in quarts. Add boiling water to cover. Release trapped air. Wipe rim of jar. Attach lid. Place in canner. Fill and close remaining jars.

Hot Pack: Place carrots in a large pot. Add hot water to cover. Bring to a boil; boil 3 minutes. Pack hot carrots into 1 hot jar at a time, leaving 1 inch headspace. Add salt as in cold pack, if desired. Add boiling cooking liquid to cover. Release trapped air. Wipe rim of jar. Attach lid. Place in canner. Fill and close remaining jars.

Process in a pressure canner at 10 pounds pressure, page 17.

   Cold pack or hot pack:
     Pints: 25 minutes
     1-1/2-pints or quarts: 30 minutes

Adjust pressure for altitude, page 21.

How to Use: Combine carrots with peas and onion slices for a vegetable side dish. Or drain carrots, then sauté in butter; sprinkle with a little sugar. Cook and stir over low heat until glazed.

1/Cut off beet tops 1 to 2 inches above beet. Leave root attached. Cook 10 to 15 minutes.

2/Slip off skins, stems and roots. Leave small beets whole; slice or dice larger beets.

Cauliflower

Cauliflower loses its snow-white appearance with canning, and develops a strong flavor. Canning is not recommended. For pickling recipes, see pages 93 and 96.

Celery

Selection: Choose medium-thick stalks that are brittle, light green and glossy. Inside of stalks should be smooth. Avoid soft, wilted celery.
Yield: 1-1/2 to 2-1/2 pounds (2 large bunches) = 1 quart.
Canning Method: *Hot pack.* Process in a pressure canner.
Preparation: Wash pint, 1-1/2-pint or quart jars in hot soapy water; rinse. Keep hot until needed. Prepare lids as manufacturer directs. Break off stalks from bunch. Wash under running cold water. Trim off leaves and base of stalks. Cut into 1/4- to 1-inch diagonal slices. Place in a large pot. Add hot water to cover. Bring to a boil; boil 3 minutes. Drain, reserving cooking liquid. Return cooking liquid to pot; keep hot. Pack hot celery into 1 hot jar at a time, leaving 1 inch headspace. Add salt, if desired, using 1/2 teaspoon in pints, 3/4 teaspoon in 1-1/2-pints and 1 teaspoon in quarts. Add boiling cooking liquid to cover. Release trapped air. Wipe rim of jar. Attach lid. Place in canner. Fill and close remaining jars.
Process in a pressure canner at 10 pounds pressure, page 17.

Pints, 1-1/2-pints or quarts: 35 minutes
Adjust pressure for altitude, page 21.
How to Use: Use in soups and stews. Mix with other vegetables, such as onions, carrots and tomatoes, for an interesting side dish. Bake drained celery in a cheese sauce or creamy mustard sauce.

Chard

Also called *Swiss Chard,* this vegetable is a variety of beet. Only the leaves and stalk are eaten. See Greens, page 50.

Chilies

See Peppers, Chile, page 52.

Collard Greens

See Greens, page 50.

Corn, Cream-Style

Varieties Best for Canning: The tender sweet corn you enjoy fresh generally does not can well. More mature or more starchy varieties have better flavor, color and texture when canned.
Selection: Can as soon after harvest as possible. Harvest or purchase only what can be canned at one time. Choose corn with fresh, green husks and plump kernels that extend to tip of cob. There should be no space between rows. Milky, firm kernels will pop if pressure is applied. The milky juice from scraping the half-kernels makes the "cream" in cream-style corn.
Yield: 3 to 6 pounds (8 to 12 medium ears) = 2 pints.
Canning Method: To be safe, *cold pack or hot pack only in pint jars.* Process in a pressure canner.
Preparation: Wash pint jars in hot soapy water; rinse. Keep hot until needed. Prepare lids as manufacturer directs. Remove and discard husks and silk. Wash corn under running cold water. Cut ends from ears. Cut corn from cob, removing about 1/2 of each kernel. Working over a large bowl, use a spoon to scrape milk from cob and remaining half-kernels. In a large pot, bring about 1 gallon water to a boil over high heat; keep hot.
Cold Pack: Pack kernels and juice loosely into 1 hot jar at a time, leaving 1-1/2 inches headspace. Add 1/2 teaspoon salt, if desired. Add boiling water to within 1/2 inch of rim and 1 inch over kernels. Release trapped air. Wipe rim of jar. Attach lid. Place in canner. Fill and close remaining jars.
Hot Pack: Measure kernels and juice into a large pot. For each 4 cups, add 2 cups boiling water. Bring to a boil; boil 3 minutes. Pack hot mixture loosely into 1 hot jar at a time, leaving 1 inch headspace. Be sure corn kernels are covered with liquid. Add 1/2 teaspoon salt, if desired. Release trapped air. Wipe rim of jar. Attach lid. Place in canner. Fill and close remaining jars.
Process in a pressure canner at 10 pounds pressure, page 17.

Cold pack: Pints: 95 minutes
Hot pack: Pints: 85 minutes
Adjust pressure for altitude, page 21.
How to Use: Home-canned cream-style corn is thinner than commercially canned corn. To thicken: In a small bowl, make a smooth paste with 1 tablespoon flour and 2 tablespoons cold water. In a small saucepan, stir flour mixture into corn. Stirring constantly, bring to a boil. Add to a corn-muffin mix for Southern spoonbread or use to make corn pudding or corn chowder.

Corn, Whole-Kernel

Varieties Best for Canning: More mature or more starchy varieties have better flavor, color and texture when canned.

Selection: Pick or purchase only as much corn as can be processed at one time. Sugar in sweet corn quickly changes to starch after harvesting. To keep sweet flavor, process corn immediately. Choose corn with fresh, green husks and close rows of plump kernels that extend to tip of cob.

Yield: 3 to 6 pounds (8 to 12 medium ears) = 1 quart.

Canning Method: *Cold pack or hot pack.* Process in a pressure canner.

Preparation: Wash pint, 1-1/2-pint or quart jars in hot soapy water; rinse. Keep hot until needed. Prepare lids as manufacturer directs. Remove and discard husks and silk; wash corn under running cold water. Cut ends from ears. Cut corn from cob, removing about 2/3 of each kernel. Avoid cutting into cob. In a large pot, bring about 1 gallon water to a boil over high heat; keep hot.

Cold Pack: Pack corn loosely into 1 hot jar at a time, leaving 1 inch headspace. Do not shake or push down kernels. Add salt, if desired, using 1/2 teaspoon in pints, 3/4 teaspoon in 1-1/2-pints and 1 teaspoon in quarts. Add boiling water to cover. Release trapped air. Wipe rim of jar. Attach lid. Place in canner. Fill and close remaining jars.

Hot Pack: Measure corn kernels; place in a large pot. Add 2 cups boiling water for each 4 cups corn. Bring to a boil. Drain corn, reserving cooking liquid. Return liquid to pot; bring back to a boil. Pack hot corn into 1 hot jar at a time, leaving 1 inch headspace. Add salt as in cold pack, if desired. Pour boiling cooking liquid over corn to cover. Release trapped air. Wipe rim of jar. Attach lid. Place in canner. Fill and close remaining jars.

Process in a pressure canner at 10 pounds pressure, page 17.

   Cold pack or hot pack:
     Pints: 55 minutes
     1-1/2-pints or quarts: 85 minutes

Adjust pressure for altitude, page 21.

How to Use: Toss with green beans and serve as a vegetable dish. Add to casseroles, soups and main dishes.

Cucumbers

See *Pickles & Relishes,* pages 104-115.

1/Use a corn cutter or knife to remove about 2/3 of each kernel for whole-kernel corn.

2/For cream-style corn, cut off half of each kernel. Over a bowl, scrape milk from remaining half-kernels.

Eggplant

Selection: Eggplant darkens with canning and becomes unattractive. Results are better with freezing. If you do can them, choose heavy, firm eggplants 3 to 6 inches in diameter. Deep-purple color should be glossy and cover entire surface. Avoid soft or withered eggplant.

Yield: 1-1/2 to 2 pounds (2 medium) = 1 quart.

Canning Method: *Hot pack.* Process in a pressure canner.

Preparation: Wash pint, 1-1/2-pint or quart jars in hot soapy water; rinse. Keep hot until needed. Prepare lids as manufacturer directs. Wash and peel eggplant. Cut in 1/2-inch cubes. Place in a large bowl. Sprinkle with 1 teaspoon salt for each 2 pounds eggplant. Add cold water to cover. Let stand 45 minutes. Drain; discard brine. In a large pot, bring about 1 gallon water to a boil. Place eggplant cubes in a metal basket or sieve or on a large piece of cheesecloth. Tie cheesecloth over eggplant. Submerge in boiling water 5 minutes. Lift eggplant from water. Pack tightly into 1 hot jar at a time, leaving 1 inch headspace. Do not add salt. Add boiling cooking liquid to cover. Release trapped air. Wipe rim of jar. Attach lid. Place in canner. Fill and close remaining jars.

Process in a pressure canner at 10 pounds pressure, page 17.

Pints: 30 minutes

1-1/2-pints or quarts: 40 minutes

Adjust pressure for altitude, page 21.

How to Use: For a quick side dish, combine drained eggplant cubes with chopped onion, green-pepper squares and chopped tomatoes. Sprinkle with Italian seasoning. Top with a mushroom sauce or cheese sauce.

Greens

Varieties Best for Canning: All garden greens can well: chard, collard greens, kale, mustard greens, turnip tops, beet tops and spinach.

Selection: Use bright-green, small, young, tender, crisp greens. Avoid wilted, yellow or brown leaves. Leaves with coarse or fibrous stems will be tough. Greens deteriorate quickly. Process immediately after harvesting or purchasing. If they must be held, wrap loosely in damp paper towels and store in refrigerator vegetable crisper. Do not store more than 24 hours.

Yield: 2 to 3 pounds = 1 quart.

Canning Method: *Hot pack.* Process in a pressure canner.

Preparation: Wash pint, 1-1/2-pint or quart jars in hot soapy water; rinse. Keep hot until needed. Prepare lids as manufacturer directs. Wash greens in cold water. Lift out of water; wash again. Cut out and discard tough stems and large midribs. Use a sharp knife to cut through mound of leaves several times. In a large pot, bring 1 gallon water to a boil. Place greens in a metal basket or sieve or on a large piece of cheesecloth. Tie edges of cheesecloth over greens. Submerge in boiling water until greens are wilted, about 5 minutes. Lift greens from water. Pack loosely into 1 hot jar at a time, leaving 1 inch headspace. Add salt, if desired, using 1/4 teaspoon in pints and 1-1/2-pints and 1/2 teaspoon in quarts. Add boiling cooking liquid to cover. Release trapped air. Wipe rim of jar. Attach lid. Place in canner. Fill and close remaining jars.

Process in a pressure canner at 10 pounds pressure, page 17.

Pints: 70 minutes

1-1/2-pints or quarts: 90 minutes

Adjust pressure for altitude, page 21.

How to Use: Heat greens; season with butter, crisp fried bacon, Italian salad dressing, blue cheese or Parmesan cheese. Greens make an unusual addition to quiches or a filling for omelets. Also bake with a cream sauce.

Mushrooms

Selection: Use only fresh, cultivated mushrooms. *Do not can wild mushrooms.* Select medium to small, white or light-brown mushrooms. Underside of cap should be closed around stem. Discard dark, withered mushrooms.

Yield: 1-1/2 pounds = 2 pints.

Canning Method: *Hot pack only in 1/2-pint or pint jars.* Process in a pressure canner.

Preparation: Wash 1/2-pint or pint jars in hot soapy water; rinse. Keep jars hot until needed. Prepare lids as manufacturer directs. Soak mushrooms in cold water to cover, 2 minutes, agitating water several times. Lift mushrooms from water; trim stems. Leave small mushrooms whole. Cut larger mushrooms in half or quarter. *Do not slice mushrooms.* Bring a large pot of water to a boil over high heat. In another large pot, steam mushrooms over boiling water, 4 minutes. Pack hot mushrooms into 1 hot jar at a time, leaving 1/2 inch headspace. Add salt, if desired, using 1/4 teaspoon in 1/2-pints, and 1/2 teaspoon in pints. For better color, add crystalline ascorbic acid, using 1/16 teaspoon in 1/2-pints and 1/8

teaspoon in pints. Add boiling water to cover. Release trapped air. Wipe rim of jar. Attach lid. Place in canner. Fill and close remaining jars.
Process in a pressure canner at 10 pounds pressure, page 17.

   1/2-pints or pints: 30 minutes
Adjust pressure for altitude, page 21.
How to Use: Add to meat dishes, casseroles, soups and stews.

Okra

Selection: Commonly called *gumbo*. Choose young, tender, green pods 2 to 4 inches long that snap easily. Avoid dry, soft or rust-spotted pods.
Yield: 1-1/2 pounds = 1 quart.
Canning Method: *Hot pack* whole or cut in pieces. Process in a pressure canner.
Preparation: Wash pint, 1-1/2-pint or quart jars in hot soapy water; rinse. Keep hot until needed. Prepare lids as manufacturer directs. Wash okra pods in cold water; trim stems. If canning whole, do not cut off cap. To can pieces, remove cap; cut pods in 1/2- to 1-inch pieces. In a large pot, bring 1/2 gallon water to a boil; add whole or cut okra. Return to a boil. Boil 1 minute; drain. In a large saucepan, bring another 1/2 gallon water to a boil. Pack hot okra into 1 hot jar at a time, leaving 1 inch headspace. Add salt, if desired, using 1/2 teaspoon in pints, 3/4 teaspoon in 1-1/2-pints and 1 teaspoon in quarts. Add boiling water to cover. Release trapped air. Wipe rim of jar. Attach lid. Place in canner. Fill and close remaining jars.
Process in a pressure canner at 10 pounds pressure, page 17.

   Pints: 25 minutes
   1-1/2-pints or quarts: 40 minutes
Adjust pressure for altitude, page 21.
How to Use: Combine okra and tomatoes; serve as a vegetable side dish. Add canned okra to meat or bean stews.

Olives

To be edible, olives must be lye-cured. This is a detailed process when done in the home. If you have fresh olives available and desire to cure and can them, University of California leaflet 2758, *Home Pickling of Olives,* gives directions for pickling, canning and curing olives in the home. Send $1.26 to Public Service, University of California, Davis, CA 95616.

Onions

Because of year-round availability, large onions are not recommended for canning. For pickled onions, see page 99.

Peas: Blackeyed or Cowpeas, Crowder & Field

Selection: Select fresh, firm, well-filled pods. Avoid pods that are shriveled or soft.
Yield: 3 to 6 pounds in the pod = 1 quart; 1 bushel (30 pounds) = 5 to 10 quarts.
Canning Method: *Cold pack or hot pack.* Process in a pressure canner.
Preparation: Wash pint, 1-1/2-pint or quart jars in hot soapy water; rinse. Keep hot until needed. Prepare lids as manufacturer directs. Shell peas by pressing pod on opposite sides along seam. Wash peas in cold water. In a large pot, bring about 1 gallon water to a boil over high heat.
Cold Pack: Loosely pack washed peas into 1 hot jar at a time, leaving 1-1/2 inches headspace. Do not shake jar or press peas down. They swell during processing. Add salt, if desired, using 1/2 teaspoon in pints, 3/4 teaspoon in 1-1/2-pints and 1 teaspoon in quarts. Add boiling water to cover. Release trapped air. Wipe rim of jar. Attach lid. Place in canner. Fill and close remaining jars.
Hot Pack: Add peas to boiling water. Boil uncovered 3 minutes. Drain; reserving liquid. Bring liquid back to a boil. Loosely pack hot peas into 1 hot jar at a time, leaving 1-1/2 inches headspace. Add salt as in cold pack, if desired. Add boiling cooking liquid to cover. Release trapped air. Wipe rim of jar. Attach lid. Place in canner. Fill and close remaining jars.
Process in a pressure canner at 10 pounds pressure, page 17.

   Cold pack or hot pack:
    Pints: 35 minutes
    1-1/2-pints or quarts: 40 minutes
Adjust pressure for altitude, page 21.
How to Use: Season peas with sautéed onion and bacon bits, or herb-flavored tomato sauce.

Peas, Green

Selection: Choose fresh, firm, dark-green pea pods that are plump with peas. Avoid pods that are shriveled or soft. Can peas immediately after harvesting to assure sweet flavor.

Yield: 3 to 6 pounds in the pod = 1 quart; 1 bushel (30 pounds) = 5 to 10 quarts.

Canning Method: *Cold pack or hot pack.* Process in a pressure canner.

Preparation: Wash pint, 1-1/2-pint or quart jars in hot soapy water; rinse. Keep hot until needed. Prepare lids as manufacturer directs. Shell peas; wash in cold water. Lift peas out of water. In a large pot, bring about 1 gallon water to a boil.

Cold Pack: Loosely pack peas into 1 hot jar at a time, leaving 1 inch headspace. Add salt, if desired, using 1/2 teaspoon in pints, 3/4 teaspoon in 1-1/2-pints and 1 teaspoon in quarts. Add boiling water to cover. Release trapped air. Wipe rim of jar. Attach lid. Place in canner. Fill and close remaining jars.

Hot Pack: Place peas in a metal basket or sieve or on a large piece of cheesecloth. Tie edges of cheesecloth over peas. Submerge in boiling water. Or, add loose peas to boiling water. Boil uncovered 3 minutes. Lift peas from water or drain, reserving cooking liquid. Bring cooking liquid back to a boil. Loosely pack hot peas into 1 hot jar at a time, leaving 1 inch headspace. Add salt as in cold pack, if desired. Add boiling cooking liquid to cover. Release trapped air. Wipe rim of jar. Attach lid. Place in canner. Fill and close remaining jars.

Process in a pressure canner at 10 pounds pressure, page 17.

Cold pack or hot pack:
Pints, 1-1/2-pints or quarts: 40 minutes
Adjust pressure for altitude, page 21.

How to Use: Add to seafood or chicken noodle casseroles or fricassees. Combine with chopped celery in tomato aspic. Season with onion and curry or cook with fresh mushrooms and pimiento-stuffed olives.

Peppers, Bell

Selection: Bell peppers lose their snappy flavor and texture and become soft and unappealing when canned. If you want to can them, choose glossy, medium- to dark-green peppers with firm walls that are heavy for their size. Red peppers should be bright red. Avoid thin-walled, light peppers or wilted, soft peppers. Do not use peppers with large soft spots.

Yield: 12 ounces (about 3 medium peppers) = 1 pint.

Canning Method: *Hot pack with added vinegar.* Process in a pressure canner.

Preparation: Wash 1/2-pint or pint jars in hot soapy water; rinse. Keep hot until needed. Prepare lids as manufacturer directs. Wash peppers; cut in half. Remove stem, seeds and inner membranes. Cut in 1-inch squares or leave in halves. In a large pot, bring 1 gallon water to a boil over high heat. Place peppers in a metal basket or sieve or on a large piece of cheesecloth. Tie edges of cheesecloth over peppers. Submerge in boiling water, 3 minutes. Lift peppers from water. Pack hot pepper pieces into 1 hot jar at a time, leaving 1 inch headspace. Add vinegar, using 1-1/2 teaspoons in 1/2-pints and 1 tablespoon in pints. Add salt, if desired, using 1/4 teaspoon in 1/2-pints and 1/2 teaspoon in pints. Add boiling cooking liquid to cover. Release trapped air. Wipe rim of jar. Attach lid. Place in canner. Fill and close remaining jars.

Process in a pressure canner at 10 pounds pressure, page 17.

1/2-pints or pints: 35 minutes
Adjust pressure for altitude, page 21.

How to Use: Add canned pepper pieces to stews and main dishes. For a quick vegetable side dish, toss with canned tomatoes seasoned with onions and herbs.

Peppers, Chile

Varieties Best for Canning: Mild Anaheim peppers are best for canning. Hot jalapeño peppers are usually pickled.

Selection: Choose medium-green, firm and glossy chilies. Avoid those with soft, dark spots or wilted, shriveled or soft chilies.

Yield: 12 ounces (about 4 large Anaheim peppers) = 1/2 pint.

Canning Method: *Hot pack with added vinegar. Do not dice.* Process in a pressure canner.

Preparation: Wash 1/2-pint or pint jars in hot soapy water; rinse. Keep hot until needed. Prepare lids as manufacturer directs. Wash peppers. To peel, bake chilies in a 500F (260C) oven, 10 to 12 minutes, until skins blister. Immediately place in a paper bag to cool. When cool, pull off peels. *See caution.* Cut off stem; remove seeds, if desired. In a large saucepan, bring 6 to 8 cups water to a boil. *Loosely* pack peeled chilies into 1 hot jar at a time, leaving 1 inch headspace. Add vinegar, using 1-1/2 teaspoons in 1/2-pints and 1 tablespoon in pints. Add salt, if desired, using 1/4 teaspoon in 1/2-pints and 1/2 teaspoon in pints. Add boiling water to cover. Release trapped air. Wipe rim of jar. Attach lid. Place in canner. Fill and close remaining jars.

Process in a pressure canner at 10 pounds pressure, page 17.

1/2-pints and pints: 35 minutes

Adjust pressure for altitude, page 21.

How to Use: Fold chopped chilies, cheese and diced tomato into an omelet; add to a chicken-noodle casserole. Place shredded cheese on tortilla chips; top with a strip of pepper; bake.

Caution

Wear rubber or plastic gloves when handling chilies. Capsaicin, an alkaloid substance in the veins of chilies, is irritating to skin. After handling chilies, wash your hands thoroughly with soap and water before touching your face.

Potatoes, Sweet

See Sweet Potatoes & Yams, page 54.

Potatoes, White

Varieties Best for Canning: Chippewa, Red Lasoda, Red Pontiac, Kennebec and White Rose can well. Waxy varieties that are suitable for boiling can better than mealy types.

Selection: Choose firm, smooth potatoes, round to oblong in shape and uniform in size. Avoid potatoes with large cuts or bruises. Do not use sprouted or shriveled potatoes. Greening on the surface is from exposure to light. Remove small green areas; do not use potatoes with large green areas, they will taste bitter.

Yield: 2-1/2 to 3 pounds (7 to 9 medium potatoes) = 1 quart; 1 bushel (50 pounds) = 20 quarts.

Canning Method: *Hot pack.* Process in a pressure canner.

Preparation: Wash pint, 1-1/2-pint or quart jars in hot soapy water; rinse. Keep hot until needed. Prepare lids as manufacturer directs. Scrub potatoes with a vegetable brush under running cold water. Peel; wash again. Small potatoes, 1 to 1-1/2 inches in diameter, may be left whole. Cut larger potatoes in 1/2- to 1-inch cubes. To prevent darkening, immerse in a solution of 4 teaspoons salt and 4 quarts water. Bring 2 quarts water to a boil in a large pot. Lift potatoes from solution. Add to boiling water. Bring back to a boil. Boil whole potatoes 10 minutes, cubed potatoes 3 to 5 minutes. Drain potatoes, reserving cooking liquid. Pack hot potatoes into 1 hot jar at a time, leaving 1 inch headspace. Add salt, if desired, using 1/2 teaspoon in pints, 3/4 teaspoon in 1-1/2-pints and 1 teaspoon in quarts. Add boiling cooking liquid to cover. Release trapped air. Wipe rim of jar. Attach lid. Place in canner. Fill and close remaining jars.

Process in a pressure canner at 10 pounds pressure, page 17.

Whole potatoes:
Pints: 30 minutes
1-1/2-pints or quarts: 40 minutes
Cubed potatoes:
Pints: 35 minutes
1-1/2-pints or quarts: 40 minutes

Adjust pressure for altitude, page 21.

How to Use: Add canned potatoes to soups and stews. Heat potatoes; toss with butter and parsley or a creamy cheese sauce for an easy side dish.

Pumpkins

Varieties Best for Canning: Pumpkin varieties with dry, sweet meat can best. Scrape surface of pumpkin with your fingernail. If skin is easily cut, pumpkin is too moist.

Selection: Choose pumpkins that are hard and evenly colored. Avoid those with soft spots.

Yield: 3 pounds = 1 quart; 15 to 20 pounds (1 medium) = 5 to 7 quarts.

Canning Method: *Hot pack cubes. Do not mash or puree.* Process in a pressure canner.

Preparation: Wash pint, 1-1/2-pint or quart jars in hot, soapy water; rinse. Keep hot until needed. Prepare lids as manufacturer directs. Wash pumpkin; cut in 8 to 10 pieces. Remove seeds. Cut off peel. Cut pieces into 1-inch cubes. In a large pot, cover cubes with hot water. Bring to a boil. Drain, reserving cooking liquid. Bring liquid back to a boil. Pack cubes into 1 hot jar at a time, leaving 1 inch headspace. Add salt, if desired, using 1/2 teaspoon in pints, 3/4 teaspoon in 1-1/2-pints and 1 teaspoon in quarts. Add boiling cooking liquid to cover. Release trapped air. Wipe rim of jar. Attach lid. Place in canner. Fill and close remaining jars.

Process in a pressure canner at 10 pounds pressure, page 17.

Pints: 55 minutes
1-1/2-pints or quarts: 90 minutes

Adjust pressure for altitude, page 21.

How to Use: Drain pumpkin cubes; mash and use in pies, bread, muffins, cakes or cookies. Add butter and spices to cubes; serve as a side dish.

Rutabagas

Not recommended for canning. They discolor and develop a strong flavor.

Squash, Summer

Selection: Choose yellow squash that are firm and heavy for their size. Skins should be tender and light-yellow color. Zucchini squash should be 6 to 8 inches long, firm and heavy, with tender skins that are dark green over pale-yellow. Select squash with no blemishes or soft spots. Avoid soft squash or those with shriveled skins.
Yield: 1-1/2 to 2 pounds = 1 quart; 1 bushel (about 40 pounds) = 16 to 20 quarts.
Canning Method: *Cold pack or hot pack.* Process in a pressure canner.
Preparation: Wash pint, 1-1/2-pint or quart jars in hot soapy water; rinse. Keep hot until needed. Prepare lids as manufacturer directs. Rub squash gently under running cold water. Trim ends; do not peel. Cut into 1/2-inch slices. Or cut into 2-inch crosswise pieces, then lengthwise into quarters. In a large pot, bring about 2 quarts water to a boil over high heat.
Cold Pack: Pack squash pieces tightly into 1 hot jar at a time, leaving 1 inch headspace. Add salt, if desired, using 1/2 teaspoon in pints, 3/4 teaspoon in 1-1/2-pints and 1 teaspoon in quarts. Add boiling water to cover. Release trapped air. Wipe rim of jar. Attach lid. Place in canner. Fill and close remaining jars.
Hot Pack: Place squash in a wire basket, metal sieve or on a large piece of cheesecloth. Tie edges of cheesecloth together over squash. Blanch by submerging in boiling water, 2 minutes. Remove from water. Loosely pack hot squash pieces into 1 hot jar at a time, leaving 1 inch headspace. Add salt as in cold pack, if desired. Add boiling blanching liquid to cover. Release trapped air. Wipe rim of jar. Attach lid. Place in canner. Fill and close remaining jars.
Process in a pressure canner at 10 pounds pressure, page 17.
> *Cold pack:*
> Pints: 25 minutes
> 1-1/2-pints or quarts: 30 minutes
> *Hot pack:*
> Pints: 30 minutes
> 1-1/2-pints or quarts: 40 minutes

Adjust pressure for altitude, page 21.
How to Use: Add canned summer squash to soups, stews or casseroles.

Squash, Winter

Varieties Best for Canning: Hard-shelled, mature squash, including Acorn or Table Queen, Buttercup, Butternut, Banana and Hubbard. Winter squash must be cut into cubes.
Selection: Choose squash that are hard and evenly colored. Avoid those with soft spots.
Yield: 3 pounds = 1 quart; 15 to 20 pounds = 5 to 7 quarts.
Canning Method: *Hot pack cubes. Do not mash or puree.* Process in a pressure canner.
Preparation: See Pumpkins, page 53.

Sweet Potatoes & Yams

Varieties Best for Canning: Sweet potatoes and yams are tubers of different plants. Sweet-potato varieties are either dry or moist. Moist varieties, such as Centennial, Nemagold, Goldrus and Puerto Rico are the most popular. Moist sweet potatoes are often called *yams*. True yam varieties are grown in Africa and South America, and are shipped to other places in the world. These are generally larger than sweet potatoes. Skins of all varieties are dark orange to dark red-orange.
Selection: Choose medium sweet potatoes and yams that are thick and chunky rather than slender. Avoid those with blemishes or signs of decay.
Yield: 2-1/2 to 3 pounds (3 medium) = 1 quart.
Canning Method: *Hot pack.* Process in a pressure canner.
Preparation: Wash pint, 1-1/2-pint or quart jars in hot soapy water; rinse. Keep hot until needed. Prepare lids as manufacturer directs. Under running water, scrub sweet potatoes or yams with a brush. Boil in 1 inch water, or steam until skins come off easily, about 20 minutes. Drop cooked potatoes or yams in cold water. Rub and pull skins off.
Dry Hot Pack: Cut cooked potatoes or yams into cubes. Pack into 1 hot jar at a time, leaving 1 inch headspace. Press firmly to fill all space. Do not add salt or water. Wipe rim of jar. Attach lid. Place in canner. Fill and close remaining jars.
Wet Hot Pack: In a large pot, bring about 2 quarts water to a boil over high heat. Cut cooked potatoes or yams into cubes or elongated pieces. Pack into 1 hot jar at a time, leaving 1 inch headspace. Add boiling water to cover. Release trapped air. Wipe rim of jar. Attach lid. Place in canner. Fill and close remaining jars.
Process in a pressure canner at 10 pounds pressure, page 17.

Dry hot pack:
    Pints: 65 minutes
    1-1/2-pints or quarts: 95 minutes
Wet hot pack:
    Pints: 55 minutes
    1-1/2-pints or quarts: 90 minutes
Adjust pressure for altitude, page 21.
How to Use: Substitute sweet potatoes or yams for white potatoes in soups, stews and casseroles. Mash and use in breads, biscuits, cookies or spice cakes.

Swiss Chard

See Greens, page 50.

Tomatoes

Varieties Best for Canning: Most tomato varieties can well. Check with your county cooperative extension agent or farm service office for the names of firm, meaty varieties that are grown in your area.
Selection: Choose firm-ripe, red-orange tomatoes that are not quite ready for eating fresh. Current research has shown all firm-ripe varieties are acidic enough to water-bath process. Seeds for low-acid tomatoes are not available to home gardeners in the United States. If you purchase tomatoes of an unknown acidity, add lemon juice as directed below. *Do not can soft, overripe tomatoes or those from dead vines.* Their acid content is not high enough for safe water-bath processing. Do not can tomatoes with soft spots or split skins.
Yield: 2-1/2 to 3 pounds (5 to 6 medium) = 1 quart; 1 lug (30 pounds) = 10 quarts; 1 bushel (53 pounds) = 15 to 20 quarts.
Canning Method: *Cold pack or hot pack.* You may add lemon juice to increase the acidity. Process in a boiling-water bath.
Preparation: Wash pint, 1-1/2-pint or quart jars in hot soapy water; rinse. Keep hot until needed. Prepare lids as manufacturer directs. In a large pot, bring 8 cups water to a boil; keep hot. Wash tomatoes in cold water. Immerse tomatoes in boiling water, 30 seconds. Remove from boiling water; immerse in cold water. Slip off skins, page 25. Cut out core; trim away any green spots. Cut large tomatoes in halves or quarters.
Cold Pack: Pack tomatoes into 1 hot jar at a time, pressing with a spoon until juices begin to flow. Leave 1/2 inch headspace. Add lemon juice, if desired, using 1 tablespoon in pints, 1-1/2 tablespoons in 1-1/2-pints and 2 tablespoons in quarts. Add salt, if desired, using 1/2 teaspoon in pints, 3/4 teaspoon in 1-1/2-pints and 1 teaspoon in quarts. Release trapped air. Wipe rim of jar. Attach lid. Place in canner. Fill and close remaining jars.
Hot Pack: Place 5 or 6 tomatoes in a large pot. Mash with a potato masher. Add remaining tomatoes. Bring to a boil; boil 5 minutes. Stir occasionally to prevent scorching. Ladle hot tomatoes and juice into 1 hot jar at a time, leaving 1/2 inch headspace. Add lemon juice and salt as in cold pack. Release trapped air. Wipe rim of jar. Attach lid. Place in canner. Fill and close remaining jars.
Process in a boiling-water bath, page 17.
    Cold pack or hot pack:
        Pints: 35 minutes
        1-1/2-pints or quarts: 45 minutes
Adjust times for altitude, page 20.
To process tomatoes in a pressure canner: Place filled jars in canner. Exhaust air. Bring pressure to 15 pounds. Immediately remove canner from heat. Let pressure drop, undisturbed. Remove canner lid. After 10 minutes, remove jars from canner. Cool jars. Label and store in a cool dark place.
How to Use: Use canned tomatoes in sauces, soups, stews, casseroles and main dishes. Combine with other vegetables for a side dish. To make quick scalloped tomatoes, stir seasoned croutons and chopped onions into canned tomatoes. Bake 20 minutes at 350F (175C).

Turnips

Not recommended for canning. They discolor and develop a strong flavor.

Basic Canning:
Jams & Jellies

Jam and jelly making is easy and rewarding for first-time canners if commercial pectins are used. Because you use fully ripe fruit and a short cooking time, you are almost guaranteed fresh, full-fruit flavor. You no longer have to guess how thick a jam or jelly will be.

Jelly is made from fruit juice and is tender yet firm enough to hold its shape when turned out onto a plate. It is usually clear and bright colored. *Jam* contains pieces of fruit, is softer and does not hold its shape, but spreads easily without running.

Fruit or fruit juice gives flavor and color to jams and jellies. It also provides some or all of the pectin and acid necessary to form a gel.

Pectin is a substance found in all parts of plants. When heated with the necessary amounts of sugar and acid, it causes a gel to form. Some fruits, such as apples, quince, cranberries and plums, have enough natural pectin to form a gel without added pectin. Others do not. All fruits have more pectin when they are underripe. When no pectin is added, some fruit in the mixture should be underripe. Often fruit is not peeled, pitted or cored because these normally discarded parts contain the most pectin.

Commercial pectin is made from apples or citrus. It can be used with any fruit and assures gel formation. Dry and liquid pectin cannot be substituted for one another.

Sugar adds flavor, acts as a preservative and must be present for fruit pectin to form a gel. Do not decrease sugar in recipes except as directed below. Decreasing sugar retards gelling and reduces the shelf life of sweet spreads.

You can use artificial sweeteners or less sugar if you use vegetable gums, low methoxy-pectin or gelatin instead of pectin. With these thickeners, jams and jellies can be unsweetened, artifically sweetened or sweetened with small amounts of sugar or honey. However, spreads made with these products have a different flavor and texture than regular jams and jellies. Follow package directions exactly. Process low-sugar and unsweetened spreads in a boiling-water bath. After they have been opened, store them in the refrigerator.

Honey or corn syrup may be substituted for some of the sugar, page 61. Use a light, mild-flavored honey or light corn syrup to avoid overpowering the fruit flavor.

Acid present in some fruits is sufficient to cause gelling. Others require the addition of lemon or lime juice or vinegar. Freshly squeezed, strained lemon and lime juices have excellent flavor, but bottled juice can be used.

SPECIAL EQUIPMENT

Some special equipment is needed to make jams and jellies. Use a *flat-bottom, 6- to 8-quart enamel, aluminum or stainless-steel pot* large enough for jams and jellies to boil vigorously.

Use a *jelly bag or colander lined with cheesecloth* to separate and clarify fruit juice for jelly.

A *timer, clock or watch with a second hand* will let you time 1 minute exactly when making jam or jelly with added pectin.

A *candy thermometer* tests doneness of jams and jellies made without added pectin. A *jelmeter* tests the pectin content of a fruit juice.

Make jams during the peak of fruit season; prepare only as much as can be used in 6 months. Even when stored properly in a cool dark place, jams begin to lose their fresh-fruit flavor and color beyond this time. Canned or frozen fruit make excellent jam when your supply runs low. Can or freeze the fruit with or without added sugar. You may also can fruits in their own juice or water. Label the jars so you know they are for making jam. When making jam, subtract the amount of sugar in the jar from what is called for in the jam recipe. Use both fruit and its own juice. Do not use water in which fruit was canned. Thaw frozen fruit, using it and the juice as though they were fresh.

Select fully ripe fruit. Use odd-shaped or small pieces. Do not use overripe or badly bruised fruit.

Handle the fruit gently to avoid bruising it. Follow directions for each fruit in *Quick Guide to Making Jams,* pages 62-63. A food processor or blender is helpful for chopping. Turn it on and off at low speed until the fruit is uniformly chopped. When using a blender, process a small amount of fruit at a time. If you are short 1/4 or 1/2 cup fruit, add water to make up the shortage.

To make jam with added dry pectin, combine crushed fruit, lemon juice if called for, and dry pectin. Sugar is added later.

In a 6- to 8-quart pot, combine the ingredients as directed. The pot should be no more than one-third full so the jam can boil vigorously.

Jams must be processed in a boiling-water bath to guarantee keeping quality. Jam or jelly will thicken and gel as it cools. It may look thin in the pot even though it has actually boiled long enough.

Making jelly *without* added pectin requires skill and experience and more time than jelly made *with* added pectin. To make jellies from fruits low in natural pectin, dry or liquid pectin must be added. Use fully ripe fruit for best flavor.

Preparing Fruit Juice—Wash the fruit and prepare it as directed in *Quick Guide to Making Jellies,* page 64. Cut firm fruit into small pieces or chop in a blender or food processor. Crush soft fruit and berries. To extract juices from firm fruits, bring the fruit to a boil with water, if indicated; reduce the heat. Cover and simmer until the fruit is tender, 5 to 30 minutes.

Pour the fruit mixture into a dampened jelly bag or a colander lined with 3 thicknesses of damp cheesecloth. If your jelly bag does not have its own holder, tie the bag at the top and hang it from a cupboard knob or faucet, letting the juice drip into a bowl. If you use a colander, set it in a bowl. Let the juice drip at least 4 hours or overnight. Squeezing the bag causes cloudy jelly. *Do not squeeze the bag* unless the juice is not dripping regularly. After squeezing juice from the bag, rinse the pulp out of the bag. Strain the juice through the bag again without squeezing.

Measure the extracted juice. If there is not enough juice, add the needed amount of water to the pulp in the bag. Let it drip into the other juice.

When making jelly without added pectin, *test the extracted juice* to be sure there is enough natural pectin. A simple instrument called a *jelmeter* measures the pectin present in a juice by measuring the rate the juice flows through a glass tube.

An *alcohol test* will also indicate whether there is enough pectin in the juice. Gently stir 1 teaspoon of the extracted juice into 1 tablespoon of denatured rubbing alcohol. Juice with enough pectin will form a jelly-like mass that can be picked up in 1 piece. Juice low in pectin will form small jelly-like particles. Discard the test juice and alcohol. Do not add it to the remaining juice.

If the extracted juice does not contain enough pectin, use a recipe with dry or liquid pectin.

Extracted grape juice contains tartaric acid that crystallizes in jelly, causing graininess. Chill the juice overnight before making jelly. The acid will form crystals that can be strained out.

A maximum of 4 to 5 cups of extracted juice can be made into jelly at one time. Recipes should not be doubled because larger amounts of juice sometimes do not gel. Use a 6- to 8-quart pot so the mixture will have space to boil.

Jellies may be poured into regular canning jars and then processed exactly 5 minutes in a boiling-water bath. Or, they may be safely canned in jars or glasses as directed on pages 60-61.

TESTS FOR DONENESS

Overcooking jams and jellies causes changes in flavor, color and consistency. When commercial pectins are added, cooking times are standardized and it is not necessary to test for gelling consistency. Making jam or jelly without added pectin requires testing by one of the following methods:

Plate Test: The plate test is not as reliable for jellies as it is for jams, preserves, conserves and butters. Chill a small plate in the refrigerator. When the jam has thickened slightly, 10 to 15 minutes, remove the pot from the heat to prevent overcooking. Place a spoonful of the hot mixture on the chilled plate. Place in the freezer for 1 minute. After 1 minute, there should be no watery ring around the mound. Draw your finger through the mixture. It should retain its shape and not flow into the trough.

Temperature Test: Testing with a thermometer is the most accurate and reliable method. Test the accuracy of your thermometer by holding the bulb in boiling water, not touching the bottom or side of the pan. To get an accurate reading, look straight at the thermometer, not at an angle. Record the temperature at which water boils at your altitude. Combine recipe ingredients according to directions. Boil 10 to 15 minutes, then begin checking the temperature with your thermometer. Cook *jellies* until the thermometer registers 8F (4C) above the temperature of boiling water. At sea level where water boils at 212F (100C), this finished temperature would be 220F (104C). *Jams* will be soft and spreadable when cooked to 6F (3C) above the temperature of boiling water, or 218F (103C) at sea level.

Sheeting Test: This test is widely used but is not dependable because there are degrees of sheeting. The test is not suited to jams. To test by sheeting, cool a large metal spoon in the refrigerator. Dip the spoon into the boiling jelly, taking a spoonful. Lift the spoon above the steam of the pot and turn it so the jelly runs off the side. At first, the jelly may drip off the spoon in light, syrupy drops. The jelly is done if drops flow together and fall off the spoon in a sheet.

Selecting Fruit for Jelly Making

Use in recipes with or without added pectin:

Apples	Gooseberries
Blackberries	Concord Grapes
Boysenberries	Lemons
Crab apples	Loganberries
Cranberries	Sour Plums
Currants	Quince

Use only in recipes with added dry or liquid pectin:

Apricots	Pears
Blueberries	Raspberries
Cherries	Strawberries
Peaches	

To extract juice, pour crushed or cooked fruit into a damp jelly bag or cheesecloth-lined colander set over a bowl. Let drip at least 4 hours.

How to Make Jam—At a Glance

Jams Without Added Pectin

1. Wash jars in hot soapy water; rinse. Keep hot until needed. Prepare lids as manufacturer directs.
2. Wash fruit. Remove stems, hulls and blossom ends. Cut out bruised parts.
3. Peel, pit, chop or crush fruit as directed in *Quick Guide to Making Jams*, page 62.
4. In a 6- to 8-quart pot, combine fruit, sugar and lemon juice if used. Let stand 20 minutes until juices form. Stirring constantly, cook over low heat until sugar dissolves.
5. Bring to a boil over medium-high heat. Boil until jam begins to thicken, 10 to 15 minutes.
6. Test doneness by temperature or plate test. To measure temperature, hold a thermometer in boiling jam so bulb is covered but not touching bottom of pan. Read temperature. Jam will be done at 6F (3C) above temperature of boiling water at your altitude.
7. For plate test, remove jam from heat. Place a spoonful of jam on a chilled plate. Put plate in freezer 1 minute. There should be no thin, watery ring around mound of jam on plate. Draw your finger through jam. Jam should not flow into trough made by finger.
8. Stir jam in pot; skim.
9. Ladle into dry hot jars to within 1/4 inch of top. Fill and close 1 jar at a time. Wipe rim of jar with a clean damp cloth. Put lid on jar as manfacturer directs.
10. Process jars in a boiling-water bath, 10 minutes, or time adjusted for altitudes of 1000 feet or higher, page 20.

Jams With Added Dry Pectin

1. Wash jars in hot soapy water; rinse. Keep hot until needed. Prepare lids as manufacturer directs.
2. Wash fruit. Remove stems, hulls and blossom ends. Cut out bruised parts. Prepare fruit as directed in *Quick Guide to Making Jams*, pages 62-63.
3. Combine fruit, lemon juice if called for and dry pectin in a 6- to 8-quart pot. Stir.
4. Measure sugar; set aside.
5. Stirring constantly, bring fruit mixture to a full rolling boil over high heat.
6. Add sugar all at once. Continue heating until jam comes to a rolling boil that cannot be stirred down.
7. Stirring constantly, boil *exactly* 1 minute. Remove from heat.
8. Stir and skim.
9. Ladle into hot jars to within 1/4 inch of top. Fill and close 1 jar at a time. Wipe rim of jar with a clean damp cloth. Put lid on jar as manufacturer directs.
10. Process jars in a boiling-water bath, 10 minutes, or time adjusted for altitudes of 1000 feet or higher, page 20.

Jams With Added Liquid Pectin

1. Wash jars in hot soapy water; rinse. Keep hot until needed. Prepare lids as manufacturer directs.
2. Wash fruit. Remove stems, hulls and blossom ends. Cut out bruised parts. Prepare fruit as directed in *Quick Guide to Making Jams*, page 63.
3. Combine fruit, lemon juice if called for and sugar in a 6- to 8-quart pot. Stir.
4. Open liquid pectin. Measure amount needed or open individual pouches as needed. Put in a measuring cup or glass, ready to pour.
5. Stirring constantly over high heat, bring fruit mixture to a rolling boil that cannot be stirred down. Do not reduce heat. Stirring constantly, boil *exactly* 1 minute.
6. Remove from heat. Stir in liquid pectin.
7. Stir and skim.
8. Ladle into hot jars to within 1/4 inch of top. Fill and close 1 jar at a time. Wipe rim of jar with a clean damp cloth. Put lid on jar as manufacturer directs.
9. Process jars in a boiling-water bath, 10 minutes, or time adjusted for altitudes of 1000 feet or higher, page 20.

1/To make jelly with liquid pectin, combine sugar, juice and acid if called for. Add liquid pectin after mixture comes to a boil.

2/Jams and jellies must be brought to a rolling boil that cannot be stirred down.

How To Make Jelly—At a Glance

Jellies Without Added Pectin

1. Wash jars or special glasses in hot soapy water; rinse. Sterilize by boiling 15 minutes in a large pot of water. Prepare lids as manufacturer directs.
2. Select about 1/3 underripe and 2/3 firm-ripe fruit. Wash fruit; remove stems, hulls and blossom ends.
3. Prepare fruit juice as directed in *Quick Guide to Making Jellies*, page 64.
4. Strain fruit juice through a dampened jelly bag or cheesecloth-lined colander, 4 hours to overnight.
5. If sealing with paraffin, melt paraffin in a double boiler or in a jar or can in a saucepan of simmering water, page 118. *Do not melt over direct heat*. Keep warm.
6. Test pectin content of the fruit juice with a jelmeter. Or use alcohol test by combining 1 teaspoon juice and 1 tablespoon denatured alcohol; stir. If a jelly-like mass forms, juice has enough pectin.
7. In a 6- to 8-quart pot, combine fruit juice, sugar and lemon juice if called for. Bring to a boil over high heat, stirring until sugar dissolves.
8. Boil jelly mixture 10 to 15 minutes, then begin testing for gelling point by temperature or sheeting test. To measure temperature, hold thermometer in boiling jelly so bulb is covered but not touching bottom of pot. Jelly is done at 8F (4C) above temperature of boiling water at your altitude.
9. For sheeting test, dip a chilled metal spoon into boiling jelly. Lift spoon above steam from pot. Tip so jelly drips off side of spoon into pot. When jelly no longer falls off spoon in drops but in a sheet, gel point has been reached.
10. Remove jelly from heat. Skim off bubbles. Ladle jelly into hot, sterilized containers, 1 at a time. Fill to within 1/8 inch of top if using self-sealing lids. Fill to within 1/2 inch of top if sealing with paraffin.
11. Wipe rim of jar or glass with a clean damp cloth.
12. If using self-sealing lid, place hot lid on jar. Tighten screwband firmly. Invert jar 30 seconds. Stand jar upright to cool. Or, process in a boiling-water bath, 5 minutes.
13. If sealing with paraffin, spoon a 1/8-inch layer of melted paraffin over jelly, covering completely. Cool 5 to 10 minutes until paraffin hardens. Place another spoonful of melted paraffin on top. Tilt and turn container so paraffin runs 1/4 inch or more up side. Cool 24 hours. Cover with lid or foil.

Jellies With Added Dry Pectin

1. Wash jars or special glasses in hot soapy water; rinse. Sterilize by boiling 15 minutes. Prepare lids.
2. Select fully ripe, flavorful fruit. Wash fruit; remove stems, hulls and blossom ends.
3. Prepare fruit juice as directed in *Quick Guide to Making Jellies*, pages 64-65.
4. Strain fruit juice through a dampened jelly bag or cheesecloth-lined colander, 4 hours to overnight.
5. If sealing with paraffin, melt paraffin in a double boiler or in a jar or can in a saucepan of simmering water, page 118. *Do not melt over direct heat.* Keep warm.
6. Stir fruit juice, lemon juice if called for, and dry pectin in a 6- to 8-quart pot until pectin dissolves.
7. Measure sugar; set aside.
8. Stirring constantly, bring juice mixture to a boil over high heat.
9. Add sugar all at once. Cook and stir as mixture comes to a rolling boil that cannot be stirred down.
10. Stirring constantly, boil *exactly* 1 minute.
11. Remove jelly from heat. Skim off bubbles. Ladle jelly into hot, sterilized containers, 1 at a time. Fill to within 1/8 inch of top if using self-sealing lids. Fill to within 1/2 inch of top if sealing with paraffin.
12. Wipe rim of jar or glass with a clean damp cloth.
13. If using self-sealing lid, place hot lid on jar. Tighten screwband firmly. Invert jar 30 seconds. Stand upright to cool. Or, process in a boiling-water bath, 5 minutes.
14. If sealing with paraffin, spoon a 1/8-inch layer of melted paraffin over jelly, covering completely. Cool 5 to 10 minutes until paraffin hardens. Place another spoonful of melted paraffin on top. Tilt and turn container so paraffin runs 1/4 inch or more up side. Cool 24 hours. Cover with lid or foil.

Jellies With Added Liquid Pectin

1. Wash jars or special glasses in hot soapy water; rinse. Sterilize by boiling 15 minutes. Prepare lids.
2. Select fully ripe, flavorful fruit. Wash fruit; remove stems, hulls and blossom ends.
3. Prepare fruit juice as directed in *Quick Guide to Making Jellies*, page 65.
4. Strain fruit juice through a dampened jelly bag or cheesecloth-lined colander, 4 hours to overnight.
5. If sealing with paraffin, melt paraffin in a double boiler or in a jar or can in a saucepan of simmering water, page 118. *Do not melt over direct heat.* Keep warm.
6. Stir fruit juice, sugar and lemon juice if called for, in a 6- to 8-quart pot until sugar dissolves.
7. Stirring constantly, bring to a boil over high heat.
8. Stir in liquid pectin. Cook and stir until jelly comes to a rolling boil that cannot be stirred down.
9. Stirring constantly, boil *exactly* 1 minute.
10. Remove from heat. Skim off foam. Ladle jelly into hot, sterilized containers. Fill to within 1/8 inch of top if using self-sealing lids. Fill to within 1/2 inch of top if sealing with paraffin.
11. Wipe rim of container with a clean damp cloth.
12. If using self-sealing lid, place hot lid on jar. Tighten screwband firmly. Invert jar 30 seconds. Stand upright to cool. Or, process in a boiling-water bath, 5 minutes.
13. If using paraffin, spoon a 1/8-inch layer of melted paraffin over jelly, covering completely. Cool 5 to 10 minutes or until paraffin hardens. Place another spoonful of melted paraffin on top. Tilt and turn container so paraffin runs 1/4 inch or more up side. Cool 24 hours. Cover with a lid or foil.

Substitutions for Sugar in Jams & Jellies

Corn Syrup:
Without Added Pectin: Corn syrup may be substituted on an equal basis for up to 1/4 the total amount of sugar.
With Added Dry Pectin: Corn syrup may be substituted on an equal basis for up to 1/2 the total amount of sugar.
With Added Liquid Pectin: Up to 2 cups of the total amount of sugar may be replaced with 2 cups of corn syrup.

Honey:
Without Added Pectin: Honey may be substituted on an equal basis for up to 1/2 the total amount of sugar.
With Added Dry or Liquid Pectin: Up to 2 cups of the total amount of sugar may be replaced with 2 cups of honey.

Quick Guide to Making Jams

Fruit	Ingredients	Approximate Cooking Time	Processing Time	Yield
No Added Pectin				
Apricot	4-1/2 cups chopped, pitted, apricots 4 cups sugar 2 tablespoons lemon juice	25 min.	10 min.	5-6 (8-oz.) jars
Berry	4 cups crushed blackberries, boysenberries, dewberries, gooseberries, loganberries raspberries, strawberries or youngberries 3 cups sugar 2-4 tablespoons lemon juice	20 min.	10 min.	3-4 (8-oz.) jars
Peach or Pear	6 cups chopped, peeled, cored or pitted peaches or pears 4-5 cups sugar 2 tablespoons lemon juice	20 min.	10 min.	6-7 (8-oz.) jars
Plum	5 cups chopped, pitted, red plums 4 cups sugar	15 min.	10 min.	5-6 (8-oz.) jars
Added Dry Pectin				
Apricot	5 cups chopped, pitted, apricots 1/4 cup lemon juice 1 (1-3/4-oz.) pkg. dry pectin 7 cups sugar	1 min. at rolling boil after sugar is added.	10 min.	7-8 (8-oz.) jars
Berry	5 cups crushed blackberries, boysenberries, dewberries, gooseberries, loganberries, raspberries, strawberries or youngberries 1 (1-3/4-oz.) pkg. dry pectin 7 cups sugar	1 min. at rolling boil after sugar is added.	10 min.	8-9 (8-oz.) jars
Blueberry	4 cups crushed blueberries 1 (1-3/4-oz.) pkg. dry pectin 2 tablespoons lemon juice 4 cups sugar	1 min. at rolling boil after sugar is added.	10 min.	5-6 (8-oz.) jars
Cherry	4 cups pitted, chopped sour or sweet cherries 1 (1-3/4-oz.) pkg. dry pectin 2 tablespoons lemon juice, with sweet cherries 5 cups sugar	1 min. at rolling boil after sugar is added.	10 min.	5-6 (8-oz.) jars
Peach	4 cups chopped, pitted, peeled peaches 1 (1-3/4-oz.) pkg. dry pectin 2 tablespoons lemon juice 5-1/2 cups sugar	1 min. at rolling boil after sugar is added.	10 min.	6-7 (8-oz.) jars
Pear	4 cups chopped, cored, peeled pears 1 (1-3/4-oz.) pkg. dry pectin 2 tablespoons lemon juice 5 cups sugar	1 min. at rolling boil after sugar is added.	10 min.	6-7 (8-oz.) jars

Fruit	Ingredients	Approximate Cooking Time	Processing Time	Yield
Added Dry Pectin (cont.)				
Plum	6 cups chopped, pitted plums 1 (1-3/4-oz.) pkg. dry pectin 8 cups sugar	1 min. at rolling boil after sugar is added.	10 min.	9-10 (8-oz.) jars
Rhubarb	6 cups trimmed, thinly sliced rhubarb. Simmer in 1 cup water until tender. Use 4-1/2 cups cooked rhubarb 1 (1-3/4-oz.) pkg. dry pectin 6-1/2 cups sugar	1 min. at rolling boil after sugar is added.	10 min.	6-7 (8-oz.) jars
Added Liquid Pectin				
Apricot	3-1/2 cups chopped, pitted apricots 1/3 cup lemon juice 6-1/2 cups sugar 1 (3-oz.) pouch liquid pectin	1 min. at rolling boil before pectin is added.	10 min.	6-7 (8-oz.) jars
Berry	4 cups crushed blackberries, boysenberries, dewberries, gooseberries, loganberries, raspberries, strawberries or youngberries 7 cups sugar 1 (3-oz.) pouch liquid pectin	1 min. at rolling boil before pectin is added.	10 min.	8-9 (8-oz.) jars
Cherry	2 cups chopped, pitted sour or sweet cherries 2 tablespoons lemon juice, with sweet cherries 3-1/2 cups sugar 1 (3-oz.) pouch liquid pectin	1 min. at rolling boil before pectin is added.	10 min.	4-5 (8-oz.) jars
Fig	4 cups chopped or ground figs 1/2 cup lemon juice 7-1/2 cups sugar 1 (3-oz.) pouch liquid pectin	1 min. at rolling boil before pectin is added.	10 min.	9-10 (8-oz.) jars
Grape	3-4 lbs. Concord grapes Remove, chop and reserve skins. Simmer grapes in 1/2 cup water, 5 minutes. Press through sieve; discard seeds. Add chopped skins to make 5 cups. 7-1/2 cups sugar 1 (3-oz.) pouch liquid pectin	1 min. at rolling boil before pectin is added.	10 min.	9-10 (8-oz.) jars
Peach or Pear	4 cups chopped, peeled peaches or pears 1/4 cup lemon juice 7 cups sugar 1 (3-oz.) pouch liquid pectin	1 min. at rolling boil before pectin is added.	10 min.	8-9 (8-oz.) jars
Plum	4-1/2 cups pitted, chopped plums 7-1/2 cups sugar 1 (3-oz.) pouch liquid pectin	1 min. at rolling boil before pectin is added.	10 min.	8-9 (8-oz.) jars

Quick Guide to Making Jellies

Fruit	Extracting the Juice	Cooking Ingredients	Approximate Cooking Time	Yield
No Added Pectin				
Apple	3 lbs. whole apples, finely chopped. Simmer in 3 cups water until tender, 20-30 min. Drip through jelly bag or cheesecloth-lined sieve.	4 cups juice 3 cups sugar 2 tablespoons lemon juice if apples not tart	15 min.	4-5 (8-oz.) jars
Berry	Crush 10 cups blackberries, boysenberries, gooseberries or loganberries. Simmer in 3/4 cup water, 5 min. Drip through jelly bag or cheesecloth-lined sieve.	4 cups juice 3 cups sugar	20 min.	3-4 (8-oz.) jars
Crab Apple	Simmer 3 lbs. chopped crab apples in 3 cups water until tender, 20 min. Drip through jelly bag or cheesecloth-lined sieve.	4 cups juice 3 cups sugar	15 min.	4-5 (8-oz.) jars
Currant	Boil 2 qts. currants in 2 cups water until soft, 10 min. Drip through jelly bag or cheesecloth-lined sieve.	4 cups juice 3-1/2 cups sugar	20 min.	5-6 (8-oz.) jars
Grape	Crush 3-1/2 lbs. Concord grapes. Simmer in 1/2 cup water, 10 min. Drip through jelly bag or cheesecloth-lined sieve. Refrigerate 8 to 10 hours; drip again.	4 cups juice 3 cups sugar	20 min.	3-4 (8-oz.) jars
Mint	Pour 1/2 cup boiling water over 1/2 cup packed chopped fresh mint leaves; steep 30 min. Strain; discard mint. Extract juice from 3 lbs. apples. See *Apple,* above.	1/2 cup mint extract 4 cups apple juice 3 cups sugar 2 drops green food coloring	15 min.	5-6 (8-oz.) jars
Added Dry Pectin				
Berry	Crush 10 cups blackberries, boysenberries, dewberries, strawberries or youngberries. Drip through jelly bag or cheesecloth-lined sieve.	3-1/2 cups juice 1 (1-3/4-oz.) pkg. dry pectin 5 cups sugar	1 min. at rolling boil after sugar is added.	5-6 (8-oz.) jars
Cherry, sour	Remove stems from 3-1/2 lbs. cherries. Do not pit; crush. Simmer in 1/2 cup water, 10 min. Drip through jelly bag or cheesecloth-lined sieve.	3-1/2 cups juice 1 (1-3/4-oz.) pkg. dry pectin 4-1/2 cups sugar	1 min. at rolling boil after sugar is added.	5-6 (8-oz.) jars
Grape	Crush 4 lbs. Concord grapes. Simmer in 1 cup water, 10 min. Drip through jelly bag or cheesecloth-lined sieve. Refrigerate 8 to 10 hours; drip again.	5 cups juice 1 (1-3/4-oz.) pkg. dry pectin 7 cups sugar	1 min. at rolling boil after sugar is added.	8-9 (8-oz.) jars

Fruit	Extracting the Juice	Cooking Ingredients	Approximate Cooking Time	Yield
Added Dry Pectin (cont.)				
Peach	Pit 3-1/2 lbs. unpeeled peaches; chop or grind. Simmer in 1/2 cup water, 10 min. Drip through jelly bag or cheesecloth-lined sieve.	3 cups juice 1 (1-3/4-oz.) pkg. dry pectin 1/2 cup lemon juice	1 min. at rolling boil after sugar is added.	5-6 (8-oz.) jars
Plum	Pit 5 lbs. plums; crush. Simmer fruit and pits in 1-1/2 cups water, 10 min. Drip through jelly bag or cheesecloth-lined sieve.	5-1/2 cups juice 1 (1-3/4-oz.) pkg. dry pectin 7-1/2 cups sugar	1 min. at rolling boil after sugar is added.	8-9 (8-oz.) jars
Raspberry, Loganberry	Crush 12 cups raspberries or loganberries. Drip through jelly bag or cheesecloth-lined sieve.	4 cups juice 1 (1-3/4-oz.) pkg. dry pectin 5-1/2 cups sugar	1 min. at rolling boil after sugar is added.	5-6 (8-oz.) jars
Added Liquid Pectin				
Berry	Crush 12 cups blackberries, boysenberries, dewberries, loganberries, red raspberries, strawberries or youngberries. Drip through jelly bag or cheesecloth-lined sieve.	3-3/4 cups juice 1/4 cup lemon juice 7-1/2 cups sugar 2 (3-oz.) pouches liquid pectin	1 min. at rolling boil after pectin is added.	7-8 (8-oz.) jars
Blueberry	Crush 8 cups blueberries. Simmer 5 min. Drip through jelly bag or cheesecloth-lined sieve.	4 cups juice 7-1/2 cups sugar 2 (3-oz.) pouches liquid pectin	1 min. at rolling boil after pectin is added.	7-8 (8-oz.) jars
Cherry	Remove stems from 3-1/2 lbs. sweet or sour cherries. Do not pit; crush. Simmer in 1/2 cup water, 10 min. Drip through jelly bag or cheesecloth-lined sieve.	3-1/2 cups juice 7 cups sugar 2 (3-oz.) pouches liquid pectin	1 min. at rolling boil after pectin is added.	7-8 (8-oz.) jars
Grape	Crush 3-1/2 lbs. Concord grapes. Simmer in 1/2 cup water, 10 min. Drip through jelly bag or cheesecloth-lined sieve. Refrigerate 8 to 10 hours; drip again.	4 cups grape juice 7 cups sugar 1 (3-oz.) pouch liquid pectin	1 min. at rolling boil after pectin is added.	8-9 (8-oz.) jars
Mint	Pour 2 cups boiling water over 1-1/2 cups chopped, packed, fresh mint leaves; steep 30 minutes. Strain; discard leaves.	1-3/4 cups mint extract 2 tablespoons lemon juice 1 (3-oz.) pouch liquid pectin	1 min. at rolling boil after pectin is added.	3-4 (8-oz.) jars
Plum	Pit 4-1/2 lbs. plums; crush. Simmer fruit and pits in 1/2 cup water, 10 min. Drip through jelly bag or cheesecloth-lined sieve.	4 cups juice 7-1/2 cups sugar 1 (3-oz.) pouch liquid pectin	1 min. at rolling boil after pectin is added.	7-8 (8-oz.) jars

Tip

If the color of your jams or jellies fades during storage, the room may be too warm, or they may have been stored too long.

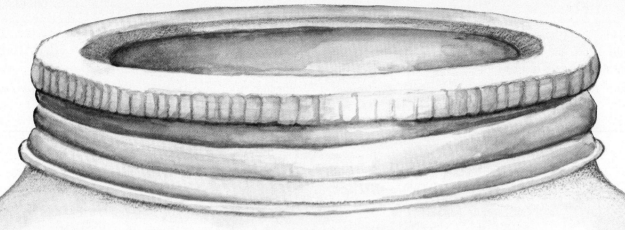

Basic Canning:
Meats, Poultry & Fish

Canned meats are convenient and safe when processed correctly. Fresh meats, poultry and fish are extremely perishable. Can them with careful attention to cleanliness and recipe directions.

Meats, poultry and fish must be processed in a pressure canner. Do not use any other method to can meats, poultry and fish. These low-acid foods must be heated to 240F (116C) to kill any Clostridium botulinum spores and other organisms that cause food poisoning. Because meats are dense, they require 75 to 90 minutes processing time. Keep an accurate account of processing time to ensure a safe product.

Use lean meats or trim off all visible fat. Fat develops a strong, undesirable flavor during processing.

Veal, pork, lamb and large game such as venison and elk may be canned using the directions for beef. Turkey, duck and rabbit are canned like chicken. Shellfish including shrimp, crab, oysters and clams may also be canned, though directions are not included here. Considering the scarcity and cost of shellfish, freezing is a better method of preservation. *Do not use directions for canning tuna, salmon, trout or whitefish to can shellfish.* For information on canning shellfish, write to U.S. Department of the Interior, Division of Fisheries Industries, Washington, D.C. 20402, or ask your county cooperative extension agent for *Canning Seafood,* a Pacific Northwest Extension Publication, PNW 194.

Bacteria grow rapidly on meat, poultry and fish. Prepare and process meat the same day of purchase if possible. Process fish within 24 hours after it is caught. Keep all meat, poultry and fish refrigerated or frozen until ready to process. Work with small amounts at a time.

Scrub cutting boards and utensils with hot soapy water *before and after each use.* Rinse well with boiling water, then disinfect cutting surfaces and wooden utensils. Stir 2 tablespoons chlorine bleach into 2 cups water. Pour onto surfaces and utensils. Cover with a clean cloth to hold the disinfectant solution on surfaces, if necessary. Leave 15 minutes. Wash thoroughly with boiling water to remove the disinfectant.

Salt does not act as a preservative, but does bring out the flavor of the meat. Its presence or absence does not change the method of canning or the processing time. If salt is included, use ordinary table salt. *Do not use salt substitutes* because they may create undesirable flavors in the meat. Process the meat without salt and add the salt substitute at serving time.

Check canned meats, poultry and fish for spoilage. A bulging lid, gas bubbles in the jar, unpleasant odors, foaming and spurting liquid as the jar is opened, indicate spoilage. The inside enameled surface of jar lids may darken because of the sulfur in meat, but this does not mean there is spoilage.

Always cover and boil canned meats 20 minutes before serving or tasting. This will destroy small amounts of toxins if present in the meat. It will also intensify any unpleasant odors and alert you to spoilage. If the meat is spoiled, destroy it as directed on page 19. *Do not just throw it in the garbage or put it in the food disposal.*

Canned meat or poultry to be used *in a cold salad* must be boiled 20 minutes, then refrigerated until it is chilled. Fish will keep its shape better if it is baked. Bake it in a 350F (175C) oven by this method developed at Oregon State University: Insert a meat thermometer in the center of the jar of fish after the lid has been removed. Cover loosely with foil. Place in the preheated oven until the thermometer registers 185F (85C). This will require about 30 minutes. Remove from the oven, cover and let stand at room temperature 30 minutes. Then refrigerate the fish until it is chilled.

When meat, poultry or fish are used in a casserole or stew, check the jar for signs of spoilage. If there are none, combine with other ingredients. *Boil stews at least 30 minutes. Bake casseroles at 350F (175C) at least 45 minutes.*

HOW TO CAN MEATS, POULTRY & FISH

Meats and poultry may be canned in pint, 1-1/2-pint or quart jars. Pints are convenient for families of two or three. Quarts and 1-1/2-pints are best for families of four or more. A 1-1/2-pint jar will hold 1 pound of ground beef using the *Ground Beef Mix* recipe. The boned meat from a 3-pound chicken will fill a pint jar. A 1-1/2-pint jar holds 2 pounds of beef cubes.

Fish, because of its density and extreme low acidity, must be packed in either 1/2-pint or pint jars.

Cut cubes of meat as uniformly as possible so they will cook evenly. Coarsely ground meat will keep its shape better than regular grind. To grind meat coarsely, use your meat grinder and the grinding plate with the largest holes, or ask a butcher to grind it for you. Use lean beef. Do not add any fat.

Cut poultry into frying pieces, leaving the bones in. If you want to remove the bones, it is easier to do so after cooking. When cutting frying pieces, leave the skin on legs and thighs, but remove it from breasts. Pack raw or cooked frying pieces into hot jars according to recipe directions.

Fish must be freshly caught and cleaned. Remove the backbone and cut the flesh into pieces that will fit in the jars without folding. Soak fish in a salt-water brine. This prevents white protein curds from forming on the fish during processing. See recipes for brine ingredients.

Pack all meats *loosely* so heat will penetrate evenly. Leave 1 inch headspace at the top of the jar. If there is too little headspace, liquid may boil out. If too much headspace is left, the jars may not seal. Meat shrinks during processing, so finished jars may be only three-fourths full. Meats not covered with liquid after processing will not spoil, although they may darken somewhat. Do not open jars to add more liquid.

Droplets of fat on the rim of the jar may prevent a seal from forming. After filling, wipe the rim with a clean, dry, absorbent cloth or paper towel. Place filled jars in a pressure canner.

A constant and steady pressure must be maintained throughout the canning process. If pressure is lost, processing time must be started again from the beginning. Watch the dial gauge or listen for the constant jiggle of the weighted regulator on your canner. Adjust the heat if necessary, then check the pressure frequently. When processing is completed, cool the canner as directed on page 18.

Label jars with the recipe title, batch number and the date. Store them in a cool dark place.

It is possible to process meats and vegetables together for a ready-to-heat-and-serve stew, but the vegetables will be greatly overcooked. *Whenever two or more foods are combined, the processing time is the longest time required for any one of the foods.* We suggest you open separate jars of vegetables and meats and combine them as you prepare meals.

To make casseroles, season and thicken the liquid from canned meats, fish or poultry. Combine meats and thickened liquid with home-canned vegetables and freshly cooked pasta or rice. By using separately canned meats and vegetables, there are more possibilities for combinations.

Chicken Broth

Save an hour by making the broth in a pressure cooker. See the variation below.

6 lbs. chicken backs, wings or carcasses
Water
4 chicken bouillon cubes
1 medium onion, sliced
2 celery stalks with leafy tops, chopped
2 medium carrots, sliced

2 garlic cloves, peeled
2 bay leaves
1/2 teaspoon dried leaf thyme
2 teaspoons dried leaf basil
10 black peppercorns

In a large pot, cover chicken backs, wings or carcasses with water. Bring to a gentle boil over medium heat. Boil 5 minutes, skimming foam from surface. Add remaining ingredients. Bring back to a boil. Reduce heat until mixture just simmers. Cover; simmer 2 hours. Wash 6 pint jars in hot soapy water; rinse. Keep hot until needed. Prepare lids as manufacturer directs. Strain broth, discarding bones, vegetables and herbs. Set broth aside 15 minutes to let fat droplets come to surface. Spoon fat from surface. Draw strips of paper towel across surface of broth to blot up remaining fat droplets. Heat broth to a simmer. Ladle into 1 hot jar at a time, leaving 1 inch headspace. Wipe rim of jar with a clean dry cloth or paper towel. Attach lid. Place in canner. Fill and close remaining jars. *Process in a pressure canner at 10 pounds pressure,* page 17.

   Pints: 20 minutes
Adjust pressure for altitude, page 21. Makes about 6 pints.

Variation

Place chicken in a large pressure canner until no more than 2/3 full. Cover with water. Add remaining ingredients. Process at 10 pounds pressure for 1 hour. Strain, pack and process as above.

Beef Broth

Ask your butcher for meaty beef bones. Freeze bones and trimmings until you have 8 pounds.

8 lbs. meaty beef bones or
   meat scraps and trimmings
Water
4 beef bouillon cubes
2 medium carrots, sliced
1 medium onion, sliced
1 celery stalk with leafy top, sliced

2 garlic cloves, minced
2 bay leaves
1/2 teaspoon dried leaf thyme
1 teaspoon dried leaf basil
1/4 cup chopped fresh parsley or
   1 tablespoon dried leaf parsley
1/2 cup red wine

Place bones or scraps and trimmings in a large pot. Cover with water. Bring to a boil over medium-high heat. Boil 5 minutes, skimming foam from surface. Add remaining ingredients. Bring back to a simmer. Cover; simmer 6 hours. Wash 6 pint jars in hot soapy water; rinse. Keep hot until needed. Prepare lids as manufacturer directs. Strain broth, discarding bones, meat scraps, vegetables and herbs. Set broth aside 15 minutes to let fat droplets come to surface. Spoon fat from surface. Draw strips of paper towel across surface of broth to blot up remaining fat droplets. Bring broth to a boil over high heat. Ladle hot broth into 1 hot jar at a time, leaving 1 inch headspace. Wipe rim of jar with a clean dry cloth or paper towel. Attach lid. Place in canner. Fill and close remaining jars. *Process in a pressure canner at 10 pounds pressure,* page 17.

   Pints: 20 minutes
Adjust pressure for altitude, page 21. Makes about 6 pints.

1/Cut lean, well-trimmed meat into uniform-size cubes. Brown cubed meat in a skillet.

2/Add onion to browned meat. Pack into jars. Add boiling stock or juice, leaving 1 inch headspace.

Stew Beef

Use in Creamy Burgundy Beef or Hungarian Goulash, page 162, or your favorite stew.

16 lbs. beef chuck or beef round, **cut 1-inch thick**	**2 teaspoons dried leaf basil**
3-3/4 cups Beef Broth, opposite page, or	**1/2 teaspoon dried leaf thyme**
3 (10-1/2-oz.) cans beef broth	**2 teaspoons salt**
6 cups water	**1/4 teaspoon pepper**
2 bay leaves	**1/2 cup vegetable oil**
	2 medium onions, chopped

Wash 12 pint, eight 1-1/2-pint or 6 quart jars in hot soapy water; rinse. Keep hot until needed. Prepare lids as manufacturer directs. Cut meat from bone. In a 4-quart pot, combine bones, broth, water, bay leaf, basil, thyme, salt and pepper. Bring to a boil over medium-high heat. Cover and simmer 20 minutes. While broth simmers, trim fat from beef. Cut beef into 1-inch cubes, making them as uniform as possible; set aside. Strain broth through a cheesecloth-lined sieve. Discard bones and spices. Return broth to pot; keep hot. In a large skillet, heat 2 tablespoons oil. Brown about 3 pounds beef cubes in hot oil. Add 1/2 cup chopped onion. Stirring constantly, cook until onion is soft. Pack beef mixture into 1 hot jar at a time, leaving 1-1/2 inches headspace. Pour hot broth over meat to cover, leaving 1 inch headspace. Wipe rim of jar with a clean dry cloth or paper towel. Attach lid. Place filled jar in canner; keep hot. Repeat, browning 3 pounds beef cubes at a time, adding 1/2 cup onion as above. Fill and close remaining jars. *Process in a pressure canner at 10 pounds pressure,* page 17.

    Pints: 75 minutes
    1-1/2-pints or quarts: 90 minutes
Adjust pressure for altitude, page 21. Makes 12 pints, eight 1-1/2-pints or 6 quarts.

Corned Beef

For a brighter red color, see the variation.

12 lbs. Corned Beef, see below	**1 medium onion, sliced**
Cold water	**2 bay leaves**
2 tablespoons pickling spices	**1 teaspoon black peppercorns**
2 garlic cloves, peeled, flattened	**1 dried hot red pepper, if desired**

Corned Beef:

12 lbs. beef brisket, bottom round, rump or eye of round	**2 tablespoons granulated sugar**
2 cups coarse salt	**1 tablespoon cream of tartar**
4 qts. water	**2 tablespoons pickling spices**
2 tablespoons brown sugar	**3 garlic cloves, peeled, flattened**

Prepare Corned Beef. Wash 8 pint, five 1-1/2-pint or 4 quart jars in hot soapy water; rinse. Keep hot until needed. Prepare lids as manufacturer directs. Remove fat from corned beef. Cut meat into pieces 1-1/2 inches shorter than canning jars. Place meat pieces in a 6- or 8-quart pot. Cover with cold water. Bring to a boil over medium-high heat. Skim foam from surface. Taste broth. If very salty, pour off broth; discard. Again cover with cold water. Bring to a boil. Add remaining ingredients. Reduce heat until mixture just simmers. Cover; simmer 30 minutes. Use a slotted spoon to remove meat from broth. Pack into hot jars, leaving 1-1/2 inches headspace. Strain broth; discard spices. Return broth to pot; bring back to a boil. Ladle hot broth over meat to cover. Release trapped air. Wipe rims of jars with a clean dry cloth or paper towel. Attach lids. Place in canner. *Process in a pressure canner at 10 pounds pressure,* page 17.

    Pints: 75 minutes

    1-1/2-pints or quarts: 90 minutes

Adjust pressure for altitude, page 21. Makes 8 pints, five 1-1/2-pints or 4 quarts.

Corned Beef:

Trim visible fat from beef. Sprinkle 1/2 to 1 cup coarse salt evenly over meat. Use your hand to rub in salt. In a 6- or 8-quart pot, combine remaining ingredients. Bring to a boil, stirring until sugar and salt dissolve. Cool to room temperature. Wash a 6- to 8-quart glass or plastic container in hot soapy water; rinse. Scald by pouring in boiling water to top of container. Place a clean plate and pint jar in container to scald. After 10 minutes, remove plate and jar. Fill jar with water from container. Attach lid; set aside. Drain water from container. Place meat in sterile container; add cooled brine. Place scalded plate on top to keep meat submerged in brine. Place scalded jar filled with water on plate, if necessary. Store in refrigerator 10 to 14 days. After 3 days, remove meat; stir brine. Turn meat over; return to brine. Repeat every 3 days. After 10 days, cut into beef to determine whether brine has penetrated to center. If necessary, continue process remaining 4 days. Remove meat from brine. Rinse under running cool water.

Variation

Corned Beef with Sodium Nitrate: Add 1 teaspoon sodium nitrate (saltpeter) to brine; omit cream of tartar. Follow directions as above.

Tip

If canning jars are hard to clean, fill them with soda water, using 2 tablespoons baking soda per quart of water. Let stand 20 minutes, then scrub the jars in hot soapy water. Never use a wire brush or anything that might scratch jars.

Ground-Beef Mix

Ask the butcher to grind lean beef coarsely.

6 cups or 1 (48-oz.) can tomato juice
1-1/4 cups Beef Broth, page 68, or
   1 (10-1/2-oz.) can beef broth
1 tablespoon salt

1/2 teaspoon pepper
6 lbs. lean beef, coarsely ground
3 cups chopped onions
1 garlic clove, minced

Wash 9 pint jars or six 1-1/2-pint jars in hot soapy water; rinse. Keep hot until needed. Prepare lids as manufacturer directs. In a 6- or 8-quart pot, combine tomato juice, broth, salt and pepper. Bring to a boil over high heat. Reduce heat to medium-low; keep broth mixture hot. Brown 2 pounds ground beef in a large heavy skillet. When meat is no longer pink, spoon into broth mixture. Discard pan drippings. Repeat browning meat, 2 pounds at a time. After last 2 pounds beef is cooked, sauté onions and garlic in pan drippings. Add to broth mixture. Bring broth mixture to a boil over medium-high heat. Cover and simmer 5 minutes. Pack into 1 hot jar at a time, leaving 1 inch headspace. Wipe rim of jar with a clean dry cloth or paper towel. Attach lid. Place in canner. Fill and close remaining jars. *Process in a pressure canner at 10 pounds pressure,* page 17.
   Pints: 75 minutes
   1-1/2-pints: 90 minutes
Adjust pressure for altitude, page 21. Makes 9 pints or six 1-1/2-pints.

Chunk Chicken   Photo on page 73.

One pint jar of this boneless chicken is equivalent to a 3-pound chicken.

6 to 8 stewing chickens (24 lbs.)
10 cups water
4 chicken bouillon cubes
1 medium onion, chopped
2 celery stalks with leafy tops, chopped

2 carrots, sliced
2 bay leaves
1 teaspoon dried leaf basil
1/4 teaspoon dried leaf thyme
2 teaspoons salt, if desired

Wash 8 pint jars in hot soapy water; rinse. Keep hot until needed. Prepare lids as manufacturer directs. Cut chickens into backs, breasts, wings and legs. In a 10-quart pot, combine chicken pieces and remaining ingredients. Bring to a boil over medium-high heat. Cover; simmer over low heat until chicken is barely pink next to bones, about 20 minutes. Lift chicken from broth. Strain broth through a cheesecloth-lined sieve. Return broth to pot; keep hot. Remove and discard skin and bones from chicken. Pack meat pieces tightly into 1 hot jar at a time, leaving 1-1/4 inches headspace. Pour hot broth over chicken to cover, leaving 1 inch headspace. Wipe rim of jar with a clean dry cloth or paper towel. Attach lid. Place in canner. Fill and close remaining jars. *Process in a pressure canner at 10 pounds pressure,* page 17.
   Pints: 75 minutes
Adjust pressure for altitude, page 21. Makes 8 pints.

Chicken Pieces

Canned chicken makes casseroles quick and easy to prepare.

3 to 4 frying chickens (12 lbs.)
1 tablespoon salt, if desired

Wash six 1-1/2-pint or 3 quart jars in hot soapy water; rinse. Keep hot until needed. Prepare lids as manufacturer directs. Use a sharp knife to cut legs and wings from each chicken, at joints. Remove skin from breasts; leave skin on legs and thighs. Cut breast meat from carcass by cutting down 1 side of center bone from wishbone to end of breast bone. Continue cutting meat away from ribs down side of breast to end of ribs. Repeat with other side of breast. Cut legs into thighs and drumsticks. Use wings and remaining carcass to make broth. Pack raw chicken pieces tightly into 1 hot jar at a time, with thighs and drumsticks on outside. Pack boneless breast in center. Leave 1 inch headspace at top of jar. Sprinkle salt over chicken if desired, using 3/4 teaspoon in 1-1/2-pints and 1 teaspoon in quarts. Add no liquid. Wipe rim of jar with a clean dry cloth or paper towel. Attach lid. Place in canner. Fill and close remaining jars. *Process in a pressure canner at 10 pounds pressure,* page 17.

    1-1/2-pints or quarts: 80 minutes
Adjust pressure for altitude, page 21. Makes six 1-1/2-pints or 3 quarts.

Tuna

You must precook this oily fish in a brine to remove some of the oil.

7 lbs. fresh tuna fillets   **2 gallons cool water**
1-1/2 cups salt

Cut fish into pieces 1 inch shorter than pint jars. Fish must not be folded over in jar. In a large nonmetal container, stir 1 cup salt into 4 quarts water until dissolved. Place fish pieces in brine; cover. Refrigerate 1 hour. Wash twelve 1/2-pint or 6 pint jars in hot soapy water; rinse. Keep hot until needed. Prepare lids as manufacturer directs. Drain fish; discard brine. In an 8-quart pot, combine remaining 1/2 cup salt and 4 quarts water. Bring to a boil over high heat. Add soaked fish pieces. Bring back to a slow boil. Reduce heat until mixture just simmers. Simmer 15 minutes. Drain. Pack hot fish into 1 hot jar at a time, leaving 1 inch headspace. Wipe rim of jar with a clean dry cloth or paper towel. Attach lid. Place in canner. Fill and close remaining jars. *Process in a pressure canner at 10 pounds pressure,* page 17.

    1/2-pints or pints: 100 minutes
Adjust pressure for altitude, page 21. Makes twelve 1/2-pints or 6 pints.

How to Make Chicken Pieces and Chunk Chicken

1/Pack raw chicken pieces with thighs and drumsticks to outside of jars. Pack boneless breast meat in center of jar.

2/Hot pack cooked, boned and skinned chicken in hot jars. Add boiling strained cooking broth, leaving 1 inch headspace.

Salmon, Trout & Whitefish

Keep freshly caught fish refrigerated until ready to process.

**7 lbs. salmon, trout or
   other white fish fillets**

**1 cup salt
4 qts. cool water**

Cut fish into pieces 1 inch shorter than pint jars. Fish must not be folded over in jar. In a large nonmetal container, stir salt into water until dissolved. Place fish pieces in brine; cover. Refrigerate 1 hour. Wash 9 pint jars in hot soapy water; rinse. Keep hot until needed. Prepare lids as manufacturer directs. Remove fish from brine; drain in a colander or on paper towels. Pack drained fish pieces into 1 hot jar at a time, leaving 1 inch headspace. Wipe rim of jar with a clean dry cloth or paper towel. Attach lid. Place in canner. Fill and close remaining jars. *Process in a pressure canner at 10 pounds pressure,* page 17.

   Pints: 100 minutes

Adjust pressure for altitude, page 21. Makes 9 pints.

Canning with Flair:

In this section, you'll find recipes for 6- to 8-quart batches of specially prepared food—fruit combinations, seasoned vegetables, unusual sweet spreads, crisp tart pickles and relishes and flavor-enhancing sauces. They will add flair to any meal. The techniques of pickling and fermenting are used to give special tart flavors and crisp textures to fruits and vegetables. Follow directions exactly to ensure safety. These canned foods make wonderful gifts.

Fruits & Syrups

Specialty fruits and fruit combinations have no substitutes in commercially canned fruits. Combinations such as Apple-Pear Sauce, Fruit Mélange and Pears in Red Wine, are attractive and colorful. Growing seasons overlap, making canning of these combinations possible.

Some specialty fruits are seasoned with ginger, honey or brandy. Some are tart with vinegar, giving a sweet-and-sour flavor. Spicy Summer Fruit combines peaches, pears and grapes in a vinegar syrup. Serve this especially tasty trio with beef, pork or lamb. Spiced Apple Rings or Minty

Pears will add a colorful and exotic touch to a platter of roasted chicken.

Home-canned pie fillings make baked desserts simple. Make a cobbler by arranging biscuits on top of a hot pie filling. Bake the cobbler in a 425F (220C) oven about 15 minutes until the biscuits are lightly browned. Or, spoon warmed pie filling over cake or cheesecake to create a fast and delicious treat.

Fruit syrups have a variety of uses. The family will be early to breakfast when Berry Syrup is served over steaming stacks of pancakes.

Ginger Pears

Fresh gingerroot doesn't darken the fruit.

8 lbs. pears
Antioxidant solution, page 25

1 (2-inch) piece gingerroot
4 cups unsweetened pineapple juice

Wash 6 pint, four 1-1/2-pint or 3 quart jars in hot soapy water; rinse. Keep hot until needed. Prepare lids as manufacturer directs. Peel pears, or immerse 4 or 5 at a time in boiling water, 30 seconds. Plunge into cold water; slip or pull off skins. Cut in halves; remove cores. To prevent darkening, immerse in antioxidant solution. Peel gingerroot; cut in thin slices. Pour pineapple juice into a large saucepan. Add sliced gingerroot; bring to a boil over medium-high heat. Reduce heat to low; simmer 10 minutes. Remove about one-third of pear halves from solution; rinse. Using a slotted spoon, carefully lower rinsed pear halves into hot pineapple juice. Bring juice back to a simmer; simmer 2 minutes. Use slotted spoon or tongs to layer pear halves, cut-side down, in 1 hot jar at a time, leaving 1/2 inch headspace. Remove 1 or 2 gingerroot slices from pineapple juice. Insert at side of jar. Add hot juice to cover. Release trapped air. Wipe rim of jar with a clean damp cloth. Attach lid. Place in canner. Fill and close remaining jars, cooking one-third of pears at a time. *Process in a boiling-water bath,* page 17.

    Pints: 20 minutes   1-1/2-pints or quarts: 25 minutes

Adjust times for altitude, page 20. Makes 6 pints, four 1-1/2-pints or 3 quarts.

Variation

Substitute 1 teaspoon ground ginger for gingerroot.

Minty Pears

Winter D'Anjou pears and summer Bartletts make excellent mint-flavored pears.

8 lbs. pears
Antioxidant solution, page 25
3 cups sugar

4 cups water
3/4 cup green crème de menthe
3 or 4 drops green food coloring

Wash 6 pint, four 1-1/2-pint or 3 quart jars in hot soapy water; rinse. Keep hot until needed. Prepare lids as manufacturer directs. Peel pears, or immerse 4 or 5 at a time in boiling water, 30 seconds. Plunge into cold water; slip or pull off skins. Cut in halves; remove cores. To prevent darkening, immerse in antioxidant solution. In a 4-quart pot, combine sugar and water; bring to a boil over high heat, stirring until sugar dissolves. Reduce heat until syrup boils gently. Lift pear halves 1 at a time from solution; rinse in fresh water. As pears are rinsed, lower with a slotted spoon into boiling syrup until bottom of pot is covered with a single layer of pears. Cook until pears are heated through, 3 to 5 minutes. Using slotted spoon, place hot pears in a large hot bowl. Cover; set aside. Continue heating pears, 1 layer at a time, until all pears are hot. Attach a candy thermometer to side of pot. Increase heat under syrup to medium-high. Boil until syrup reaches 220F (105C) or until beginning to thicken. Add crème de menthe and food coloring, 1 drop at a time until syrup is bright green. Use a slotted spoon or tongs to layer pears, cut-side down, into 1 hot jar at a time, leaving 1/2 inch headspace. Add hot syrup to cover. Release trapped air. Wipe rim of jar with a clean damp cloth. Attach lid. Place in canner. Fill and close remaining jars. *Process in a boiling-water bath,* page 17.

    Pints: 20 minutes   1-1/2-pints or quarts: 25 minutes

Adjust time for altitude, page 20. Makes 6 pints, four 1-1/2-pints or 3 quarts.

Pears in Red Wine
Photo on cover.

Rich enough to serve on their own as a warm or cold dessert.

7 lbs. pears	6 (2-1/2-inch) cinnamon sticks
Antioxidant solution, page 25	1 medium lemon
3 cups red wine	1 teaspoon red food coloring
3 cups water	6 tablespoons brandy
4-1/2 cups sugar	

Wash 6 pint, five 1-1/2-pint or 3 quart jars in hot soapy water; rinse. Keep hot until needed. Prepare lids as manufacturer directs. Peel pears, or immerse 4 or 5 pears at a time in boiling water, 30 seconds. Plunge into cold water; slip or pull off skins. Cut in halves; remove cores. To prevent darkening, immerse in antioxidant solution. In a 4-quart pot, combine wine, water, sugar and cinnamon sticks. Stir over medium-high heat until sugar dissolves; set aside. Wash lemon; use a vegetable peeler to peel half of lemon, removing only yellow portion. Cut peel into thin slivers; add to wine mixture. Stir in food coloring. Bring to a boil over high heat; reduce heat to low. Remove about one-third of pears from solution; rinse in fresh water. As pears are rinsed, lower with a slotted spoon into boiling syrup until bottom of pot is covered with a single layer of pears. Cook until heated through, about 3 minutes. Use a slotted spoon or tongs to layer hot pears, cut-side down, into 1 hot jar at a time, leaving 1/2 inch headspace. Add brandy, using 1 tablespoon in pints, 1-1/2 tablespoons in 1-1/2-pints and 2 tablespoons in quarts. Add hot syrup to cover. Release trapped air. Wipe rim of jar with a clean damp cloth. Attach lid. Place in canner. Fill and close remaining jars, heating one-third of pears at a time. *Process in a boiling-water bath,* page 17.

Pints: 20 minutes   1-1/2-pints or quarts: 25 minutes

Adjust time for altitude, page 20. Makes 6 pints, five 1-1/2-pints or 3 quarts.

Fruit Mélange

A rich dessert to serve in a sherbet dish topped with whipped cream and chopped nuts.

3 lbs. peaches	2 cups water
Antioxidant solution, page 25	1 cup raisins
1 lb. seedless green grapes	1/3 cup cherry brandy
3 lbs. prune plums	2/3 cup port
2-1/2 cups sugar	

Wash 6 pint, four 1-1/2-pint or 3 quart jars in hot soapy water; rinse. Keep hot until needed. Prepare lids as manufacturer directs. Wash peaches. Immerse 4 or 5 peaches at a time in boiling water, 30 seconds. Plunge into cold water; slip off skins. Cut peaches in halves; discard pits. To prevent darkening, immerse in antioxidant solution. Wash grapes and plums; set aside. In a 6-quart pot, combine sugar and 2 cups water. Bring to a boil over high heat, stirring to dissolve sugar. Lift peaches from solution; rinse. Add peaches to boiling syrup. Bring syrup back to a boil. Reduce heat to low; simmer 2 minutes. Add grapes, plums and raisins to syrup; bring back to a boil. Stir in cherry brandy and port. Ladle hot syrup and fruit into 1 hot jar at a time, leaving 1/2 inch headspace. Release trapped air. Wipe rim of jar with a clean damp cloth. Attach lid. Place in canner. Fill and close remaining jars. *Process in a boiling-water bath,* page 17.

Pints: 20 minutes   1-1/2-pints or quarts: 25 minutes

Adjust time for altitude, page 20. Makes 6 pints, four 1-1/2-pints or 3 quarts.

How to Make Pears in Red Wine

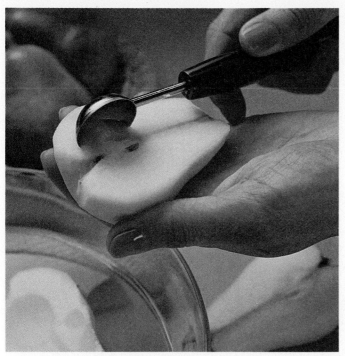

1/Use a melon baller or pear corer to cut cores from peeled pears. This gives a smooth indentation where core was removed.

2/Heat pears in a single layer in wine mixture. Arrange colored pears in overlapping layers in hot jars.

Regal Plums

Rich and full of flavor—elegant served flaming with brandy.

4 lbs. ripe prune plums
2 cups water
3/4 cup granulated sugar

3/4 cup packed brown sugar
4 (1-inch) cinnamon sticks
2 tablespoons grated orange peel

Wash 4 pint jars in hot soapy water; rinse. Keep hot until needed. Prepare lids as manufacturer directs. Wash plums. Prick skins with a fork or wooden pick to keep plums from bursting. If desired, cut in half; remove pits. Set whole or cut plums aside. In a 4-quart pot, combine water and sugars. Bring to a boil over medium-high heat, stirring until sugars dissolve. Reduce heat to low; simmer, uncovered, 10 minutes. Add plums; return syrup to a boil. In each hot jar, place 1 cinnamon stick and 1-1/2 teaspoons orange peel. Add hot plums to 1 hot jar at a time, leaving 1/2 inch headspace. Add boiling syrup to cover. Release trapped air. Wipe rim of jar with a clean damp cloth. Attach lid. Fill and close remaining jars. Place in canner. *Process in a boiling-water bath,* page 17.

　　Pints: 20 minutes
Adjust time for altitude, page 20. Makes 4 pints.

Spicy Summer Fruit

Tart and spicy! The perfect complement for meats or other main dishes.

3 lbs. peaches
Antioxidant solution, page 25
3 lbs. pears
1-1/2 lbs. seedless green grapes
3-1/2 cups sugar

1-3/4 cups distilled white vinegar
3/4 cup water
3 (2-1/2-inch) cinnamon sticks
1 tablespoon whole cloves
1 teaspoon whole allspice

Wash 6 pint jars in hot soapy water; rinse. Keep hot until needed. Prepare lids as manufacturer directs. Wash peaches in water to cover. Immerse 4 or 5 peaches at a time in boiling water, 30 seconds. Plunge into cold water; slip off skins. Cut peaches in half; remove pits. Cut in 1-1/2-inch pieces. To prevent darkening, immerse in antioxidant solution. Peel pears. Cut in halves; remove cores. Cut in fourths lengthwise. Immerse in antioxidant solution with peaches. Wash grapes; remove stems. Set grapes aside. In a 6- to 8-quart pot, combine remaining ingredients. Bring to a boil over high heat, stirring to dissolve sugar. Reduce heat to low. Cover; simmer 10 minutes. Strain syrup; discard spices. Return syrup to pot. Remove peaches and pears from solution; rinse in fresh water. Add peaches, pears and grapes to vinegar syrup. Bring to a boil again over medium-high heat; reduce heat to low. Cover; simmer 2 minutes. Ladle hot fruit into 1 hot jar at a time, leaving 1/2 inch headspace. Add syrup to cover. Release trapped air. Wipe rim of jar with a clean damp cloth. Attach lid. Place in canner. Fill and close remaining jars. *Process in a boiling-water bath,* page 17.
   Pints: 20 minutes
Adjust time for altitude, page 20. Makes 6 pints.

Spiced Apple Rings

Garnish a platter of roast meat or poultry with these sweet-tart rings.

4 lbs. small tart apples
Antioxidant solution, page 25
3 cups sugar
3/4 cup distilled white vinegar
3/4 cup water

1/4 cup light corn syrup
1/4 cup red-hot cinnamon candies
1/4 teaspoon red food coloring
1 tablespoon whole cloves
3 (2-inch) cinnamon sticks

Wash 4 wide-mouth pint jars in hot soapy water; rinse. Keep hot until needed. Prepare lids as manufacturer directs. Wash apples; peel. Cut crosswise into 1/2-inch slices. Cut out core to make rings. To prevent darkening, immerse in antioxidant solution. In a 6-quart pot, combine sugar, vinegar, water, corn syrup, candies and red food coloring. Lay cloves and cinnamon on a 6-inch square of cheesecloth. Tie edges together over spices. Or break up cinnamon and place spices in a tea ball. Add to syrup. Bring to a boil over medium heat. Reduce heat to low. Cover; simmer 10 minutes. Remove apple rings from solution; rinse in fresh water. Use a slotted spoon to lower rinsed apples carefully into syrup. Bring syrup back to a boil. Remove and discard spice bag. Pack hot apple rings into 1 hot jar at a time, leaving 1/2 inch headspace. Add boiling syrup to cover. Release trapped air. Wipe rim of jar with a clean damp cloth. Attach lid. Place in canner. Fill and close remaining jars. *Process in a boiling-water bath,* page 17.
   Pints: 10 minutes
Adjust time for altitude, page 20. Makes 4 pints.

Chunky Salad Fruit

Use the fruit in a salad or make a gelatin salad using fruit and juice.

3 lbs. peaches	**1 medium pineapple**
Antioxidant solution, page 25	**5 cups orange-pineapple juice**
3 lbs. pears	**Water**

Wash 6 pint, four 1-1/2-pint or 3 quart jars in hot soapy water; rinse. Keep hot until needed. Prepare lids as manufacturer directs. Wash peaches. Immerse 4 or 5 peaches at a time in boiling water, 30 seconds. Plunge into cold water; slip off skins. Cut peaches in half; discard pits. Cut each half in quarters by cutting lengthwise and crosswise. To prevent darkening, immerse in antioxidant solution. Peel pears, or immerse 4 or 5 at a time in boiling water, 30 seconds. Plunge in cold water; slip off skins. Cut in halves; remove cores. Cut in 1-inch cubes. Immerse in antioxidant solution with peaches. Use a sharp knife to cut a slice off top and bottom of pineapple. Stand pineapple top-side up. Slicing from top to bottom, cut off shell. Use a paring knife to remove *eyes,* page 38. With pineapple standing on end, cut in half top to bottom. Cut each half lengthwise into 1/2- to 3/4-inch wedges. Cut about 3/4 inch from wedge point to remove core; discard core. Cut wedges in 2-inch pieces. In a medium saucepan, bring orange-pineapple juice to a boil over medium heat; keep hot. Pour water 2 inches deep into a 4-quart pot. Add half of pineapple pieces; return to a boil. Boil 3 minutes. Remove half of peaches and pears from solution; rinse in fresh water. Use a slotted spoon to lower peaches and pears into boiling water with pineapple. Return to a boil; reduce heat to low. Cover; simmer 1 minute. Use a slotted spoon to lift fruit from water. Pack equal amounts of peaches, pears and pineapple into 1 hot jar at a time, leaving 1/2 inch headspace. Add hot orange-pineapple juice to cover. Release trapped air. Wipe rim of jar with a clean damp cloth. Attach lid. Place in canner. Fill and close remaining jars, heating fruit as above. *Process in a boiling-water bath,* page 17.

Pints: 20 minutes   1-1/2-pints or quarts: 25 minutes

Adjust time for altitude, page 20. Makes 6 pints, four 1-1/2-pints or 3 quarts.

Spiced Bananas

Excellent as a condiment with curried meats, seafood or spicy bean dishes.

1/2 cup white-wine vinegar	**1 teaspoon ground cinnamon**
1/2 cup lemon juice	**1 teaspoon ground ginger**
1-1/4 cups sugar	**12 green-tipped bananas**
3/4 cup honey	**1 cup lightly salted cocktail peanuts**
1 teaspoon ground mace	

Wash 4 pint jars in hot soapy water; rinse. Keep hot until needed. Prepare lids as manufacturer directs. In a 4-quart pot, combine vinegar, lemon juice, sugar, honey, mace, cinnamon and ginger. Bring to a boil over medium heat, stirring until sugar dissolves. Peel bananas; cut diagonally into 1-inch slices. Add sliced bananas and peanuts to syrup. Gently stir until bananas are heated through, but are still firm. Ladle hot bananas and peanuts into 1 hot jar at a time, leaving 1/2 inch headspace. Add syrup to cover. Release trapped air. Wipe rim of jar with a damp cloth. Attach lid. Place in canner. Fill and close remaining jars. *Process in a boiling-water bath,* page 17.

Pints: 10 minutes

Adjust time for altitude, page 20. Makes 4 pints.

Tropical Fruit Cocktail

A pretty dessert in stemmed glasses or use like fruit cocktail in salads and desserts.

1 cup sugar	**2 tablespoons lime juice**
1-1/3 cups water	**1 cup grated fresh coconut**
1 medium pineapple	**3 tablespoons Amaretto or**
1 large papaya	**1-1/2 teaspoons almond extract**
2 mangoes	

Wash 3 pint jars in hot soapy water; rinse. Keep hot until needed. Prepare lids as manufacturer directs. In a 4-quart pot, combine sugar and water. Stir over high heat until sugar dissolves; keep hot. Cut a slice off top and bottom of pineapple. Stand pineapple top-side up. Slicing from top to bottom, cut off shell. Use a paring knife to remove *eyes,* page 38. Lay pineapple on its side; cut crosswise into 1/2-inch slices. Use center of a doughnut cutter or a knife to cut core from each slice; discard. Cut each slice into 1/2-inch pieces. Add pineapple pieces to hot syrup. Bring to a simmer. Cover; simmer 10 minutes. Peel papaya; cut in half. Remove and discard seeds. Cut in 1/2-inch cubes. Add papaya pieces and lime juice to syrup. Simmer another 5 minutes. Peel mangoes; slice thinly. Divide mango slices and coconut among hot jars. Fill jars with pineapple-papaya mixture, being sure fruit is covered with syrup. Leave 1/2 inch headspace. Add 1 tablespoon Amaretto or 1/2 teaspoon almond extract to each jar. Release trapped air. Wipe rims of jars with a clean damp cloth. Attach lids. *Process in a boiling-water bath,* page 17.

Pints: 15 minutes

Adjust time for altitude, page 20. Makes 3 pints.

Honey-Melon Balls

Pineapple and coconut add a tropical flavor.

2 medium cantaloupe, about 3 lbs. each	**1-1/2 cups honey**
1 medium pineapple	**1/4 cup lemon juice**
1 cup water	**1 cup shredded coconut**

Wash 4 pint jars in hot soapy water; rinse. Keep hot until needed. Prepare lids as manufacturer directs. Cut cantaloupe in half; remove seeds. Use a melon baller to cut cantaloupe into balls, making 8 cups. Cut a slice off top and bottom of pineapple. Stand pineapple top-side up. Slicing from top to bottom, cut off shell. Use a paring knife to remove *eyes,* page 38. Lay pineapple on its side; cut crosswise into 1/2-inch slices. Use center of a doughnut cutter or a knife to cut core from each slice; discard. Cut each slice into 1/2-inch pieces. In a 4-quart pot, combine water, honey and lemon juice. Bring to a boil over medium-high heat. Add melon balls and pineapple pieces. Simmer 2 minutes. Remove from heat. Sprinkle about 1/4 cup coconut among hot melon balls and pineapple as they are packed into 1 hot jar at a time, leaving 1/2 inch headspace. Add honey syrup to cover. Release trapped air. Wipe rim of jar with a clean damp cloth. Attach lid. Place in canner. Fill and close remaining jars. *Process in a boiling-water bath,* page 17.

Pints: 20 minutes

Adjust time for altitude, page 20. Makes 4 pints.

Serving Suggestion: Pour syrup from jar into a small saucepan. Stir in 1 tablespoon cornstarch. Stir over medium heat until thickened. Add pineapple and melon balls; heat to serving temperature. Spoon fruit and syrup over pound cake, vanilla ice cream or cheesecake.

Apricots & Pears in White Grape Juice

A good way to can fruit without added sugar.

3 lbs. pears
Antioxidant solution, page 25
3 lbs. apricots

3 cups white grape juice
Water

Wash 6 pint, four 1-1/2-pint or 3 quart jars in hot soapy water; rinse. Keep hot until needed. Prepare lids as manufacturer directs. Peel pears, or lower 4 or 5 at a time into boiling water, 30 seconds. Immerse in cold water; slip or pull off skins. Cut into halves. Remove cores. To prevent darkening, immerse pear halves in antioxidant solution. Wash apricots. Cut in halves; discard pits. Immerse in antioxidant solution with pears. In a small saucepan, bring grape juice to a boil over medium heat; keep hot. Pour water 2 inches deep in a 6-quart pot; bring to a boil over high heat. Remove about half of pears and apricots from solution; rinse in fresh water. Use a slotted spoon to lower fruit carefully into boiling water. Return water to a gentle boil; simmer 2 minutes. Use slotted spoon or tongs to layer pears and apricots in 1 hot jar at a time, leaving 1/2 inch headspace. Add hot grape juice to cover. Release trapped air. Wipe rim of jar with a clean damp cloth. Attach lid. Place in canner. Fill and close remaining jars, cooking remaining fruit as above. *Process in a boiling-water bath,* page 17.

    Pints: 20 minutes   1-1/2-pints or quarts: 25 minutes

Adjust time for altitude, page 20. Makes 6 pints, four 1-1/2-pints or 3 quarts.

Plum Good Applesauce

Plums give this applesauce a pretty rose color.

3 lbs. red plums or prune plums
6 lbs. Golden Delicious or
  Rome Beauty apples

1-1/2 cups white wine
1-1/2 to 2 cups sugar or to taste

Wash 8 pint, five 1-1/2-pint or 4 quart jars in hot soapy water; rinse. Keep hot until needed. Prepare lids as manufacturer directs. Wash plums. Cut in half; discard pit. Wash apples; peel. Cut in quarters; remove cores. In an 8-quart pot, combine apples, plums and wine. Bring to a boil over medium-high heat. Reduce heat to low. Simmer until fruits are tender, about 30 minutes. Stir occasionally; add water if necessary to prevent scorching. Press fruit through a food mill or sieve. Return to pot. Sweeten to taste with sugar. Stirring constantly, bring to a boil over medium heat. Ladle hot sauce into 1 hot jar at a time, leaving 1/2 inch headspace. Release trapped air. Wipe rim of jar with a clean damp cloth. Attach lid. Place in canner. Fill and close remaining jars. *Process in a boiling-water bath,* page 17.

    Pints: 20 minutes   1-1/2-pints or quarts: 25 minutes

Adjust time for altitude, page 20. Makes 8 pints, five 1-1/2-pints or 4 quarts.

Apple-Pear Sauce

This mild-flavored sauce looks like applesauce, but has a different flavor.

4 lbs. juicy tart apples
4 lbs. pears
Antioxidant solution, page 25
1 cup orange juice

1/4 to 1/2 cup water, if desired
2 tablespoons grated orange peel
2/3 cup sugar

Wash 8 pint, five 1-1/2-pint or 4 quart jars in hot soapy water; rinse. Keep hot until needed. Prepare lids as manufacturer directs. Wash apples and pears; cut in quarters. To prevent browning, immerse in antioxidant solution. Lift apples and pears from solution; rinse. Place in a 6-quart pot. Pour orange juice over fruit; cover. Stirring occasionally, cook over low heat until fruit is tender. If mixture is too dry, add 1/4 to 1/2 cup water as mixture cooks. Press through a food mill or sieve into a large bowl; discard seeds and skins. Return puree to pot. Stir in orange peel and sugar. Stirring constantly over medium heat, bring to a boil. Ladle into 1 hot jar at a time, leaving 1/2 inch headspace. Release trapped air. Wipe rim of jar with a clean damp cloth. Attach lid. Place in canner. Fill and close remaining jars. *Process in a boiling-water bath,* page 17.

    Pints: 20 minutes   1-1/2-pints or quarts: 25 minutes
Adjust time for altitude, page 20. Makes 8 pints, five 1-1/2-pints or 4 quarts.

Variation

Peel and core apples and pears. Immerse in antioxidant solution. After cooking with orange juice, puree in blender. Cook with grated peel and sugar as above. Fill jars and process as above.

Cranberry-Pineapple Sauce

Serve warm or cold with poultry, or use in Cranberry-Nut Bread, page 169.

1 (20-oz.) can crushed pineapple in juice
Water
2 cups sugar
4 cups fresh or frozen cranberries

1 teaspoon ground cinnamon
1/2 teaspoon ground cloves
1 tablespoon grated orange peel

Wash 3 pint jars in hot soapy water; rinse. Keep hot until needed. Prepare lids as manufacturer directs. Drain pineapple, reserving juice in a 2-cup measure. Press to remove as much juice as possible. Add water to make 2 cups liquid. In a large saucepan, combine juice and sugar. Bring to a boil over high heat, stirring until sugar dissolves. Add drained pineapple, cranberries and remaining ingredients. Return to a boil; reduce heat to low. Cover; simmer until cranberries stop popping, about 15 minutes. Ladle hot sauce into 1 hot jar at a time, leaving 1/2 inch headspace. Release trapped air. Wipe rim of jar with a clean damp cloth. Attach lid. Place in canner. Fill and close remaining jars. *Process in a boiling-water bath,* page 17.

    Pints: 15 minutes
Adjust time for altitude, page 20. Makes 3 pints.

Peach Pie Filling

Enjoy a sunny peach pie in the middle of winter with your own pie filling.

10 lbs. peaches
Antioxidant solution, page 25
3 cups sugar
2 teaspoons ground cinnamon

1/2 teaspoon ground mace
2 tablespoons grated lemon peel
1/4 cup lemon juice
1 to 1-1/4 cups tapioca

Wash 10 pint or 5 quart jars in hot soapy water; rinse. Keep hot until needed. Prepare lids as manufacturer directs. Wash peaches. Immerse 4 or 5 peaches at a time in gently boiling water, 30 seconds. Plunge into cold water; slip off skins. Slice peaches; discard pits. Immerse slices in antioxidant solution; set aside. In a small bowl, combine 2 cups sugar, cinnamon, mace and lemon peel; set aside. Remove peaches from solution; rinse in fresh water. Place rinsed sliced peaches in a 10-quart pot. Add sugar mixture and lemon juice. Let stand 15 minutes until juices begin to flow. Attach a candy thermometer to side of pot so bulb is covered with peach mixture. Stirring frequently, bring to a boil over medium-low heat. Continue boiling until mixture reaches 212F (100C). In a small bowl, combine remaining 1 cup sugar and 1 cup tapioca. Add remaining tapioca if peaches are very juicy. Stir into peaches. Stirring constantly, heat until temperature is again 212F (100C). Ladle hot filling into 1 hot jar at a time, leaving 1/2 inch headspace. Release trapped air. Wipe rim of jar with a clean damp cloth. Attach lid. Place in canner. Fill and close remaining jars. *Process in a boiling-water bath,* page 17.

 Pints: 20 minutes   Quarts: 25 minutes

Adjust time for altitude, page 20. Makes 10 pints or 5 quarts.

Variation

Apricot Pie Filling: Substitute apricots for peaches. Do not peel. Substitute 1/2 teaspoon nutmeg for mace.

Cherry Pie Filling

If you have a large pot, this recipe can be doubled.

6 lbs. fresh sour cherries
3 cups sugar
1/2 cup cornstarch or 1 cup tapioca

1 teaspoon almond extract
1/4 teaspoon red food coloring

Wash 6 pint, four 1-1/2-pint or 3 quart jars in hot soapy water; rinse. Keep hot until needed. Prepare lids as manufacturer directs. Wash cherries. Lift from water; remove stems and pits. Combine cherries and 2 cups sugar in an 8-quart pot. Let stand 15 minutes or until juices begin to flow. Attach a candy thermometer to side of pot so bulb is covered with cherry mixture. Stirring frequently, bring to a boil over medium-low heat. Continue boiling until mixture reaches 212F (100C). In a small bowl, combine remaining 1 cup sugar and cornstarch or tapioca. Stir into cherry mixture. Stir in almond extract and food coloring. Stirring constantly, heat until temperature is again 212F (100C). Ladle hot filling into 1 hot jar at a time, leaving 1/2 inch headspace. Release trapped air. Wipe rim of jar with a clean damp cloth. Attach lid. Place in canner. Fill and close remaining jars. *Process in a boiling-water bath,* page 17.

 Pints: 15 minutes   1-1/2-pints or quarts: 20 minutes

Adjust time for altitude, page 20. Makes 6 pints, four 1-1/2-pints or 3 quarts.

Mincemeat

You'll need a pressure canner to process this fruit-and-meat mixture.

2 lbs. boneless lean beef (round or arm)
1/2 lb. suet
2 medium oranges
4 lbs. tart apples
1 lb. dark raisins
1 lb. golden raisins
8 oz. chopped candied citron
4 cups packed dark-brown sugar

1 tablespoon salt
1 tablespoon ground cinnamon
1 tablespoon ground allspice
1 teaspoon ground nutmeg
1 teaspoon ground cloves
4 cups apple cider or apple juice
1 cup brandy, if desired

Trim all fat from meat. Grind meat and suet together, using coarse blade of food processor or coarse plate of food grinder. Grate only colored part of orange peel. Remove remaining peel, including all white membrane. Section oranges by cutting on both sides of each section membrane. See photo, page 121. Add sections to meat mixture. Peel and core apples; chop coarsely. To meat mixture, add chopped apples, raisins, citron, brown sugar, salt, cinnamon, allspice, nutmeg, cloves and apple cider or apple juice. Mix well. Stirring constantly, bring to a boil over medium-high heat. Reduce heat to low. Simmer, uncovered, 15 minutes, stirring frequently to prevent scorching. Wash 10 pint, seven 1-1/2-pint or 5 quart jars in hot soapy water; rinse. Keep hot until needed. Prepare lids as manufacturer directs. Stir brandy into meat mixture, if desired. Ladle hot mincemeat into 1 hot jar at a time, leaving 1 inch headspace. Release trapped air. Wipe rim of jar with a clean damp cloth. Attach lid. Place in canner. Fill and close remaining jars. Place lid on canner. Exhaust air. *Process in a pressure canner at 10 pounds pressure,* page 17.

Pints, 1-1/2-pints or quarts: 20 minutes
Adjust pressure for altitude, page 21. Makes 10 pints, seven 1-1/2-pints or 5 quarts.

Pie Apples

Select firm, dry apples; juicy apples are too soft.

6 lbs. firm baking apples
Antioxidant solution, page 25
2 cups sugar
1/3 cup all-purpose flour

1 teaspoon ground cinnamon
1/4 teaspoon ground nutmeg
1 tablespoon grated lemon peel
2 tablespoons lemon juice

Wash 6 pint, four 1-1/2-pint or 3 quart jars in hot soapy water; rinse. Keep hot until needed. Prepare lids as manufacturer directs. Wash apples; peel, core and slice. To prevent darkening, immerse sliced apples in antioxidant solution. In a small bowl, combine sugar, flour, cinnamon and nutmeg; mix well. Lift apples from solution; rinse in fresh water. Place in an 8-quart pot. Sprinkle with sugar mixture; stir gently. Let stand until juices begin to flow, about 30 minutes. Stir in lemon peel and lemon juice; cover. Stirring frequently, cook over medium heat until mixture thickens. Continue cooking until mixture reaches 212F (100C) on a candy thermometer. Ladle hot filling into 1 hot jar at a time, leaving 1/2 inch headspace. Release trapped air. Wipe rim of jar with a clean damp cloth. Attach lid. Place in canner. Fill and close remaining jars. *Process in a boiling-water bath,* page 17.

Pints: 20 minutes   1-1/2-pints or quarts: 25 minutes
Adjust time for altitude, page 20. Makes 6 pints, four 1-1/2-pints or 3 quarts.

Brandied Fruit Cocktail

These pretty jars of fruit cocktail could win a prize at the State Fair.

4 lbs. peaches
Antioxidant solution, page 25
6 lbs. pears
2 lbs. green grapes

2 (10-oz.) jars maraschino cherries
2 cups sugar
2 cups water
1-1/2 cups peach brandy

Wash 8 pint, six 1-1/2-pint or 4 quart jars in hot soapy water; rinse. Keep hot until needed. Prepare lids as manufacturer directs. Wash peaches. Immerse 4 or 5 peaches at a time in gently boiling water, 30 seconds. Plunge into cold water; slip off skins. Cut peaches in half; discard pits. Cut each half into 4 pieces by cutting in half lengthwise, then crosswise. To prevent darkening, immerse in antioxidant solution. Peel pears. Immerse in solution with peaches. Wash grapes; remove stems. Set aside in a large bowl. Drain cherries; set aside. In a 4-quart pot, combine sugar and 2 cups water. Bring to a boil over high heat. Reduce heat until syrup boils gently. Remove peaches and pears from solution; rinse in fresh water. Toss lightly with grapes. Spoon peaches, pears and grapes into boiling syrup until bottom of pot is covered. Without stirring, cook until heated through, about 3 minutes. Using a slotted spoon, lift hot fruit from boiling syrup into another large bowl. Cover; set aside. Repeat heating fruit 1 layer at a time until all fruit has been heated. Attach a candy thermometer to side of pot. Increase heat under syrup to medium-high. Boil until syrup reaches 220F (105C). Adding a few cherries to each jar, pack hot fruit into 1 hot jar at a time, leaving 1/2 inch headspace. Add peach brandy, using 3 tablespoons in pints, 1/4 cup in 1-1/2-pints and 6 tablespoons in quarts. Add boiling syrup to cover. Release trapped air. Wipe rim of jar with a clean damp cloth. Attach lid. Place in canner. Fill and close remaining jars. *Process in a boiling-water bath,* page 17.

Pints: 20 minutes   1-1/2-pints or quarts: 25 minutes

Adjust time for altitude, page 20. Makes 8 pints, six 1-1/2-pints or 4 quarts.

Spiced Crab Apples

Serve with a pork roast or with a holiday dinner.

2-1/2 pounds crab apples
3 cups sugar
1-1/2 cups distilled white vinegar
1-1/2 cups water
1/2 cup light corn syrup

1/4 cup red-hot cinnamon candies
1/4 teaspoon red food coloring
1 tablespoon whole cloves
3 (2-inch) cinnamon sticks

Wash crab apples, wiping off fuzzy blossom ends. Do not remove stems. Prick skins with a sterile needle to prevent fruit from bursting. Wash 4 pint jars in hot soapy water; rinse. Keep hot until needed. Prepare lids as manufacturer directs. In a 6-quart pot, combine sugar, vinegar, water, corn syrup, candies and red food coloring. Tie whole cloves and cinnamon sticks in a 3-inch square of cheesecloth. Add spice bag to syrup. Bring to a boil over medium-high heat, stirring until sugar dissolves. Cover pot. Reduce heat to medium-low. Simmer 10 minutes. Add crab apples. Simmer just until tender, about 10 minutes. Remove and discard spice bag. Pack cooked crab apples into 1 hot jar at a time to within 1/2 inch of top. Ladle syrup over crab apples to cover. Release trapped air. Wipe rim of jar with a clean damp cloth. Attach lid. Place in canner. Fill and close remaining jars. *Process in a boiling-water bath,* page 17.

Pints: 10 minutes.

Adjust time for altitude, page 20. Makes 4 pints.

1/Peaches peel easily after being dipped in boiling water for 30 seconds. Quickly cool in cold water before peeling.

2/Spoon brandy into jars packed with layers of peaches, grapes and cherries. Add boiling syrup to cover.

Rhubarb Pie Filling   Photo on pages 182-183.

Use for a pie, or heat and serve as a topping for dessert waffles or crepes.

12 cups sliced rhubarb (about 5 pounds)
3 cups sugar
1 tablespoon grated orange peel

1/4 cup orange juice
1/2 cup tapioca

Wash 5 pint jars in hot soapy water; rinse. Keep hot until needed. Prepare lids as manufacturer directs. In a 6-quart pot, combine rhubarb, 2 cups sugar, orange peel and orange juice. Let stand 15 minutes or until juices begin to flow. Attach a candy thermometer to side of pot so bulb is covered with rhubarb mixture. Stirring frequently, bring to a boil over medium-low heat. Continue boiling until mixture reaches 212F (100C). In a small bowl, combine remaining 1 cup sugar and tapioca. Stir into rhubarb mixture. Stirring constantly, heat until temperature is again 212F (100C). Ladle hot filling into 1 hot jar at a time, leaving 1/2 inch headspace. Release trapped air. Wipe rim of jar with a clean damp cloth. Attach lid. Place in canner. Fill and close remaining jars. *Process in a boiling-water bath,* page 17.

Pints: 15 minutes

Adjust time for altitude, page 20. Makes 5 pints.

Variation
Strawberry-Rhubarb Pie Filling: Substitute 2-1/2 pounds hulled strawberries for half of rhubarb. Omit orange peel and orange juice.

Praline Dessert Sauce

Spoon warmed sauce over vanilla ice cream for a luscious dessert.

3 cups light corn syrup	**1 cup sugar**
1/2 cup molasses	**3 cups pecan halves**
3 cups water	**1/2 cup bourbon**

Wash eight 1/2-pint or 4 pint jars in hot soapy water; rinse. Keep hot until needed. Prepare lids as manufacturer directs. In a 4-quart pot, combine corn syrup, molasses, water and sugar. Bring to a boil over medium-high heat, stirring until sugar dissolves. Stir in nuts. Reduce heat to low. Cover; simmer 15 minutes, stirring occasionally. Slowly stir in bourbon. Ladle syrup and some of nuts into 1 hot jar at a time, leaving 1/4 inch headspace. Wipe rim of jar with a clean damp cloth. Attach lid. Place in canner. Fill and close remaining jars. *Process in a boiling-water bath,* page 17.

    1/2-pints or pints: 20 minutes

Adjust time for altitude, page 20. Makes eight 1/2-pints or 4 pints.

Grenadine Syrup

Rosy-red syrup adds color and delicate flavor to cocktails, soft drinks and dessert sauces.

6 cups pomegranate seeds and	**2 cups sugar**
pulp (about 8 large fruit)	**1/2 cup corn syrup**

Wash pomegranates under running water. Cut away peel down to seeds. Pull apart, releasing seeds. Measure seeds and any red pulp. Place in a large bowl. Do not include tough cream-colored membranes. Use a potato masher to crush seeds. Stir in sugar. Cover with waxed paper, then a towel; let stand 10 to 12 hours. Wash six 1/2-pint or 3 pint jars in hot soapy water; rinse. Keep hot until needed. Prepare lids as manufacturer directs. Line a colandar or large sieve with 2 layers of cheesecloth; set aside. Pour pomegranate mixture into a large saucepan. Over medium heat, slowly bring to a boil. Place a large bowl under cheesecloth-lined colandar or sieve. Pour hot pomegranate mixture into colander or sieve to remove seeds and pulp. Strain again through a jelly bag or cheesecloth for a clearer syrup. Return syrup to saucepan; add corn syrup. Stirring occasionally, bring to a simmer over medium heat. Ladle hot syrup into 1 hot jar at a time, leaving 1/4 inch headspace. Wipe rim of jar with a clean damp cloth. Attach lid. Place in canner. Fill and close remaining jars. *Process in a boiling-water bath,* page 17.

    1/2-pints or pints: 10 minutes

Adjust time for altitude, page 20. Makes six 1/2-pints or 3 pints.

Tip

Use a damp cloth to wipe jar rims when canning with a sugar syrup. Use a dry cloth with water-packed foods or vinegar solutions.

Brandied Fruit Syrup

Spoon this rich sauce over ice cream or pound cake as a special dessert for guests.

1-1/2 teaspoons butter or margarine
1 cup filberts
3 cups granulated sugar
1-1/2 cups packed brown sugar
3 cups water
1 cup light corn syrup
2 medium oranges

2 medium lemons
1 (6-oz.) pkg. dried apricot halves,
** cut in quarters**
1 (12-oz.) pkg. dried figs,
** sliced crosswise**
1 cup golden raisins
1 cup brandy

Wash 4 pint jars in hot soapy water; rinse. Keep hot until needed. Prepare lids as manufacturer directs. Melt butter or margarine in a heavy skillet over low heat. Add filberts; stir frequently until toasted, about 3 minutes. Drain on paper towels. In a 4-quart pot, combine granulated sugar, brown sugar, water and corn syrup. Use a vegetable peeler to cut colored peel from oranges and lemons. Add peel to sugar mixture. Juice oranges and lemons; add juice to sugar mixture. Attach a candy thermometer to pot so bulb is covered with juice mixture. Bring to a boil over high heat, stirring until sugar dissolves. Reduce heat until mixture boils gently. Continue boiling until mixture reaches 220F (105C), about 15 minutes. Use a slotted spoon to skim syrup to remove peel. Add apricots, figs and raisins. Reduce heat to low. Cover; simmer 2 minutes. Stir in brandy and toasted filberts. Ladle hot syrup and fruit into 1 hot jar at a time, leaving 1/2 inch headspace. Release trapped air. Wipe rim of jar with a clean damp cloth. Attach lid. Place in canner. Fill and close remaining jars. *Process in a boiling-water bath,* page 17.

   Pints: 20 minutes
Adjust time for altitude, page 20. Makes 4 pints.

Berry Syrup

A real treat on pancakes and waffles.

8 cups blackberries, blueberries,
** raspberries or strawberries**
1/4 cup lemon juice

3 cups sugar
1 cup corn syrup

Wash berries; remove stems or hulls. Lift berries from water; place in a 4- or 6-quart pot. Crush berries with a potato masher. Stirring occasionally, bring to a boil over medium heat. Pour berries and juice into a damp jelly bag set over a bowl or into a colander lined with a double thickness of damp cheesecloth. Let juice drip at least 2 hours. Squeeze bag or cheesecloth to extract remaining juice. There should be 3 to 4 cups juice. Wash 3 pint jars in hot soapy water; rinse. Keep hot until needed. Prepare lids as manufacturer directs. In 4- or 6-quart pot, combine berry juice and remaining ingredients. Stirring constantly, bring to a rolling boil over high heat. Boil 1 minute; remove from heat. Pour syrup into 1 hot jar at a time, leaving 1/4 inch headspace. Wipe rim of jar with a clean damp cloth. Attach lid. Place in canner. Fill and close remaining jars. *Process in a boiling-water bath,* page 17.

   Pints: 10 minutes
Adjust time for altitude, page 20. Makes 3 pints.

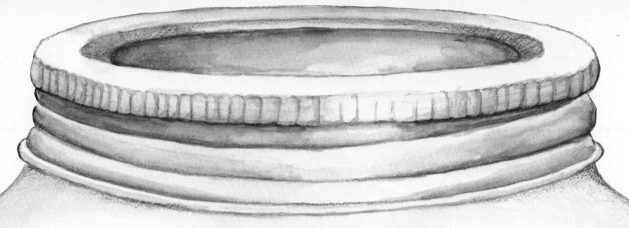

Canning with Flair:
Vegetables

A creative combination of vegetables in a spirited sauce makes a vegetable dish the center of attraction at a meal. However, the processing time of mixed vegetables must be that of the vegetable requiring the highest temperature and longest time. Pressure canning of combinations sometimes causes overprocessing of some ingredients.

Combined with tomatoes or high-acid fruits, the vegetables remain colorful and tasty. Though the processing time is not changed, the vegetables hold their shape and have a pleasingly heightened flavor. Spanish Green Beans have an *Ole!* flair because of the colorful, spritely seasoned tomato sauce. Lemon-Fruited Beets have a mellow, less-sharp flavor than beets canned alone.

Some delicate vegetables sacrifice their flavor and texture when pressure canned. Pickling vegetables maintains crisp texture and fresh flavor. Vegetables canned in vinegar may be safely processed in a boiling-water bath because the acidity is raised.

Do not change the amount of vinegar called for in any of these recipes. Altering the vinegar level may result in an unsafe food. Use only commercial, standardized vinegars of 4% to 6% acidity. Do not use homemade vinegar.

Use pickled vegetables in salads, as appetizers, or serve a variety with crackers and assorted cheeses. Dilly Beans make a fun stirrer to nibble on while sipping a tomato-juice cocktail.

Creole Vegetables

Tomatoes help the okra keep its shape during processing.

16 cups chopped peeled tomatoes (12 lbs.)
4 cups chopped onions
2 cups chopped green bell peppers
4 garlic cloves, minced
1/4 cup Worcestershire sauce

2 teaspoons sugar
4 teaspoons salt
1 teaspoon hot red-pepper flakes
16 cups sliced okra,
   1/2-inch thick (8 lbs.)

Wash 10 pint or 5 quart jars in hot soapy water; rinse. Keep hot until needed. Prepare lids as manufacturer directs. In an 8- to 10-quart pot, combine all ingredients except okra. Bring to a boil over medium heat; reduce heat to low. Cover; simmer 30 minutes, stirring frequently. Stir in okra. Bring mixture back to a boil. Spoon hot okra mixture into 1 hot jar at a time, leaving 1 inch headspace. Release trapped air. Wipe rim of jar with a clean damp cloth. Attach lid. Place in canner. Fill and close remaining jars. *Process in a pressure canner at 10 pounds pressure,* page 17.

Pints: 30 minutes   Quarts: 35 minutes
Adjust pressure for altitude, page 21. Makes 10 pints or 5 quarts.

Lemon-Fruited Beets

Pineapple mellows the sharp beet flavor without making it sweet.

6 lbs. fresh beets
1 fresh medium pineapple
4 cups water

2 cups sugar
1/4 cup lemon juice
1 tablespoon salt

Wash 6 pint, four 1-1/2-pint or 3 quart jars in hot soapy water; rinse. Keep hot until needed. Prepare lids as manufacturer directs. Cut off all but 1 inch of beet tops. Do not remove root. Wash beets; lift from water. In a large pot, cook beets in gently boiling water to cover, 15 minutes. While beets cook, use a brush to scrub pineapple under running water. Using a sharp knife, cut a slice off top and bottom of pineapple. Stand pineapple stem-end down. Slicing from top to bottom, cut off shell. Remove *eyes* with a paring knife, page 38. Lay pineapple on its side. Cut in 1/4-inch slices. Cut core from center of each slice. Cut slices in 1/2-inch pieces; set aside. Drain cooked beets. Immerse beets in cold water. Slip off skins, roots and stems. Cut beets into 1/2-inch cubes; set aside. In a 6- or 8-quart pot, combine 4 cups water and sugar. Bring to a boil over medium-high heat, stirring until sugar dissolves. Add pineapple pieces; cover and simmer 5 minutes. Add lemon juice and cubed beets. Simmer 5 minutes longer. Ladle hot beet mixture into 1 hot jar at a time, leaving 1 inch headspace. Add liquid from pot to cover beet mixture. Add salt, using 1/2 teaspoon in pints, 3/4 teaspoon in 1-1/2-pints and 1 teaspoon in quarts. Release trapped air. Wipe rim of jar with a clean damp cloth. Attach lid. Place in canner. Fill and close remaining jars. *Process in a pressure canner at 10 pounds pressure,* page 17.

Pints: 30 minutes   1-1/2-pints or quarts: 35 minutes

Adjust pressure for altitude, page 21. Makes 6 pints, four 1-1/2-pints or 3 quarts.

Tiny Toms   Photo on page 102.

A fun way to use the excess production of a cherry-tomato plant.

2 qts. small green cherry tomatoes
2-1/2 cups cider vinegar
2-1/2 cups water
3 tablespoons salt

4 garlic cloves, flattened
4 teaspoons mustard seeds
4 fresh dill heads, trimmed
1 medium onion, sliced

Wash 4 pint jars in hot soapy water; rinse. Keep hot until needed. Prepare lids as manufacturer directs. Wash tomatoes; lift from water. Remove stems; set aside. In a medium saucepan, combine vinegar, water and salt. Bring to a boil over high heat. Reduce heat to low; cover. Place 1 garlic clove in 1 hot jar. Add 1 teaspoon mustard seeds and 1 dill head. Tightly pack one-fourth of tomatoes and one-fourth of onion slices in jar, leaving 1/2 inch headspace. Add hot vinegar mixture to cover. Release trapped air. Wipe rim of jar with a clean damp cloth. Attach lid. Place in canner. Fill and close remaining jars. *Process in a boiling-water bath,* page 17.

Pints: 10 minutes

Adjust time for altitude, page 20. Makes 4 pints.

How to Make Marinated Button Mushrooms

1/Mushroom caps should be less than 1 inch in diameter. Trim stems of mushrooms even with cap.

2/Place spices, garlic, peppercorns, olive oil and mushrooms in each jar, leaving 1/2 inch headspace. Add hot vinegar to cover.

Spanish Green Beans

Simple to serve—just heat and top with garlic croutons, bacon or onion rings.

1/4 cup olive oil or vegetable oil	1/4 cup prepared mustard
2 cups chopped onions	2 tablespoons dried leaf oregano
1-1/2 cups chopped green bell peppers	2 teaspoons sugar
4 garlic cloves, minced	2 tablespoons salt
12 cups chopped peeled tomatoes (9 lbs.)	16 cups cut fresh green beans (5-1/2 lbs.)

Wash 8 pint or 4 quart jars in hot soapy water; rinse. Keep hot until needed. Prepare lids as manufacturer directs. In an 8- to 10-quart pot, heat oil over medium heat. Add onions, green peppers and garlic. Sauté until onion is soft. Stir in tomatoes, mustard, oregano, sugar and salt; mix well. Bring to a boil over medium heat; add green beans. Stirring occasionally, bring back to a gentle boil. Boil 3 to 5 minutes until beans are hot. Pack hot bean mixture into 1 hot jar at a time, leaving 1 inch headspace. Release trapped air. Wipe rim of jar with a clean damp cloth. Attach lid. Place in canner. Fill and close remaining jars. *Process in a pressure canner at 10 pounds pressure,* page 17.

Pints: 30 minutes   Quarts: 35 minutes

Adjust pressure for altitude, page 21. Makes 8 pints or 4 quarts.

Marinated Button Mushrooms   Photo on page 102.

Try making your own Tarragon Vinegar, page 137.

6 cups small button mushrooms (2 lbs.)
1/4 cup lemon juice
Water
1 teaspoon salt
1 cup tarragon vinegar
1 teaspoon dried leaf oregano
1 teaspoon dried leaf basil

1/2 teaspoon salt
2 garlic cloves, peeled, cut in half
12 black peppercorns
3/4 cup olive oil or
   1/4 cup olive oil and
   1/2 cup vegetable oil

Wash four 1/2-pint jars in hot soapy water; rinse. Keep hot until needed. Prepare lids as manufacturer directs. Wash mushrooms briefly in cold water, agitating water; lift from water. Trim stems flat to mushroom cap. Use stems for another purpose. Place trimmed mushrooms in a 4-quart pot. Sprinkle with lemon juice. Add water to cover; add salt. Bring to a boil over medium-high heat. Reduce heat to low; simmer, uncovered, 5 minutes. Drain mushrooms; discard liquid. In a small saucepan, bring vinegar to a boil; add mushrooms. Cover; keep hot. In each hot jar, place 1/4 teaspoon oregano, 1/4 teaspoon basil, 1/8 teaspoon salt, 1/2 clove garlic, 3 peppercorns and 3 tablespoons oil. Pack mushrooms into 1 jar at a time, leaving 1/2 inch headspace. Add hot vinegar to cover. Release trapped air. Wipe rim of jar with a clean dry cloth or paper towel. Attach lid. Place in canner. Fill and close remaining jars. *Process in a boiling-water bath,* page 17.

   1/2-pints: 20 minutes
Adjust time for altitude, page 20. Makes four 1/2-pints.

Pickled Sprouts & Cauliflower   Photo on cover.

Pickling salt is available with other salt or with canning equipment in your supermarket.

2 lbs. small Brussels sprouts
2-1/2 lbs. cauliflower
2 qts. water
1/4 cup pickling salt
3 cups white-wine vinegar
1 cup water

1/3 cup sugar
3/4 teaspoon hot red-pepper flakes,
   or 1/4 teaspoon red (cayenne) pepper
2 tablespoons dried leaf tarragon
2 tablespoons mustard seeds

Wash sprouts in water to cover; remove outer leaves with blemishes. Lift from water. Wash cauliflower under running water; cut away leaves and core. Separate into flowerets. In a medium saucepan, bring 2 quarts water to a boil over high heat. Place sprouts and cauliflower in a large bowl. Sprinkle with pickling salt. Pour boiling water over vegetables to cover. Cover bowl with a towel or plastic wrap. Let stand at room temperature 2 to 3 hours. Wash six 1/2-pint jars in hot soapy water; rinse. Keep hot until needed. Prepare lids as manufacturer directs. Drain vegetables; discard brine. Immerse soaked vegetables in cold water. In a medium saucepan, combine vinegar, 1 cup water and sugar. Bring to a boil over high heat. Into each hot jar, spoon 1/8 teaspoon red-pepper flakes, 1 teaspoon tarragon and 1 teaspoon mustard seeds. Pack sprouts and cauliflower into 1 hot jar at a time, leaving 1/2 inch headspace. Add boiling vinegar mixture to cover. Release trapped air. Wipe rim of jar with a clean damp cloth. Attach lid. Place in canner. Fill and close remaining jars. *Process in a boiling-water bath,* page 17.

   1/2-pints: 15 minutes
Adjust time for altitude, page 20. Makes six 1/2-pints.

Candied Sweet Potatoes

While the Sunday roast bakes, heat these 30 minutes in a covered casserole.

12 lbs. sweet potatoes
5 medium oranges
Water

1-1/2 cups packed brown sugar
1 cup honey

Wash 8 pint, six 1-1/2-pint or 4 quart jars in hot soapy water; rinse. Keep hot until needed. Prepare lids as manufacturer directs. Wash potatoes, scrubbing with a brush. Over medium heat, boil potatoes in water to cover until skins come off easily, about 20 minutes. While potatoes cook, prepare orange sauce. Wash oranges. Grate 1/4 cup peel; set aside. Juice oranges; add water to make 2-1/2 cups. In a medium saucepan, combine orange-juice mixture, brown sugar and honey. Stirring constantly, bring to a boil over medium-high heat. Stir until sugar dissolves. Cover; keep hot. Immerse cooked potatoes in cold water. Rub and pull skins off. Cut potatoes into 3" x 2" strips. Pack potatoes into 1 hot jar at a time, leaving 1 inch headspace. Sprinkle grated orange peel over potatoes, using 1-1/2 teaspoons in pints, 2 teaspoons in 1-1/2-pints and 1 tablespoon in quarts. Pour 1/3 cup hot syrup into pints, 1/2 cup into 1-1/2-pints and 3/4 cup into quarts. Wipe rim of jar with a clean damp cloth. Attach lid. Place in canner. Fill and close remaining jars. *Process in a pressure canner at 10 pounds pressure,* page 17.

Pints: 65 minutes   1-1/2-pints or quarts: 90 minutes

Adjust pressure for altitude, page 21. Makes 8 pints, six 1-1/2-pints or 4 quarts.

Minty Cocktail Carrots   Photo on page 102.

Delicious served cold.

1 cup water
1/2 cup fresh mint leaves
1 cup distilled white vinegar
1/2 teaspoon salt

2 lbs. baby carrots or other carrots
1-1/2 cups sugar
1/2 cup corn syrup
6 fresh mint sprigs

Wash six 1/2-pint or 3 pint jars in hot soapy water; rinse. Keep hot until needed. Prepare lids as manufacturer directs. In a medium saucepan, bring 1 cup water to a boil over high heat. Add mint leaves; remove from heat. Cover; let steep 15 minutes. Remove and discard mint leaves. Add vinegar and salt to mint water. Wash carrots. Peel; rinse. Cut larger carrots into 3-inch sticks. Add whole carrots or carrot sticks to vinegar mixture. Bring to a boil over medium-high heat. Reduce heat to low. Simmer 15 minutes. Remove carrots. Add sugar and corn syrup to vinegar mixture. Attach a candy thermometer to side of pan so bulb is covered with syrup. Bring mixture to a boil over medium-high heat. Reduce heat to low. Simmer until syrup reaches 220F (105C) or begins to thicken. Add carrots; simmer 5 minutes longer. Pack hot carrots into 1 hot jar at a time, leaving 1/2 inch headspace. Add 1 mint sprig to 1/2-pint jars or 2 sprigs to pint jars. Add boiling syrup to cover. Release trapped air. Wipe rim of jar with a clean damp cloth. Attach lid. Place in canner. Fill and close remaining jars. *Process in a boiling-water bath,* page 17.

Pints or 1/2-pints: 15 minutes

Adjust time for altitude, page 20. Makes six 1/2-pints or 3 pints.

How to Make Candied Sweet Potatoes

1/Rub and pull skins from cooked sweet potatoes. Cut peeled potatoes into strips.

2/Pack potato strips into jars. Sprinkle with grated orange peel. Pour orange syrup over potatoes.

Texas Spiced Okra

Okra prepared this way has a crisp, clean bite and a tangy flavor.

**3 lbs. young tender okra,
   3 to 4 inches long
3 cups water
2 cups cider vinegar
1 cup white-wine vinegar
1/3 cup pickling salt**

**1 tablespoon mustard seeds
6 garlic cloves, peeled,
   crushed separately
3/4 teaspoon hot red-pepper flakes or
   3 dried, whole, hot red peppers**

Wash 6 pint jars in hot soapy water; rinse. Keep hot until needed. Prepare lids as manufacturer directs. Wash okra, gently rubbing to remove dirt; lift from water. Cut off stems, leaving caps. Do not cut into okra pods. Pierce each pod with a fork; set aside. In a medium saucepan, combine water, cider vinegar, wine vinegar and pickling salt. Bring to a boil over medium-high heat. In each hot jar, place 1/2 teaspoon mustard seeds, 1 garlic clove and 1/8 teaspoon red-pepper flakes or 1/2 red pepper. Pack okra lengthwise in 1 jar at a time, alternating stem ends and tips, to within 1/2 inch of top. Add boiling brine to cover, leaving 1/2 inch headspace. Release trapped air. Wipe rim of jar with a clean damp cloth. Attach lid. Place in canner. Fill and close remaining jars. *Process in a boiling-water bath,* page 17.

   Pints: 20 minutes

Adjust time for altitude, page 20. Wait 4 weeks before serving so flavors can blend. Makes 6 pints.

Cocktail Vegetable Mix

Colorful and peppy, these vegetables will perk up any buffet or cocktail table.

1 (10-oz.) pkg. frozen artichoke hearts,
   thawed
2 cups sliced carrots
2 cups diagonally sliced celery
2 cups pickling onions, peeled
2 red or green bell peppers,
   cut in 1-inch squares
2 cups cauliflower flowerets
1/2 cup pickling salt

1 qt. water
2 cups sugar
8 cups distilled white vinegar
1/4 cup mustard seeds
2 tablespoons celery seeds
1/2 teaspoon hot red-pepper flakes
5 garlic cloves, peeled,
   crushed separately
20 black peppercorns

In a 2-gallon crock or large nonmetal bowl, combine artichoke hearts, carrots, celery, pickling onions, bell peppers and cauliflower flowerets; set aside. In a large saucepan, bring pickling salt and water to a boil over high heat, stirring to dissolve salt. Pour over vegetables. Cover with a lid, plastic wrap or a clean towel. Let stand in a cool place, 10 to 12 hours. Wash 5 pint jars in hot soapy water; rinse. Keep hot until needed. Prepare lids as manufacturer directs. Drain vegetables; discard brine. In an 8-quart pot, combine sugar, vinegar, mustard seeds and celery seeds. Bring to a boil over medium-high heat. Add brined vegetables; return to a boil. Reduce heat to low. Cover; simmer 2 minutes, stirring frequently. In 1 hot jar at a time, place about 1/8 teaspoon red-pepper flakes, 1 garlic clove and 4 peppercorns. Pack hot vegetables into jar, leaving 1/2 inch headspace. Add boiling vinegar mixture to cover. Release trapped air. Wipe rim of jar with a clean damp cloth. Attach lid. Place in canner. Fill and close remaining jars. *Process in a boiling-water bath,* page 17.
   Pints: 15 minutes
Adjust time for altitude, page 20. Makes 5 pints.

Dilly Beans

Garnish Bloody Marys or vegetable-juice cocktails with these tasty beans.

2 lbs. young, slender,
   straight green beans
2 cups water
2 cups distilled white vinegar

3 tablespoons pickling salt
4 fresh dill sprigs
4 garlic cloves, peeled
1/2 teaspoon hot red-pepper flakes

Wash 4 pint jars in hot soapy water; rinse. Keep hot until needed. Prepare lids as manufacturer directs. Wash beans; snap off stems. Trim beans 1/2 inch shorter than jars. In a medium saucepan, bring water, vinegar and pickling salt to a boil over medium-high heat. In each hot jar, place 1 dill sprig, 1 garlic clove and 1/8 teaspoon red-pepper flakes. Pack beans lengthwise in 1 jar at a time. Add boiling vinegar mixture to cover, leaving 1/2 inch headspace. Release trapped air. Wipe rim of jar with a clean damp cloth. Attach lid. Place in canner. Fill and close remaining jars. *Process in a boiling-water bath,* page 17.
   Pints: 20 minutes
Adjust time for altitude, page 20. Wait 4 weeks before serving so flavors can blend. Makes 4 pints.

Chili Beans

Ready to use with hamburgers or tacos or to make a casserole.

2 lbs. dried red beans, pinto beans or
  pink beans
Water for soaking
8 cups water
2 teaspoons salt

2 cups chopped onions
1/4 cup vegetable oil
1 pint Green-Chili Salsa, page 135,
  or 2 (8-oz.) cans green-chili salsa
1 tablespoon chili powder

Sort through beans, discarding broken, discolored and damaged beans. In a large bowl or pot, cover beans with water until 3 inches above beans. Let soak 10 to 12 hours. Drain; discard soak water. In a 6- or 8-quart pot, combine drained beans, 8 cups water and salt. In a medium skillet, sauté onions in oil until tender but not browned. Stir sautéed onions and oil into beans. Bring to a boil over medium-high heat; reduce heat to low. Cover; simmer 45 minutes. Drain beans, reserving cooking liquid. In a medium bowl, combine 2-1/2 cups reserved cooking liquid, salsa and chili powder. Return beans to pot; stir in salsa mixture. Bring beans to a boil over medium-high heat; reduce heat to low. Cover; simmer 20 minutes. Wash 6 pint jars in hot soapy water; rinse. Keep hot until needed. Prepare lids as manufacturer directs. Bring remaining reserved cooking liquid to a boil. Ladle hot bean mixture into 1 hot jar at a time, leaving 1 inch headspace. Add enough liquid from pot to covers beans. If necessary, add hot reserved cooking liquid to cover beans. Release trapped air. Wipe rim of jar with a clean damp cloth. Attach lid. Place in canner. Fill and close remaining jars. *Process in a pressure canner at 10 pounds pressure,* page 17.
   Pints: 65 minutes
Adjust pressure for altitude, page 21. Makes 6 pints.

Snappy Tomato-Juice Cocktail

Serve this mildly spicy drink alone or as a cocktail mixer.

1/2 teaspoon black peppercorns
2 dried whole hot red peppers
1 garlic clove, crushed
10 lbs. firm ripe tomatoes
3 Chili Peppers, page 52, or
  1 (4-oz.) can whole green chilies
1/2 cup chopped onion

1/2 cup chopped celery with leaves
6 tablespoons lemon juice
1 tablespoon salt
1 teaspoon sugar
1 teaspoon paprika
1 teaspoon Worcestershire sauce

Wash 6 pint, four 1-1/2-pint or 3 quart jars in hot soapy water; rinse. Keep hot until needed. Prepare lids as manufacturer directs. On 3 layers of cheesecloth, combine peppercorns, red peppers and garlic. Gather sides of cheesecloth together; tie with cotton string. Set aside. Wash tomatoes. Remove stems and cores. Cut 4 to 6 tomatoes into quarters, or enough tomatoes to cover bottom of an 8-quart pot. Use a wooden spoon to stir and crush tomatoes until juices begin to flow. Cut and add remaining tomatoes. Bring to a boil over medium-high heat. Add green chilies, onion and celery. Add spice packet. Reduce heat to low; simmer until vegetables are soft, about 45 minutes. Remove and discard spice packet. Press vegetables through a food mill or sieve into a 4-quart pot. Discard pulp and seeds. Stir in remaining ingredients. Bring juice to a boil over medium-high heat. Pour hot juice into 1 hot jar at a time, leaving 1/4 inch headspace. Attach lid. Place in canner. Fill and close remaining jars. *Process in a boiling-water bath,* page 17.
   Pints, 1-1/2-pints or quarts: 35 minutes
Adjust time for altitude, page 20. Makes 6 pints, four 1-1/2-pints or 3 quarts.

How to Make Curried Onions

1/Pickling onions peel easily if boiled in water 1 minute. Cool by dipping in cold water before peeling.

2/Pack brined onions, mustard seeds, celery seeds and green-pepper rings into hot jars.

Oranged Carrots

Orange juice gives extra flavor to the carrots.

7 lbs. medium carrots
5 cups orange juice
1 cup water
1/2 cup lemon juice

1/4 cup granulated sugar
1/2 cup packed brown sugar
2 tablespoons grated orange peel
Salt, if desired

Wash 6 pint, four 1-1/2-pint or 3 quart jars in hot soapy water; rinse. Keep hot until needed. Prepare lids as manufacturer directs. Wash carrots in water to cover. Scrub gently with a brush. Peel or scrape carrots. Cut crosswise into 1/4-inch slices. In a 6-quart pot, combine orange juice, water, lemon juice, granulated sugar and brown sugar. Bring to a boil over medium-high heat. Add carrots; return to a boil. Boil 3 minutes. Pack hot carrots into 1 hot jar at a time, leaving 1 inch headspace. Add orange peel to jar, using 1 teaspoon in pints, 1-1/2 teaspoons in 1-1/2-pints and 2 teaspoons in quarts. Add hot cooking syrup to cover. Add salt if desired, using 1/4 teaspoon in pints, 1/2 teaspoon in 1-1/2-pints and 3/4 teaspoon in quarts. Release trapped air. Wipe rim of jar with a clean damp cloth. Attach lid. Place in canner. Fill and close remaining jars. *Process in a pressure canner at 10 pounds pressure,* page 17.
    Pints: 25 minutes   1-1/2-pints or quarts: 30 minutes
Adjust pressure for altitude, page 21. Makes 6 pints, four 1-1/2-pints or 3 quarts.

Curried Onions

Pale yellow in color, these onions are a nice accompaniment to roasted meats.

10 cups pickling onions (3 lbs.)	**1/2 cup sugar**
1/4 cup pickling salt	**1-1/2 teaspoons curry powder**
1 qt. hot water	**1 tablespoon mustard seeds**
2 small green bell peppers	**3/4 teaspoon celery seeds**
3 cups distilled white vinegar	

In a large pot, lower onions into boiling water; boil 1 minute. Drain; plunge into cold water. Slip peels off. Place peeled onions in a gallon crock or large nonmetal bowl. Stir pickling salt into 1 quart hot water until dissolved. Pour over onions. Cover with a lid, plastic wrap or a clean towel. Let stand at room temperature 2 days. Wash six 1/2-pint or 3 pint jars in hot soapy water; rinse. Keep hot until needed. Prepare lids as manufacturer directs. Turn onions into a colander to drain; discard brine. Rinse onions in cold water; set aside. Wash green peppers under running water. Cut crosswise into 1/4-inch rings. Remove seeds and inner membranes; set aside. In a medium saucepan, combine vinegar, sugar and curry powder. Bring to a boil over medium-high heat, stirring until sugar is dissolved. Into each 1/2-pint jar, spoon 1/2 teaspoon mustard seeds and 1/8 teaspoon celery seeds. Into each pint jar, spoon 1 teaspoon mustard seeds and 1/4 teaspoon celery seeds. Pack onions and several green-pepper rings into 1 hot jar at a time, leaving 1/2 inch headspace. Add hot brine to cover. Release trapped air. Wipe rim of jar with a clean damp cloth. Attach lid. Place in canner. Fill and close remaining jars. *Process in a boiling-water bath,* page 17.

    1/2-pints or pints: 20 minutes

Adjust time for altitude, page 20. Makes six 1/2-pints or 3 pints.

Cocktail Onions

Serve with cocktails as a low-calorie appetizer.

10 cups pickling onions (3 lbs.)	**1/2 cup sugar**
Boiling water	**2 tablespoons mixed pickling spices**
1/4 cup pickling salt	**14 black peppercorns**
1 qt. hot water	**1 (4-oz.) jar small pimiento-stuffed**
3 cups distilled white vinegar	**green olives, if desired**

In a large pot, immerse onions in boiling water; boil 1 minute. Drain; plunge into cold water. Slip peels off. Place peeled onions in a gallon crock or large nonmetal bowl. Stir salt into 1 quart hot water until dissolved. Pour over onions. Cover with a lid, plastic wrap or a clean towel. Let stand at room temperature 2 days. Wash seven 1/2-pint jars in hot soapy water; rinse. Keep hot until needed. Prepare lids as manufacturer directs. Turn onions into a colander to drain; discard brine. Rinse onions in cold water. In a medium saucepan, combine vinegar, sugar and pickling spices. Bring to a boil over medium-high heat; reduce heat to low. Cover; simmer 10 minutes. Strain vinegar mixture to remove spices. Return vinegar mixture to pan; keep hot. Place 2 peppercorns in 1 hot jar. Pack onions and a few olives, if desired, into jar, leaving 1/2 inch headspace. Add hot vinegar mixture to cover. Release trapped air. Wipe rim of jar with a clean damp cloth. Attach lid. Place in canner. Fill and close remaining jars. *Process in a boiling-water bath,* page 17.

    1/2-pints: 20 minutes

Adjust time for altitude, page 20. Makes six 1/2-pints without olives or seven 1/2-pints with olives.

Barbequed Beans

Partially cooked beans finish cooking in the canner without overcooking.

2 lbs. dried red beans, red kidney beans or pinto beans	**1/2 cup ketchup**
Water for soaking	**1/4 cup chili sauce**
8 cups water	**2 tablespoons vinegar**
1/2 lb. sliced bacon	**1/4 cup packed brown sugar**
1 cup chopped onion	**2 tablespoons prepared mustard**
4 garlic cloves, minced	**2 teaspoons salt**
1 teaspoon salt	**1 teaspoon pepper**
	3 to 4 drops liquid smoke, if desired

Sort through beans, discarding broken, discolored and damaged beans. In a 6- or 8-quart pot, cover beans with water until 3 inches above beans. Let soak 10 to 12 hours. Drain; discard soak water. Add 8 cups water; set aside. In a medium skillet, fry bacon until crisp; drain on paper towels. Crumble bacon. Sauté onion and garlic in bacon drippings until onion is tender. Add crumbled bacon, onion mixture and 1 teaspoon salt to beans. Bring to a boil. Cover; simmer over low heat 45 minutes. Drain, reserving cooking liquid. In a medium bowl, combine 3-1/2 cups cooking liquid and remaining ingredients; mix well. Stir sauce into beans. Simmer over low heat, 20 minutes. Wash 6 pint jars in hot soapy water; rinse. Keep hot until needed. Prepare lids as manufacturer directs. Bring remaining reserved cooking liquid to a boil. Ladle bean mixture into 1 hot jar at a time, leaving 1 inch headspace. Add enough sauce to covers beans. If necessary, add hot reserved cooking liquid. Release trapped air. Wipe rim of jar. Attach lid. Place in canner. Fill and cover remaining jars. *Process in a pressure canner at 10 pounds pressure,* page 17.

Pints: 65 minutes

Adjust pressure for altitude, page 21. Makes 6 pints.

Garden-Vegetable Drink

Serve ice cold in tall glasses. Stir with Quick Dill Spears, page 107.

10 lbs. firm red tomatoes	**1/2 cup chopped green bell pepper**
1 cup sliced carrots	**1 garlic clove, crushed**
1/3 cup chopped onion	**2 tablespoons chopped fresh parsley**
2 green onions, sliced	**1 tablespoon salt**
1 cup grated zucchini (1 medium)	**6 tablespoons lemon juice**
1 celery stalk with top, sliced	**1 tablespoon prepared mustard**

Wash 6 pint, four 1-1/2-pint or 3 quart jars in hot soapy water; rinse. Keep hot until needed. Prepare lids as manufacturer directs. Wash tomatoes. Remove stems and cores. Cut 4 to 6 tomatoes into quarters, or enough to cover bottom of an 8-quart pot. Use a wooden spoon to stir and crush tomatoes until juices begin to flow. Cut and add remaining tomatoes. Stir in carrots, onions, zucchini, celery, green pepper, garlic and parsley. Cover; simmer over low heat until vegetables are soft, about 45 minutes. Press vegetables through a food mill or sieve, into a 4-quart pot. Discard peels and seeds. Stir in salt, lemon juice and prepared mustard. Bring to a boil. Ladle hot juice into 1 hot jar at a time, leaving 1/4 inch headspace. Wipe rim of jar with a clean damp cloth. Attach lid. Place in canner. Fill and close remaining jars. *Process in a boiling-water bath,* page 17.

Pints, 1-1/2-pints or quarts: 35 minutes

Adjust time for altitude, page 20. Makes 6 pints, four 1-1/2-pints or 3 quarts.

Sauerkraut

Maintaining a constant fermenting temperature is very important.

20 lbs. green cabbage heads   **About 3 qts. water**
About 1-1/4 cups pickling salt

Remove and discard outer cabbage leaves. Wash cabbage under running water. Thinly shred one-fourth of cabbage. Place in a large bowl. Sprinkle with 3-1/2 tablespoons salt. Lift and turn with your hands to distribute salt. Turn into a 5-gallon crock or nonmetal container. Repeat, shredding and mixing one-fourth of cabbage at a time with 3-1/2 tablespoons salt. Cover cabbage mixture with a clean white cloth. Tuck edges down into container. Let stand at room temperature overnight to wilt. Make top level. Make a brine of 1/4 cup salt dissolved in 2 quarts water. If liquid does not cover cabbage, add brine until cabbage is covered. Place a 5-gallon plastic bag on top of cabbage. Pour remaining brine into bag. Make more brine, if necessary. Bag must be full enough to weigh down entire surface of cabbage. Twist and tie top of bag. Cover crock or container with a lid or plastic wrap and a towel. Let cabbage ferment, undisturbed, 3 weeks. After 3 weeks, begin checking sauerkraut. When liquid no longer bubbles, fermentation is complete. Mix remaining 2 tablespoons salt with 1 quart water. Cover; set aside. Wash 10 quart jars in hot soapy water; rinse. Keep hot until needed. Prepare lids as manufacturer directs. Heat sauerkraut in a large pot over medium heat until 185F (85C) or simmering. Do not boil. Pack into 1 hot jar at a time, leaving 1/2 inch headspace. Attach lid. Place in canner. Fill and close remaining jars. *Process in a boiling-water bath,* page 17.
    Quarts: 20 minutes
Adjust time for altitude, page 20. Makes 10 quarts.

Pea Pods Oriental   Photo on cover.

Fresh gingerroot supplies a special flavor to delicate pea pods.

1 tablespoon salt   **1 qt. water**
1 qt. cold water   **1/4 cup pickling salt**
3/4 lb. fresh broccoli   **2 (8-oz.) cans whole water chestnuts,**
3 cups immature pea pods or   **   drained**
**   Chinese pea pods**   **5 cups distilled white vinegar**
4 or 5 celery stalks without leaves   **1/2 cup sugar**
1 cup chopped red bell pepper   **1 tablespoon grated fresh gingerroot**
**   or 1 (4-oz.) jar diced pimiento**   **3 tablespoons mustard seeds**

In a large bowl, stir 1 tablespoon salt into 1 quart cold water; set aside. Wash broccoli. Immerse in salted water, 10 minutes. Rinse in fresh water. Cut into flowerets with 1-inch stems attached. Peel remaining stems with a vegetable peeler. Cut into 1/8-inch slices. Wash pea pods; break off stem ends. Wash celery; cut off base. Cut stalks into 1/4-inch diagonal slices, making 3 cups. In a large bowl, combine broccoli flowerets and sliced stems, pea pods, sliced celery and red pepper or pimiento; set aside. In a large saucepan, combine 1 quart water and pickling salt. Bring to a boil. Pour brine over vegetables. Cover with a towel; let stand 10 to 12 hours. Drain; discard brine. Wash 6 pint jars in hot soapy water; rinse. Keep hot until needed. Prepare lids as manufacturer directs. Stir water chestnuts into marinated vegetables. In a large saucepan, combine vinegar, sugar, gingerroot and mustard seeds. Bring to a boil. Cover; simmer 10 minutes. Pack vegetables into 1 hot jar at a time, leaving 1/2 inch headspace. Add boiling vinegar mixture to cover. Release trapped air. Wipe rim of jar with a clean damp cloth. Attach lid. Place in canner. Fill and close remaining jars. *Process in a boiling-water bath,* page 17.
    Pints: 20 minutes
Adjust time for altitude, page 20. Makes 6 pints.

Asparagus Spears with Tarragon

An elegant appetizer.

4 lbs. tender, thin green asparagus	**1-1/2 cups water**
1 medium onion, peeled	**1/4 cup sugar**
1/4 cup pickling salt	**5 teaspoons mixed pickling spices**
2 qts. water	**5 teaspoons dried leaf tarragon**
3 cups white-wine vinegar	**20 black peppercorns**

Wash asparagus. Cut off stem ends so stalks are 1/2 inch shorter than jars; set aside. Cut onion in half top to bottom. Place cut-side down on a cutting board. Cut into thin slices; separate into half rings. In a large bowl, stir pickling salt into 2 quarts water until dissolved. Add asparagus and onion; cover with a towel. Let stand 10 to 12 hours. Wash 5 pint jars in hot soapy water; rinse. Keep hot until needed. Prepare lids as manufacturer directs. Drain vegetables; discard brine. In a medium saucepan, combine vinegar, 1-1/2 cups water and sugar. Bring to a boil over high heat. Into each hot jar, spoon 1 teaspoon mixed pickling spices, 1 teaspoon tarragon and 4 peppercorns. Divide onion slices among jar. Tightly pack asparagus spears into 1 jar at a time, stem-ends down. Add boiling vinegar mixture, leaving 1/2 inch headspace. Release trapped air. Wipe rim of jar with a clean damp cloth. Attach lid. Place in canner. Fill and close remaining jars. *Process in a boiling-water bath,* page 17.

Pints: 20 minutes

Adjust time for altitude, page 20. Makes 5 pints.

Boston-Style Baked Beans

To serve, bake in a bean pot 1 hour at 350F (175C) or heat in a saucepan.

2 lbs. dried pea beans or	**1 cup molasses**
small white beans	**1/3 cup sugar**
Water for soaking	**2 teaspoons dry mustard**
10 cups water	**1 tablespoon salt**
1 medium onion, sliced	**1/2 teaspoon pepper**
1/2 lb. salt pork, cut in 1-inch cubes	

Wash and sort beans. In a large bowl or pot, cover beans with water until 3 inches above beans. Let soak 10 to 12 hours. Drain; discard soak water. Combine soaked beans and 10 cups water in a 6- or 8-quart pot. Bring to a boil. Cover; simmer over low heat 10 minutes. Drain beans, reserving cooking liquid. Preheat oven to 300F (150C). In a 4- to 6-quart casserole or bean pot, layer beans, onion and salt pork; set aside. In a medium bowl, combine 2 cups reserved cooking liquid and remaining ingredients; mix well. Pour over beans. Add enough of reserved cooking liquid to cover beans. Cover casserole or bean pot with a lid or foil. Bake 3 hours in preheated oven. Check beans every 45 minutes to be sure they are covered with liquid. Add more of reserved cooking liquid, if necessary. As beans bake, wash 6 pint jars in hot soapy water; rinse. Keep hot until needed. Prepare lids as manufacturer directs. Beans will be slightly firm. Ladle hot bean mixture into 1 hot jar at a time, leaving 1 inch headspace. Add enough liquid from pot or casserole to cover beans. Release trapped air. Wipe rim of jar with a clean damp cloth. Attach lid. Place in canner. Fill and close remaining jars. *Process in a pressure canner at 10 pounds pressure,* page 17.

Pints: 80 minutes

Adjust pressure for altitude, page 21. Makes 6 pints.

Clockwise from top left: Asparagus Spears with Tarragon; Tiny Toms, page 91; Minty Cocktail Carrots, page 94; Marinated Button Mushrooms, page 93.

Canning with Flair:
Pickles & Relishes

Originally, pickling was a method of preserving for the winter months. Today, we pickle to be able to enjoy the crisp, sour or sweet-sour flavor. Crisp, tangy pickles stimulate the taste buds and heighten enjoyment of other foods.

The Pickling Process: There are two kinds of pickles or methods of pickling: *brined or fermented* and *fresh-packed*, also called *quick-cured*.

Brined or fermented pickles ferment 3 to 4 weeks in a salt brine. Lactic acid produced during fermentation gives the pickles their snappy, sharp flavor and acts as a preservative. When bubbles stop forming in the brine, fermentation is completed. The exterior color of the pickles changes from bright green to olive-green, and the white interior becomes translucent.

Fresh-packed or quick-cured pickles soak in a brine 10 to 12 hours. Raw cucumber slices or spears are packed in jars and covered with a vinegar syrup. Because of the vinegar, fresh-packed pickles are more tart and pungent than fermented pickles. The short brining period and seasoned vinegar preserves the crisp texture and changes the color of the cucumbers to olive-green. Relishes, fruits and some vegetables are pickled using this method.

Ingredients for Pickles: *Cucumbers* must be fresh. Use them within 24 hours after picking. Wilted, shriveled cucumbers will make soft, hollow, disappointing pickles. U-pick farms, roadside markets and your own garden are the best sources for pickling cucumbers.

Use only varieties that have been developed for pickling. Slicing varieties do not pickle well. The brine or vinegar cannot penetrate waxed cucumbers.

Vinegar must be a standardized vinegar of 4% to 6% acidity. Most commercial vinegars are 5% acidity, but read the label to be sure. Recipes all depend upon this level of acidity for safe processing. Do not use vinegars of unknown acidity.

Distilled white vinegar is generally preferred for pickling. But for a more mellow flavor, wine vinegar may be used as long as its level of acidity is 5%. Cider vinegar adds an interesting flavor but darkens pickles. Follow recipe directions for the type and amount of vinegar.

Salt used in pickling should be a canning or pickling salt that contains no additives or iodine. Regular table salt contains anticaking additives that cloud the brine. Iodine in table salt and sea salt darkens the pickles and interferes with the fermentation process.

Pickling salt is usually labeled for pickling. It is available in supermarkets and in some hardware stores.

Soft water is best for making the brine. Minerals in very hard water interfere with fermentation. Use bottled water, if necessary.

Herbs should be fresh or fresh frozen. *Dried spices* are usually tied in a cheesecloth bag for easy removal so they won't darken the pickles in the jar.

Pickling additives such as *alum* and *slake lime* have been used in the past to make pickles crisp. Modern pickling methods do not use these additives. They are unnecessary, and if used in excess, may cause digestive upset. Pickles are kept crisp by using fresh-picked cucumbers, paying careful attention to sanitation during fermentation and following processing times exactly.

Equipment for Pickling: *Use 3- to 5-gallon crocks or other containers* to hold the cucumbers during fermentation. Make sure crocks are glazed, unchipped and have no lead content. If plastic containers are used, the plastic must be food-grade polyethylene. A good source is quick-food restaurants. Glass bowls or jars, nonmetal casseroles, stainless-steel pots or unchipped enamelware pots may be used as containers.

Large deep stainless-steel, aluminum or unchipped enamelware pots are also needed for heating some types of pickles before packing and processing. Do not use copper, brass, iron or galvanized pans. They will react with the pickles and brine.

Canning Method: *Pickles and relishes must be processed in a boiling-water bath to be safe.* When accurately timed, pickles remain crisp and firm.

Preparing Pickles and Relishes: Read the recipe to learn the procedures to be used and ingredients and equipment needed.

Wash the cucumbers in several changes of cool water or under running water. Use your hands or a soft brush to remove garden dirt and blossom fragments.

Use cucumbers under 2 inches long for Sweet Midgets. Medium-size cucumbers, 3 to 5 inches, are best for Bread & Butter Pickles, Quick Dill Spears and Sandwich Pickle Slices. Use large cucumbers for Crisp Cinnamon Rings.

When making relishes, uniformly chop vegetables and fruits in a blender or food processor. Process on low speed to chop vegetables rather than pureeing them. When using a blender, add water to chop firm vegetables such as onions, celery and cabbage. Pour off the water. When a measurement for chopped fruits or vegetables is given in a recipe, use only that amount.

Pickles and relishes should be stored several weeks before opening and serving. It is sometimes hard to wait, but flavors develop and mingle, making the wait worthwhile.

Bread & Butter Pickles

Tart with a touch of sweetness, these are a family favorite.

6 lbs. pickling cucumbers,	**3 cups cider vinegar**
3 to 5 inches long	**2 tablespoons mustard seeds**
2 lbs. onions	**1 teaspoon mixed pickling spices**
1/3 cup pickling salt	**1/2 teaspoon ground turmeric**
Ice cubes	**1/8 teaspoon red (cayenne) pepper,**
3 cups sugar	**if desired**

Wash cucumbers. Scrub gently with a brush to remove spines. Remove blossom fragments. Cut a thin slice from each end of cucumbers; discard. Cut cucumbers crosswise into 1/4-inch slices, making about 5 quarts sliced cucumbers. Peel onions; cut in half, top to bottom. Lay cut-side down. Cut crosswise into 1/4-inch slices, making about 1 quart onion slices. Layer cucumber slices and onion slices alternately in a large pot or bowl, sprinkling pickling salt over each layer. Cover top with ice cubes. Cover pot or bowl; let stand 3 hours. Wash 8 pint jars in hot soapy water; rinse. Keep hot until needed. Prepare lids as manufacturer directs. Turn cucumber mixture into a colander to drain; rinse well with cold water. In an 8-quart pot, combine remaining ingredients. Bring to a boil over medium-high heat; boil 5 minutes. Add drained cucumber mixture. Return to a boil. Pack hot cucumber mixture into 1 hot jar at a time, leaving 1/4 inch headspace. Add vinegar mixture to cover. Release trapped air. Wipe rim of jar with a clean damp cloth. Attach lid. Place in canner. Fill and close remaining jars. *Process in a boiling-water bath,* page 17.

Pints: 15 minutes

Adjust time for altitude, page 20. Makes 8 pints.

Quick Dill Spears   Photo on cover.

Easy, overnight process gives crisp dills with a fresh, tart flavor.

6 lbs. pickling cucumbers,
   3 to 5 inches long
4 qts. water
3/4 cup pickling salt
3 cups distilled white vinegar

4-1/2 cups water
3 tablespoons pickling salt
1 teaspoon sugar
2 tablespoons mixed pickling spices
1 bunch fresh dill

Wash cucumbers. Scrub gently with a brush to remove spines. Remove blossom fragments. Cut cucumbers lengthwise into 4 spears. Arrange cucumber spears in a large crock or nonmetal bowl. In a 6-quart pot, combine 4 quarts water and 3/4 cup pickling salt; stir to dissolve salt. Pour over cucumbers. Cover crock or bowl; let stand overnight or 10 to 12 hours at room temperature. Wash 5 quart jars in hot soapy water; rinse. Keep hot until needed. Prepare lids as manufacturer directs. Drain cucumbers; discard brine. Set drained cucumbers aside. In a 4-quart pot, combine vinegar, 4-1/2 cups water, 3 tablespoons pickling salt and sugar. Tie pickling spices in a 4-inch square of cheesecloth; add to brine. Bring to a boil over medium-high heat. Cover; simmer 15 minutes. Remove spice bag from brine; discard. Place a large sprig of dill in 1 hot jar. Pack jar with cucumber spears, leaving 1/4 inch headspace. Add boiling brine to cover. Release trapped air. Wipe rim of jar with a clean damp cloth. Attach lid. Place in canner. Fill and close remaining jars. *Process in a boiling-water bath,* page 17.

  Quarts: 15 minutes
Adjust time for altitude, page 20. Makes 4 to 5 quarts.

Green & Yellow Pickles   Photo on cover, pages 182-183.

Crisp and colorful—similar in flavor to Bread & Butter Pickles, page 105.

6 large zucchini squash
6 large straightneck yellow squash
1 large onion
1/2 cup pickling salt
Ice cubes

3 cups distilled white vinegar
3 cups sugar
1 tablespoon mustard seeds
1 teaspoon celery seeds
1/2 teaspoon turmeric

Wash zucchini and yellow squash. Trim a thin slice from both ends of each squash; discard. Cut crosswise into 1/4-inch slices. Peel onion; cut in half top to bottom. With cut-side down, cut onion halves crosswise into 1/4-inch slices. Layer squash and onion slices alternately in a large bowl or plastic container, sprinkling pickling salt over each layer. Cover top with ice cubes. Cover container; let stand 3 hours at room temperature. Wash 6 pint jars in hot soapy water; rinse. Keep hot until needed. Prepare lids as manufacturer directs. Drain vegetables; discard brine. Set aside. In a 6-quart pot, combine remaining ingredients. Bring to a boil over medium-high heat. Stir in drained squash mixture. Bring back to a boil. Pack hot squash and onions into 1 hot jar at a time, leaving 1/4 inch headspace. Add hot vinegar mixture to cover. Release trapped air. Wipe rim of jar with a clean damp cloth. Attach lid. Place in canner. Fill and close remaining jars. *Process in a boiling-water bath,* page 17.

  Pints: 10 minutes
Adjust time for altitude, page 20. Makes 5 to 6 pints.

Wine-Vinegar Pickles

In France these tiny sour pickles are known as cornichons.

2 qts. small pickling cucumbers,
   1 to 1-1/2 inches long (about 2 lbs.)
1 qt. water
3 cups pickling onions (about 1 lb.)
1/4 cup pickling salt
1 qt. hot water
1 qt. white-wine vinegar

1 cup water
3 tablespoons sugar
24 black peppercorns
6 tablespoons minced fresh tarragon or
   2 tablespoons dried leaf tarragon
1/2 cup finely chopped green bell pepper

Wash cucumbers in water to cover. Scrub gently with a brush to remove spines. Remove blossom fragments; set cucumbers aside. In a large saucepan, bring 1 quart water to a boil over medium-high heat. Add onions to boiling water; blanch 30 seconds. Drain; cover with cold water. Peel onions. In a large saucepan, combine washed cucumbers and peeled onions; set aside. Stir pickling salt and 1 quart hot water until dissolved. Pour over cucumbers and onions. Cover; let stand 2 days at room temperature. Drain; discard brine. Rinse in cold water. Wash six 1/2-pint or 3 pint jars in hot soapy water; rinse. Keep hot until needed. Prepare lids as manufacturer directs. In a medium saucepan, combine vinegar, 1 cup water and sugar. Bring to a boil; keep hot. Into each hot 1/2-pint jar, place 4 peppercorns, 1 tablespoon fresh tarragon or 1 teaspoon dried leaf tarragon and 1 heaping tablespoon green pepper. Into each pint jar, place 8 peppercorns, 2 tablespoons fresh tarragon or 2 teaspoons dried leaf tarragon and 2 heaping tablespoons green pepper. Pack cucumbers and onions into 1 jar at a time, leaving 1/4 inch headspace. Add hot vinegar mixture to cover. Release trapped air. Wipe rim of jar with a clean damp cloth. Attach lid. Place in canner. Fill and close remaining jars. *Process in a boiling-water bath,* page 17.

   1/2-pints or pints: 10 minutes

Adjust time for altitude, page 20. Makes six 1/2-pints or 3 pints.

Sandwich Pickle Slices

These thin slices are ready to put in a sandwich or hamburger.

4 lbs. pickling cucumbers,
   3 to 5 inches long
1/2 cup pickling salt
Ice cubes
2 cups distilled white vinegar

3 cups water
2 tablespoons sugar
1/4 cup dill seeds
1/4 cup dried dill weed
4 teaspoons black peppercorns

Wash cucumbers in water to cover. Scrub gently with a brush to remove spines. Remove blossom fragments. Slice cucumbers as thin as possible. Layer cucumber slices in a crock or large nonmetal bowl, sprinkling pickling salt over each layer. Cover cucumber slices with ice cubes. Cover crock or bowl. Refrigerate overnight or 10 to 12 hours. Wash 4 pint jars in hot soapy water; rinse. Keep hot until needed. Prepare lids as manufacturer directs. In a large saucepan, combine vinegar, water and sugar. Bring to a boil over high heat, stirring until sugar is dissolved. Drain cucumber slices; discard brine. Pack drained slices into 1 hot jar at a time, sprinkling one-fourth of dill seeds, dill weed and peppercorns among slices as jar is filled. Add boiling vinegar mixture to cover, leaving 1/4 inch headspace. Release trapped air. Wipe rim of jar with a clean damp cloth. Attach lid. Place in canner. Fill and close remaining jars. *Process in a boiling-water bath,* page 17.

   Pints: 10 minutes

Adjust time for altitude, page 20. Makes 4 pints.

Sweet Midgets   Photo on page 106.

Adding sugar over several days keeps pickles from shriveling.

4 qts. small pickling cucumbers,
   about 2 inches long (about 8 lbs.)
1-1/2 cups pickling salt
4 qts. hot water
Boiling water
8 cups cider vinegar
9 cups sugar

2 tablespoons whole allspice
2 teaspoons celery seeds
2 teaspoons mustard seeds
2 (2-inch) cinnamon sticks,
   each broken in 2 or 3 pieces
2 teaspoons mixed pickling spices

Wash cucumbers in water to cover. Scrub gently with a brush to remove spines. Remove blossom fragments. Wash a 3-gallon crock or glass or plastic container in hot soapy water; rinse. Pour in boiling water to top of container. Place a clean plate and pint jar in crock or plastic container to scald. Let stand 10 minutes; drain. Pack cucumbers in crock or container; set aside. In a 6-quart pot, stir pickling salt into 4 quarts hot water; cool. Pour over cucumbers. Place scalded plate on top of cucumbers to keep them submerged in brine. Brine should be about 2 inches above surface of plate. If necessary, place scalded jar filled with water on plate to keep cucumbers submerged. Cover crock; let stand 7 days at room temperature. Each day, scald a spoon in boiling water. Remove lid from container. Use scalded spoon to skim off foam from surface. Do not stir pickles. If mold grows on plate or weight, remove from crock. Wash and scald them. Replace plate and weight; cover crock again. After 7 days, drain and discard brine. Wash crock, plate and weight; scald each again. Rinse cucumbers; return to crock. Pour boiling water over cucumbers to cover. Add scalded plate and weight; cover crock. Repeat rinsing once each day for 2 more days. Drain; discard water. Again wash crock, plate and weight; scald as above. Rinse cucumbers; prick with a scalded fork to prevent shriveling. Return cucumbers to scalded crock; set aside. In a large saucepan, combine vinegar, 3 cups sugar, allspice, celery seeds, mustard seeds, cinnamon and pickling spices. Bring to a boil over medium-high heat. Pour over cucumbers. Place scalded plate and weight on top of cucumbers. Cover; let stand 24 hours. Drain syrup into a saucepan; add 2 cups of remaining sugar. Bring to a boil over medium-high heat; pour over cucumbers. Cover container; let stand 24 hours. Repeat this process 2 more times until all of sugar has been used. Wash 8 pint jars in hot soapy water; rinse. Keep hot until needed. Prepare lids as manufacturer directs. Drain pickles; reserve liquid in a medium saucepan. Stir syrup over high heat until mixture boils. Remove and discard cinnamon pieces. Pack drained pickles into 1 hot jar at a time, leaving 1/4 inch headspace. Add boiling syrup to cover. Release trapped air. Wipe rim of jar with a clean damp cloth. Attach lid. Place in canner. Fill and close remaining jars. *Process in a boiling-water bath,* page 17.
   Pints: 10 minutes
Adjust time for altitude, page 20. Makes 8 pints.

Tip

Do not use homemade vinegars for pickling or canning. The acidity is too variable. Use only commercial vinegars of 4% to 6% acidity.

How to Make Pickle-Barrel Dills

1/Layer pickling cucumbers, dill and spices in a scalded 5-gallon crock or plastic container.

2/Keep cucumbers submerged in brine by placing a scalded plate and weight on top.

3/Skim foam from surface of brine each day. Do not disturb pickles or stir brine.

4/Fermented cucumbers turn olive-green outside. Centers are a uniform pale-green color.

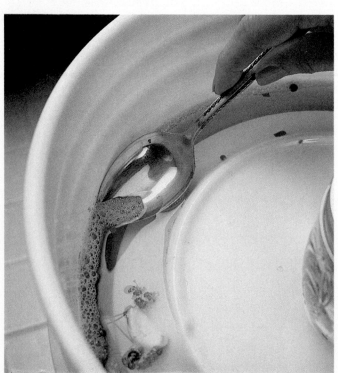

Pickle-Barrel Dills

Buy an empty 5-gallon food container from a restaurant to use for a crock.

10 lbs. pickling cucumbers, 3 to 6 inches long	**1-1/3 cups distilled white vinegar**
1 bunch fresh dill	**3/4 cup pickling salt**
1/3 cup mixed pickling spices	**1 gallon warm water**
	6 large garlic cloves, peeled

Select cucumbers of fairly uniform size. Wash cucumbers in water to cover. Scrub gently with a brush to remove spines. Remove blossom fragments. Pat dry with paper towels. Wash a 5-gallon crock or plastic container in hot soapy water; rinse. Pour in boiling water to top of container. Place a clean plate and pint jar in crock to scald. Let stand 10 minutes; drain. Spread a layer of dill in bottom of crock; sprinkle with 1 tablespoon pickling spices. Arrange about one-third of washed cucumbers over spices. Continue layering dill, cucumbers and spices, ending with dill and spices on top. In a 6-quart pot, combine vinegar, pickling salt and water; stir to dissolve salt. Pour over cucumbers. Add garlic cloves. Place scalded plate on top of cucumbers to keep them submerged in brine. Brine should be about 2 inches above surface of plate. If necessary, place scalded jar filled with water on plate to keep cucumbers submerged. Cover crock; let stand 3 weeks at room temperature. Each day, scald a spoon in boiling water. Remove lid from container. Use scalded spoon to skim off foam from surface. Do not stir pickles. If mold grows on plate or weight, remove from crock. Wash and scald them. Replace plate and weight; cover crock again. Foam and cloudiness in brine indicate pickles are fermenting as they should. Fermentation is complete when brine no longer bubbles. Pickles should be olive-green, have few or no white spots inside when cut and have a pleasing dill flavor. Wash 6 quart jars in hot soapy water; rinse. Keep hot until needed. Prepare lids as manufacturer directs. Drain brine from pickles into a 4-quart pot; bring to a boil over medium-high heat. Remove dill sprigs and garlic cloves from crock. Place some of each in 1 hot jar; pack pickles into jar, leaving 1/4 inch headspace. Add boiling brine to cover. Release trapped air. Wipe rim of jar with a clean damp cloth. Attach lid. Place in canner. Fill and close remaining jars. *Process in a boiling-water bath,* page 17.

    Quarts: 10 minutes

Adjust time for altitude, page 20. Makes 5 to 6 quarts.

Cranapple Relish

Autumn's treasures — apples and cranberries — combined in a relish.

2 medium, tart apples, peeled, minced	**1/2 teaspoon salt**
2 cups fresh cranberries, minced	**1 cup sugar**
1 cup cranapple juice	**3/4 cup distilled white vinegar**
1/2 cup golden raisins	**1/2 teaspoon ground cloves**
1/4 cup chopped onion	

Wash five 1/2-pint jars in hot soapy water; rinse. Keep hot until needed. Prepare lids as manufacturer directs. In a 4-quart pot, combine all ingredients. Bring to a boil over medium-high heat; reduce heat to low. Cover; simmer 15 minutes. Remove cover; cook until mixture thickens slightly, 10 to 15 minutes. Ladle hot relish into 1 hot jar at a time, leaving 1/4 inch headspace. Release trapped air. Wipe rim of jar with a clean damp cloth. Attach lid. Place in canner. Fill and close remaining jars. *Process in a boiling-water bath,* page 17.

    1/2-pints: 15 minutes

Adjust time for altitude, page 20. Makes five 1/2-pints.

Crisp Cinnamon Rings

These rosy-red pickle rings are crisp and fresh.

10 large pickling cucumbers,
   about 2 inches in diameter
Boiling water
7 cups sugar

2 tablespoons pickling salt
3 cups distilled white vinegar
4 (3-inch) cinnamon sticks
1/2 cup red-hot cinnamon candies

Wash cucumbers. Scrub gently with a brush to remove spines. Remove blossom fragments. Wash a 3-gallon crock or glass or plastic container in hot soapy water; rinse. Pour in boiling water to top of container. Let stand 10 minutes; drain. Pack cucumbers in crock or container. Pour boiling water over cucumbers to cover. Cover; let stand overnight or 10 to 12 hours at room temperature. Drain; discard water. Repeat procedure of covering with boiling water, standing overnight and draining 3 more times. On 4th day, peel cucumbers; cut in 1/2-inch slices. Remove center of slices with a zucchini corer or a knife, leaving doughnut-shaped slices. Return slices to crock or container. In a medium saucepan, combine 3 cups sugar and remaining ingredients. Bring to a boil over medium-high heat, stirring until sugar dissolves. Pour syrup over cucumber rings. Cover; let stand overnight. Drain syrup into a saucepan; add 1 cup of remaining sugar. Bring to a boil; pour over cucumber rings. Repeat adding 1 cup of remaining sugar to syrup, bringing mixture to a boil and pouring over cucumbers once a day for 3 days, until all sugar has been added. On final day, wash 3 pint jars in hot soapy water; rinse. Keep hot until needed. Prepare lids as manufacturer directs. Drain syrup into a medium saucepan; bring to a boil. Remove and discard cinnamon sticks. Pack cucumber rings into 1 hot jar at a time, leaving 1/4 inch headspace. Add boiling syrup to cover. Release trapped air. Wipe rim of jar with a clean damp cloth. Attach lid. Place in canner. Fill and close remaining jars. *Process in a boiling-water bath,* page 17.
  Pints: 10 minutes
Adjust time for altitude, page 20. Makes 3 pints.

Piccalilli

Sweet-and-sour flavors combine in our traditional hamburger relish.

6 cups minced green tomatoes
6 cups minced firm red tomatoes
4 cups minced cabbage
2 cups minced onions
2 large red or green bell peppers, minced

1/3 cup pickling salt
3 cups distilled white vinegar
1-1/2 cups packed brown sugar
1/2 teaspoon ground ginger
2 tablespoons mixed pickling spices

In a large bowl or plastic container, combine tomatoes, cabbage, onions and bell peppers. Sprinkle with pickling salt; mix well. Cover; let stand 3 to 4 hours at room temperature. Drain vegetables, pressing to remove as much liquid as possible. Wash 6 pint jars in hot soapy water; rinse. Keep hot until needed. Prepare lids as manufacturer directs. In a 6- or 8-quart pot, combine vinegar, brown sugar and ginger. Tie pickling spices in a 4-inch square of cheesecloth. Add to vinegar mixture. Bring to a boil over medium-high heat; reduce heat to low. Cover; simmer 15 minutes. Stir in drained vegetables. Bring back to a boil over medium heat; reduce heat to low. Stirring frequently, simmer 5 minutes. Remove and discard spice bag. Ladle hot relish into 1 hot jar at a time, leaving 1/4 inch headspace. Release trapped air. Wipe rim of jar with a clean damp cloth. Attach lid. Fill and close remaining jars. *Process in a boiling-water bath,* page 17.
  Pints: 15 minutes
Adjust time for altitude, page 20. Makes 6 pints.

Iowa Corn Relish

Spoon over a hamburger to give it a zesty touch.

12 to 14 medium ears of corn	1 cup packed brown sugar
2 cups sliced celery	3 cups cider vinegar
1 cup chopped onion	2 tablespoons mustard seeds
2 cups chopped cabbage	1 tablespoon dry mustard
1 cup chopped red bell pepper	1 teaspoon curry powder
1/2 teaspoon ground ginger	1 tablespoon pickling salt

Husk corn; remove silk. Rinse husked corn; cut off both ends. In a large pot, bring about 2 quarts water to a boil over medium-high heat. Add corn to boiling water. Cover; boil 5 minutes. Use tongs to remove corn from boiling water; plunge into cold water. Stand ears of corn on end; cut kernels from the cob with a sharp knife or a corn cutter. In a 6-quart pot, combine 8 cups cut corn and remaining ingredients. Bring to a boil over medium-high heat; reduce heat to low. Cover; simmer 15 minutes. Wash 6 pint jars in hot soapy water; rinse. Keep hot until needed. Prepare lids as manufacturer directs. Ladle hot relish into 1 hot jar at a time, leaving 1/4 inch headspace. Release trapped air. Wipe rim of jar with a clean damp cloth. Attach lid. Place in canner. Fill and close remaining jars. *Process in a boiling-water bath,* page 17.

   Pints: 15 minutes

Adjust time for altitude, page 20. Makes 6 pints.

Variation

Substitute green bell pepper for red bell pepper. Add 1 (4-ounce) jar pimientos for color.

Hot-Dog Relish   Photo on page 106.

Mustard color and flavor make this relish the perfect complement to hot dogs.

2 cups finely chopped onions	1/4 cup all-purpose flour
2 cups finely chopped cucumbers	2 teaspoons ground turmeric
6 green or red bell peppers, finely chopped	1 cup water
4 cups finely chopped green tomatoes	1/4 cup prepared mustard
3 tablespoons pickling salt	1 tablespoon mustard seeds
3 cups sugar	2 cups cider vinegar

In a large bowl or plastic container, combine onions, cucumbers, peppers and tomatoes. Sprinkle with pickling salt; mix well. Cover; let stand overnight or 10 to 12 hours at room temperature. Turn brined vegetables into a colandar to drain; discard liquid. Rinse with clear water. Wash 4 pint jars in hot soapy water; rinse. Keep hot until needed. Prepare lids as manufacturer directs. In a 6-quart pot, combine sugar, flour and turmeric. Slowly stir in water until mixture is smooth. Stir in remaining ingredients. Over medium heat, stir frequently until mixture thickens, about 10 minutes. Stir in rinsed chopped vegetables; bring back to a boil. Reduce heat to low; simmer uncovered 20 minutes. Ladle hot relish into 1 hot jar at a time, leaving 1/4 inch headspace. Release trapped air. Wipe rim of jar with a clean damp cloth. Attach lid. Place in canner. Fill and close remaining jars. *Process in a boiling-water bath,* page 17.

   Pints: 15 minutes

Adjust time for altitude, page 20. Makes 4 pints.

India Relish

Serve with meat or fold into a mayonnaise dressing for chicken, ham or tuna salad.

6 cups minced zucchini	3 cups distilled white vinegar
4 cups minced cabbage	1 teaspoon ground ginger
1 cup minced green bell pepper	1/2 teaspoon ground turmeric
3 cups minced carrots	1 teaspoon ground coriander
3 cups minced onions	1/2 teaspoon ground cumin
1/4 cup pickling salt	1/4 teaspoon red (cayenne) pepper
2 cups sugar	

In a large bowl, combine zucchini, cabbage, bell pepper, carrots and onions. Sprinkle with pickling salt; mix well. Cover; let stand 3 to 4 hours. Drain vegetables, discarding liquid. Return drained vegetables to bowl. In a large saucepan, combine remaining ingredients. Bring to a boil over medium-high heat. Pour over vegetables; stir. Cover; let stand at room temperature until cool, about 2 hours. Wash 5 pint jars in hot soapy water; rinse. Keep hot until needed. Prepare lids as manufacturer directs. Turn vegetables and vinegar mixture into a 6-quart pot. Bring to a boil over medium-high heat. Stirring constantly, boil 15 minutes. Ladle hot relish into 1 hot jar at a time, leaving 1/4 inch headspace. Release trapped air. Wipe rim of jar with a clean damp cloth. Attach lid. Place in canner. Fill and close remaining jars. *Process in a boiling-water bath,* page 17.

   Pints: 15 minutes

Adjust time for altitude, page 20. Makes 5 pints.

Variation

Chop vegetables in blender or food processor for uniform size. In blender, process about 1 cup vegetable pieces in water to cover. Drain off water. When processing in food processor, add no water.

Spicy Sweet-Pepper Relish

A bright-red relish—make it as spicy hot as you like.

8 cups minced red, green or mixed bell peppers (about 12)	1 cup distilled white vinegar
2 cups minced onions	1 cup sugar
3 lbs. firm red tomatoes	1 tablespoon paprika
4 teaspoons pickling salt	2 dried whole hot red peppers, if desired

Wash 4 pint jars in hot soapy water; rinse. Keep hot until needed. Prepare lids as manufacturer directs. In a large bowl, combine bell peppers, onions and tomatoes. Sprinkle with pickling salt; stir well. Let stand about 10 minutes. In a 6-quart pot, combine vinegar, sugar, paprika and whole hot red peppers, if desired. Bring to a boil over medium heat. Stir in bell-pepper mixture. Stirring frequently, simmer, uncovered, until thickened, about 45 minutes. Remove and discard hot red peppers. Ladle hot relish into 1 hot jar at a time, leaving 1/4 inch headspace. Release trapped air. Wipe rim of jar with a clean damp cloth. Attach lid. Place in canner. Fill and close remaining jars. *Process in a boiling-water bath,* page 17.

   Pints: 15 minutes

Adjust time for altitude, page 20. Makes 4 pints.

How to Make India Relish

1/To chop or mince vegetables in a blender, cover vegetable pieces with water. Process until pieces are uniformly minced. Pour off water.

2/Combine minced vegetables in a large bowl. Sprinkle with pickling salt; stir in until distributed. Let stand 3 to 4 hours. Drain; discard liquid.

Ruby Relish

Deep red, sweet and spicy—perfect with a chicken salad or a roast-beef sandwich.

About 3 lbs. fresh beets
Boiling water
4 cups finely chopped peeled apples
1 cup packed brown sugar
3/4 cup light corn syrup
1 tablespoon pickling salt

1 cup cider vinegar
1/3 cup water
1 teaspoon ground cinnamon
1/2 teaspoon ground allspice
1/4 teaspoon ground cloves

Wash beets; cut off all but 2 inches of stem. Do not cut off root. Add washed beets to a large pot of boiling water. Boil until beets are just tender, about 15 minutes. Drain beets; cover with cold water. Slip off skins, stems and roots. Finely chop beets in a blender or food processor. Place 4 cups chopped beets in a large bowl. Use remaining beets for another purpose. Stir apples into chopped beets; set aside. In a 4-quart pot, combine remaining ingredients. Bring to a boil over medium-high heat. Stir in chopped beets and apples. Cook, uncovered, until mixture thickens, about 20 minutes. Wash 3 pint jars in hot soapy water; rinse. Keep hot until needed. Prepare lids as manufacturer directs. Ladle hot relish into 1 hot jar at a time, leaving 1/4 inch headspace. Release trapped air. Wipe rim of jar with a clean damp cloth. Attach lid. Place in canner. Fill and close remaining jars. *Process in a boiling-water bath,* page 17.
  Pints: 20 minutes
Adjust time for altitude, page 20. Makes 3 pints.

Canning with Flair:
Sweet Spreads

Sweet spreads capture the bright colors and fresh, sweet flavor of fruits. They are irresistible when spread on hot biscuits or rolled in a crepe and topped with whipped cream. Sweet spreads are easy to make—even for the first-time canner.

Sweet spreads include jams, jellies, marmalades, preserves, conserves and butters. A *preserve* is a spread with large pieces or whole fruit in a lightly gelled syrup. *Jam*—made from crushed or chopped fruit—is more uniform and is soft and easy to spread. Add nuts or raisins and you have a *conserve. Jelly* begins with the clear juice extracted from fruit. The juice is gelled to form a bright, shimmering mound firm enough to be unmolded and served on a plate. Sweet-tart *marmalade* has slivers of orange, lemon, lime or grapefruit peel in a clear jelly. *Fruit butter* is made from whole fruit simmered with sugar and juices or flavorings. The cooked fruit is pureed, then slow-cooked until thick.

Except for jellies, sweet spreads *must* be processed in a boiling-water bath at least 10 minutes. Jellies may also be processed for 5 minutes in a boiling-water bath. Years ago, all sweet spreads were made using the open-kettle method, page 6. Open-kettle canning is no longer considered safe, except for jellies. Paraffin should only be used to seal jellies, page 118. Follow processing directions *exactly* when making sweet spreads.

Make enough sweet spreads to supply your family for 6 months. When your supply is gone, use winter fruits or frozen or canned fruits to make more sweet spreads. You'll have jars of bright, flavorful spreads all year round.

Hot-Pepper Jelly

Sweet-Pepper Jelly, the variation given below, is a mild, green jelly.

4 canned jalapeño peppers or
   1/2 cup sliced fresh jalapeño peppers
6 large green or red bell peppers,
   cut in 1-inch squares
1-1/2 cups cider vinegar

1-1/2 cups apple juice
3/4 teaspoon salt
1 (1-3/4-oz.) pkg. dry pectin
5 cups sugar
4 to 6 drops red food coloring

Rinse jalapeño peppers under running water. Cut off stems; cut in half lengthwise. Remove and discard seeds. Puree half of bell pepper squares, half of jalapeño peppers and 3/4 cup vinegar in blender. Pour into a large bowl. Repeat with remaining peppers and vinegar. Stir apple juice into puree. Cover; let stand overnight. Wash six 1/2-pint jars in hot soapy water; rinse. Keep hot until needed. Prepare lids as manufacturer directs. Line a colander or large sieve with 2 layers of damp cheesecloth. Set colander over a 6-quart pot. Strain puree through cheesecloth; discard pulp. Measure juice. If necessary, add water to make 4 cups. Stir salt and dry pectin into juice. Stirring constantly, bring mixture to a rolling boil over high heat. Add sugar all at once. Continue to cook and stir until jelly comes to a rolling boil that cannot be stirred down. Stirring constantly, boil 1 minute. Remove from heat. Stir in food coloring. Use a metal spoon to skim off foam. Ladle hot jelly into 1 hot jar at a time, leaving 1/4 inch headspace. Wipe rim of jar with a clean damp cloth. Attach lid. Fill and close remaining jars. Invert jars 5 to 10 seconds, then stand upright to cool. Or seal with paraffin, page 118. Makes six 1/2-pints.

Variation

Sweet-Pepper Jelly: Omit jalapeño peppers. Increase green or red bell peppers to 7. Substitute green food coloring for red food coloring.

Honey-Lemon Jelly

Use a mild or flavorful honey to suit your taste.

1/2 cup strained,
   freshly squeezed lemon juice
1/2 cup water

3/4 cup honey
3 cups sugar
1 (3-oz.) pouch liquid pectin

Wash three 1/2-pint jars in hot, soapy water; rinse. Keep hot until needed. Prepare lids as manufacturer directs. In a 4-quart pot, combine lemon juice, water, honey and sugar. Bring to a boil over high heat. Stir in pectin. Continue to cook and stir until jelly comes to a rolling boil that cannot be stirred down. Stirring constantly, boil 1 minute. Remove from heat. Use a metal spoon to skim off foam. Ladle hot jelly into 1 hot jar at a time, leaving 1/4 inch headspace. Wipe rim of jar with a clean damp cloth. Attach lid. Fill and close remaining jars. Invert jars 5 to 10 seconds, then stand upright to cool. Or seal with paraffin, page 118. Makes three 1/2-pints.

Tip

Caution: If jelly or jam has mold growing on the top, discard the contents and wash the jar in hot soapy water. Do not scrape away the mold and use the rest of the contents. The mold may have caused a significant change in the acidity of the jelly or jam so other harmful organisms can grow.

Cranberry-Claret Jelly   Photo on pages 182-183.

Claret is a medium-bodied red wine, usually labeled a Bordeaux or Cabernet Sauvignon.

3 cups cranberry juice
1 cup claret or other red wine
1/4 teaspoon ground cinnamon

1/4 teaspoon ground cloves
1 (1-3/4-oz.) pkg. dry pectin
5 cups sugar

Wash six 1/2-pint jars in hot soapy water; rinse. Keep hot until needed. Prepare lids as manufacturer directs. In a 6-quart pot, combine cranberry juice, wine, cinnamon, cloves and dry pectin. Stir until pectin dissolves. Stirring constantly, bring juice mixture to a boil over medium-high heat. Add sugar all at once. Continue to cook and stir until jelly comes to a rolling boil that cannot be stirred down. Stirring constantly, boil 1 minute. Remove from heat. Use a metal spoon to skim off foam. Ladle hot jelly into 1 hot jar at a time, leaving 1/4 inch headspace. Wipe rim of jar with a clean damp cloth. Attach lid. Fill and close remaining jars. Invert jars 5 to 10 seconds, then stand upright to cool. Or seal with paraffin, below. Makes six 1/2-pints.

May-Day Jam   Photo on pages 182-183.

Strawberry and rhubarb blend their flavors with pineapple.

2 cups diced red rhubarb
2 cups fresh or
    canned crushed pineapple, drained

1 pint strawberries, washed, hulled
4 cups sugar

In a 6-quart pot, combine rhubarb, pineapple and strawberries. Gently stir in sugar. Let stand until juices begin to flow, about 15 minutes. Wash four 1/2-pint jars in hot soapy water; rinse. Keep hot until needed. Prepare lids as manufacturer directs. Stirring constantly, bring jam to a boil over medium heat. Stirring frequently, continue to boil until jam thickens, 15 to 20 minutes. Stirring occasionally, continue to boil gently until jam reaches 218F (103C) or is done according to plate test, page 58. Ladle hot jam into 1 hot jar at a time, leaving 1/4 inch headspace. Wipe rim with a clean damp cloth. Attach lid. Place in canner. Fill and close remaining jars. *Process in a boiling-water bath,* page 17.

    1/2-pints: 10 minutes

Adjust time for altitude, page 20. Makes four 1/2-pints.

How to Melt Paraffin

Never melt paraffin over direct heat. Remove paper and melt slab of paraffin in a double boiler or in a jar or clean can placed in gently boiling water. Do not let water boil into paraffin. It should remain over hot water until melted. Remove from heat before pouring over jellies or dipping lids in melted paraffin. If paraffin should ignite, cover with a lid to smother the fire. **Never throw water on a paraffin fire.**

Tarragon-Chablis Jelly

Instead of serving butter, try this herb jelly on dinner rolls for a nice treat.

**1/2 cup lightly packed fresh
  tarragon leaves or
  1/4 cup dried leaf tarragon**
3/4 cup white-wine vinegar
2 cups Chablis
6-1/2 cups sugar

2 (3-oz.) pouches liquid pectin
**1 drop yellow food coloring,
  if desired**
**1 drop orange food coloring,
  if desired**

Wash six 1/2-pint jars in hot soapy water; rinse. Keep hot until needed. Prepare lids as manufacturer directs. In a large saucepan, combine tarragon leaves, vinegar and Chablis. Bring to a boil over high heat; remove from heat. Cover; let stand 1 hour. Strain herb-flavored liquid into a 6-quart pot; discard leaves. Stir in sugar until dissolved. Bring to a boil over high heat. Stir in liquid pectin. Continue to cook and stir until jelly comes to a rolling boil. Stirring constantly, boil 1 minute. Remove from heat; stir in yellow and orange food coloring, if desired. Use a metal spoon to skim off foam. Ladle hot jelly into 1 hot jar at a time, leaving 1/4 inch headspace. Wipe rim of jar with a clean damp cloth. Attach lid. Fill and close remaining jars. Invert jars 5 to 10 seconds, then stand upright to cool. Or seal with paraffin, opposite page. Makes six 1/2-pints.

Variations

Thyme-Chablis Jelly: Substitute fresh or dried thyme for tarragon.

Marjoram-Chablis Jelly: Substitute fresh or dried marjoram for tarragon.

Pumpkin Butter

Use as a spread or to make Pumpkin Doughnuts, page 170.

1 (5- to 7-lb.) pumpkin
Hot water
3-1/2 cups sugar
1-1/2 cups honey

1-1/2 teaspoons ground cinnamon
1/4 teaspoon ground allspice
1/2 teaspoon salt

Wash pumpkin. Cut into several pieces that will fit in a 6-quart pot. Scrape out and discard seeds. In 6-quart pot, cover pumpkin pieces with hot water. Bring to a boil over medium-high heat. Reduce heat to low. Cover; simmer until tender, about 20 minutes. Drain, discarding liquid. Use a large spoon to scrape pulp from peel; discard peel. Press pulp through a food mill or puree in a blender or food processor. Measure puree. A dry pumpkin variety will yield about 5 cups puree. A more moist pumpkin will yield 6 to 8 cups puree. Return puree to pot. Bring to a boil over medium heat. Stirring frequently, boil until thickened, 10 to 20 minutes. Wash seven 1/2-pint jars in hot soapy water; rinse. Keep hot until needed. Prepare lids as manufacturer directs. When puree will mound slightly on a spoon, measure again. Use no more than 4 cups puree. Stir in remaining ingredients. Simmer uncovered until thick enough to spread. Test thickness of pumpkin butter with plate test, page 58. Ladle hot pumpkin butter into 1 hot jar at a time, leaving 1/4 inch headspace. Wipe rim of jar with a clean damp cloth. Attach lid. Place in canner. Fill and close remaining jars. *Process in a boiling-water bath,* page 17.
  Pints: 10 minutes
Adjust time for altitude, page 20. Makes seven 1/2-pints.

Tomato Marmalade

This sweet-tart orange-red marmalade has a tomato-preserve and citrus flavor.

2 medium grapefruit
Water
6 cups chopped peeled tomatoes
3 cups sugar

1/4 teaspoon salt
2 (3-inch) cinnamon sticks
4 whole cloves

Wash four 1/2-pint or 2 pint jars in hot soapy water; rinse. Keep hot until needed. Prepare lids as manufacturer directs. Use a brush to scrub grapefruit under running water. Use a vegetable peeler to cut off only colored part of peel. Do not include any white pith. Cut peel into thin strips. In a small saucepan, cover strips of peel with water. Bring to a boil over medium heat; reduce heat to low. Cover; simmer 5 minutes. Drain; set blanched peel aside. Cut outside white pith from grapefruit, cutting slightly into fruit to remove membrane. Working over a large bowl, section grapefruit by cutting on either side of membranes to make wedges. In a 4-quart pot, combine blanched peel, grapefruit wedges and remaining ingredients. Bring to a boil over medium heat, stirring until sugar dissolves. Use a spoon to skim off any foam. Stirring occasionally, continue to boil gently until marmalade reaches 218F (103C) or is done according to plate test, page 58. Ladle hot marmalade into 1 hot jar at a time, leaving 1/4 inch headspace. Release trapped air. Wipe rim of jar with a clean damp cloth. Attach lid. Place in canner. Fill and close remaining jars. *Process in a boiling-water bath,* page 17.

    1/2-pints or pints: 10 minutes

Adjust time for altitude, page 20. Makes four 1/2-pints or 2 pints.

Apricot Honey

As smooth as fruit butters—apricots and honey are a perfect combination.

4 lbs. ripe apricots
Antioxidant solution, page 25
1/2 cup water

2-1/2 cups honey
1 tablespoon lemon juice

Wash eight 1/2-pint or 4 pint jars in hot soapy water; rinse. Keep hot until needed. Prepare lids as manufacturer directs. Wash apricots. Immerse 8 or 10 apricots at a time in boiling water, 30 seconds. Use a slotted spoon to lift from boiling water. Plunge into cold water. Slip off skins. Cut apricots in half; remove and discard pits. To prevent darkening, immerse peeled, halved apricots in antioxidant solution. Lift fruit from solution; rinse. Coarsely chop. In a 4-quart pot, combine chopped apricots and 1/2 cup water. Bring to a boil. Reduce heat to low. Cover; simmer until apricots are tender, about 10 minutes. Mash fruit with a potato masher. Stir in honey and lemon juice. Stirring constantly, bring back to a boil. Stirring frequently, cook until mixture is thick enough to spread. Test thickness with plate test, page 58. Ladle hot apricot honey into 1 hot jar at a time, leaving 1/4 inch headspace. Wipe rim of jar with a clean damp cloth. Attach lid. Place in canner. Fill and close remaining jars. *Process in a boiling-water bath,* page 17.

    1/2-pints or pints: 10 minutes

Adjust time for altitude, page 20. Makes eight 1/2-pints or 4 pints.

How to Make Tomato Marmalade

1/Use a vegetable peeler to remove only yellow part of grapefruit peel. Cut peel in matchsticks.

2/Cut off white pith, cutting down to flesh. Cut on both sides of membranes to section grapefruit into wedges.

Peach-Melba Conserve

Spoon conserve over vanilla pudding for an easy dessert.

1/2 cup slivered almonds
6 cups sugar
4 cups sliced peeled peaches
1 cup raspberries

3 tablespoons lemon juice
1 teaspoon grated lemon peel
1 (1-3/4-oz.) pkg. dry pectin

Wash seven 1/2-pint jars in hot soapy water; rinse. Keep hot until needed. Prepare lids as manufacturer directs. Stirring constantly, toast almonds in a heavy skillet over medium-low heat. Set aside. Measure sugar into a large bowl, set aside. In a 6-quart pot, combine remaining ingredients; mix well. Stirring constantly, bring mixture to a rolling boil over high heat. Add sugar all at once. Continue to cook and stir until jelly comes to a rolling boil that cannot be stirred down. Stirring constantly, boil 1 minute. Remove from heat. For 5 minutes, use a metal spoon to stir and skim foam from conserve. Stir in toasted almonds. Ladle hot conserve into 1 hot jar at a time, leaving 1/4 inch headspace. Wipe rim of jar with a clean damp cloth. Attach lid. Place in canner. Fill and close remaining jars. *Process in a boiling-water bath,* page 17.

    1/2-pints: 10 minutes

Adjust time for altitude, page 20. Makes six or seven 1/2-pints.

Sunrise Marmalade

Make this marmalade during winter months when many fresh fruits are not available.

2 medium lemons
2 cups shredded carrots
2 cups fresh or
   canned crushed pineapple, drained
1 cup orange juice

1 cup water
5 cups sugar
1/2 cup maraschino cherries,
   cut in quarters

Wash four 1/2-pint jars in hot soapy water; rinse. Keep hot until needed. Prepare lids as manufacturer directs. Scrub lemons with a brush under running water. Cut a 1/4-inch-thick slice off each end of each lemon; discard. Slice remaining lemons crosswise as thin as possible; set aside. In a 6-quart pot, combine carrots, pineapple and lemon slices. Stir in orange juice and water. Bring to a boil over medium heat. Reduce heat to low. Cover; simmer 20 minutes. Stir in sugar. Stirring constantly, bring back to a boil. Stirring occasionally, boil until thickened and marmalade reaches 218F (103C) or is done according to plate test, page 58. Stir in cherries. Ladle hot marmalade into 1 hot jar at a time, leaving 1/4 inch headspace. Wipe rim of jar with a clean damp cloth. Attach lid. Place in canner. Fill and close remaining jars. *Process in a boiling-water bath,* page 17.
   1/2-pints: 10 minutes
Adjust time for altitude, page 20. Makes four 1/2-pints.

Lemon-Blueberry Marmalade   Photo on page 182.

Frozen blueberries can be used to make this treat any time.

2 medium lemons
Water
3 cups fresh or
   frozen unsweetened blueberries

3 cups sugar

Wash four 1/2-pint jars in hot soapy water; rinse. Keep hot until needed. Prepare lids as manufacturer directs. Scrub lemons with a brush under running water. Use a vegetable peeler to cut off only colored part of peel. Cut peel into thin strips. In a small saucepan, cover strips of peel with water. Bring to a boil over medium heat. Cover; simmer 10 minutes. Drain; set aside. Juice lemons. Measure juice; add water, if necessary, to make 1/2 cup. Wash fresh blueberries. Thaw frozen berries. In a 6-quart pot, crush berries with a potato masher. Add blanched peel, lemon juice and sugar. Bring to a boil over medium heat, stirring until sugar dissolves. Continue to boil gently until marmalade reaches 218F (103C) or is done according to plate test, page 58. Ladle hot marmalade into 1 hot jar at a time, leaving 1/4 inch headspace. Release trapped air. Wipe rim of jar with a clean damp cloth. Attach lid. Place in canner. Fill and close remaining jars. *Process in a boiling-water bath,* page 17.
   1/2-pints: 10 minutes
Adjust time for altitude, page 20. Makes four 1/2-pints.

Clockwise from top right: Tomato-Pineapple Preserves, page 125; Lemon-Blueberry Marmalade; Sunrise Marmalade; Cherry-Berry Preserves, page 125.

Apple Butter

For a quicker version, see the variation.

2 lbs. Rome Beauty apples
2 lbs. Golden Delicious apples
2 lbs. tart, green Newtown Pippin or
   Granny Smith apples
1/2 cup apple cider

3 cups sugar
1-1/2 teaspoons ground cinnamon
1/2 teaspoon ground allspice
1/4 teaspoon ground cloves

Wash, peel, core and slice apples. Combine apple slices and apple cider in a 6-quart pot. Bring to a boil over medium heat. Reduce heat to low. Cover. Stirring occasionally, simmer until apples are tender, about 20 minutes. Puree apple mixture in a blender or food processor until smooth. Return apple puree to pot. Add sugar, cinnamon, allspice and cloves. Bring to a boil over medium-low heat, stirring occasionally. Cover; cook until thick, stirring occasionally. Test thickness with plate test, page 58. Wash six 1/2-pint or 3 pint jars in hot soapy water; rinse. Keep hot until needed. Prepare lids as manufacturer directs. Ladle hot apple butter into 1 hot jar at a time, leaving 1/4 inch headspace. Release trapped air. Wipe rim of jar with a clean damp cloth. Attach lid. Place in canner. Fill and close remaining jars. *Process jars in a boiling-water bath,* page 17.

    1/2-pints or pints: 10 minutes

Adjust time for altitude, page 20. Makes six 1/2-pints or 3 pints.

Variation

Quick Apple Butter: Substitute 8 cups unsweetened applesauce for apples. Omit apple cider. Decrease sugar to 2-1/2 cups. Increase spices to 1 tablespoon cinnamon, 1 teaspoon allspice and 1/2 teaspoon cloves. Combine all ingredients in a 4-quart pot. Bring to a boil over medium-low heat. Stirring occasionally, simmer until thick, about 30 minutes. Test thickness with plate test, page 58. Proceed as above.

Silky Pear Butter

After opening, store in the refrigerator.

4 lbs. ripe pears
1 cup orange-pineapple juice
2 tablespoons lemon juice

2 cups sugar
2 tablespoons orange liqueur, if desired

Wash pears. Immerse 4 or 5 pears at a time in boiling water, 30 seconds. Plunge into cold water; slip or pull off skins. Cut in quarters; remove and discard cores. In a 6-quart pot, combine peeled pears, orange-pineapple juice and lemon juice. Bring to a boil over medium heat. Reduce heat to low. Cover; simmer until pears are tender, about 30 minutes. Puree cooked pear mixture in a blender or food processor. Return puree to pot. Stir in sugar. Stirring frequently, simmer over medium-low heat until pear butter thickens, 20 to 30 minutes. Wash five 1/2-pint jars in hot soapy water; rinse. Keep hot until needed. Prepare lids as manufacturer directs. Test thickness of pear butter with plate test, page 58. Stir in liqueur, if desired. Ladle pear butter into 1 hot jar at a time, leaving 1/4 inch headspace. Wipe rim of jar with a clean damp cloth. Attach lid. Place in canner. Fill and close remaining jars. *Process in a boiling-water bath,* page 17.

    1/2-pints: 10 minutes

Adjust time for altitude, page 20. Makes five 1/2-pints.

Tomato-Pineapple Preserves   Photo on page 123.

A unique sweet spread—indescribably delicious!

2 lbs. small ripe tomatoes   **1 (11-oz.) can crushed pineapple in juice**
4 cups sugar   **1/4 cup lemon juice**

Wash tomatoes. Immerse 3 or 4 tomatoes at a time in boiling water, 30 seconds. Plunge into cold water. Slip off skins. Cut large tomatoes into halves or quarters. Place cut tomatoes in a large bowl; sprinkle with sugar. Stir gently; cover with a towel. Let stand at room temperature overnight or at least 8 hours. Place a sieve over a 4-quart pot. Turn tomatoes into sieve. Let drain 10 to 15 minutes. Reserve juice and tomatoes separately. Wash four 1/2-pint jars in hot soapy water; rinse. Keep hot until needed. Prepare lids as manufacturer directs. Add pineapple with juice to tomato juice. Attach a candy thermometer to side of pan so bulb is covered with juice. Bring juice to a boil over medium-high heat. Stirring occasionally, boil until juice reaches 220F (105C). Add tomatoes; boil until thickened. Test thickness with plate test, page 58. Ladle hot preserves into 1 hot jar at a time, leaving 1/4 inch headspace. Wipe rim of jar with a clean damp cloth. Attach lid. Place in canner. Fill and close remaining jars. *Process in a boiling-water bath,* page 17.
    1/2-pints: 10 minutes
Adjust time for altitude, page 20. Makes four 1/2-pints.

Cherry-Berry Preserves   Photo on page 123.

Marvelous spooned on French toast or hot cooked cereal.

3 cups fresh dark sweet cherries   **3 tablespoons lemon juice**
2 cups fresh or frozen raspberries, thawed   **4 cups sugar**

Wash five 1/2-pint jars in hot soapy water; rinse. Keep hot until needed. Prepare lids as manufacturer directs. Wash cherries. Cut in half; discard pit. Wash raspberries. Drain thawed raspberries. In a 6-quart pot, combine cherries, raspberries, lemon juice and sugar. Stir, then let stand 15 minutes or until juices begin to flow. Stirring constantly, bring mixture to a boil over medium heat. Stirring constantly, boil until thickened, 15 to 20 minutes. Stirring occasionally, continue to boil gently until preserves reach 218F (103C) or until done according to plate test, page 58. Ladle hot preserves into 1 hot jar at a time, leaving 1/4 inch headspace. Wipe rim of jar with a clean damp cloth. Attach lid. Place in canner. Fill and close remaining jars. *Process in a boiling-water bath,* page 17.
    1/2-pints: 10 minutes
Adjust time for altitude, page 20. Makes four or five 1/2-pints.

Tip
_____

Jams and other spreads thicken as they cool. Hot spreads may be quite thin even when they have cooked enough. When no pectin is added in the recipe, rely on the plate test or temperature test, page 58, to tell when the spread is done.

Kiwi Preserves

Originally imported from New Zealand, kiwi has a delicate berry-like flavor.

4 kiwi berries
1/4 cup lime juice
3/4 cup unsweetened pineapple juice

3 cups sugar
1 (3-oz.) pouch liquid pectin

Wash three 1/2-pint jars in hot soapy water; rinse. Keep hot until needed. Prepare lids as manufacturer directs. Wash kiwi berries; peel. Slice about 1/8 inch thick; set aside. In a 4-quart pot, combine lime juice, pineapple juice and sugar. Bring to a boil over medium-high heat, stirring until sugar dissolves. Add kiwi slices. Return mixture to a boil. Stirring constantly, boil 1 minute. Remove from heat; stir in pectin. Ladle hot preserves into 1 hot jar at a time, leaving 1/4 inch headspace. Wipe rim of jar with a clean damp cloth. Attach lid. Place in canner. Fill and close remaining jars. *Process in a boiling-water bath,* page 17.
   1/2-pints: 10 minutes
Adjust time for altitude, page 20. Makes three 1/2-pints.

Pink-Champagne Jelly

Delicately flavored—perfect for a gift.

1-1/2 cups pink champagne
3 drops angostura bitters

3-1/2 cups sugar
1 (3-oz.) pouch liquid pectin

Wash three 1/2-pint jars in hot soapy water; rinse. Keep hot until needed. Prepare lids as manufacturer directs. In a 4-quart pot, combine champagne, bitters and sugar. Stir to dissolve sugar. Bring to a boil over high heat. Stir in pectin. Continue to cook and stir until jelly comes to a rolling boil that cannot be stirred down. Stirring constantly, boil 1 minute. Remove from heat. Use a metal spoon to skim off foam. Ladle hot jelly into 1 hot jar at a time, leaving 1/4 inch headspace. Wipe rim with a clean damp cloth. Attach lid. Fill and close remaining jars. Invert jars 5 to 10 seconds, then stand upright to cool. Or seal with paraffin, page 118. Makes three 1/2-pints.

Tropical Conserve   Photo on cover.

Serve on waffles with whipped cream and coconut for a tropical delight.

2 large papaya
1 cup fresh or
   canned crushed pineapple, drained
2 tablespoons lime juice

5 cups sugar
1 teaspoon grated fresh gingerroot or
   1/2 teaspoon ground ginger
1 cup golden raisins

Wash six 1/2-pint jars in hot soapy water; rinse. Keep hot until needed. Prepare lids as manufacturer directs. Wash papaya; peel. Discard seeds; cut fruit into 1/2-inch cubes. In a 4-quart pot, combine papaya, pineapple, lime juice and 1 cup sugar. Stirring constantly, bring to a boil over medium heat. Add remaining sugar and gingerroot or ground ginger. Stirring frequently, boil until thickened. Test thickness with the plate test, page 58. Stir in raisins. Ladle hot conserve into 1 hot jar at a time, leaving 1/4 inch headspace. Wipe rim with a clean damp cloth. Attach lid. Place in canner. Fill and close remaining jars. *Process in a boiling-water bath,* page 17.
   1/2-pints: 10 minutes
Adjust time for altitude, page 20. Makes six 1/2-pints.

1/Use a vegetable peeler to peel kiwi berries. Slice crosswise, 1/8 inch thick.

2/Add kiwi slices to boiling pineapple syrup. Boil 1 minute, then stir in pectin.

Rum-Raisin Conserve   Photo on pages 182-183.

Jamaica rum is dark and syrupy with a full, exotic flavor.

2 lbs. prune plums	**1 cup raisins**
3 cups sugar	**1 cup chopped Brazil nuts**
3/4 cup water	**1/4 cup dark Jamaica rum**

Wash four 1/2-pint jars in hot soapy water; rinse. Keep hot until needed. Prepare lids as manufacturer directs. Wash plums. Coarsely chop plums, discarding pits. In a 4-quart pot, combine chopped plums, sugar, water and raisins. Bring to a boil over medium-high heat, stirring until sugar dissolves. Reduce heat to low; cover. Stirring occasionally, simmer until conserve begins to thicken, about 20 minutes. Stirring constantly, continue to boil gently until conserve reaches 218F (103C) or is done according to plate test, page 58. Stir in nuts and rum. Ladle conserve into 1 hot jar at a time, leaving 1/4 inch headspace. Wipe rim of jar with a clean damp cloth. Attach lid. Place in canner. Fill and close remaining jars. *Process in a boiling-water bath,* page 17.

  1/2-pints: 10 minutes

Adjust time for altitude, page 20. Makes four 1/2-pints.

Canning with Flair:
Sauces & Condiments

These sauces and condiments are high-acid and can be processed in a boiling-water bath. Many are tomato-based with other vegetables added for flavor. To some, vinegar or lemon juice has been added to assure proper acidity. Follow recipes *exactly*, measuring or weighing ingredients accurately.

In most of the ketchups, barbecue sauces and tomato-based sauces, whole or coarsely chopped fruits and vegetables are simmered until soft. Some mixtures are forced through a sieve or food mill. Or, the mixture is pureed in a blender for a smooth sauce. Fruits and vegetables may also be left whole as the sauce boils down, making a chunky sauce.

Mustards contain dry mustard, vinegar and spices. Elegant Champagne Mustard is made with champagne and champagne vinegar or white-wine vinegar. Spicy Tomato Mustard gets its name from the tomato sauce in it.

Chutney is a highly seasoned condiment of fruit, onion and spices. Chili peppers make it peppery hot. Calcutta-Style Chutney is made with mango and papaya just as chutney is made in India. Peach-Plum Chutney is a dark, fruity yet spicy condiment that adds to the enjoyment of meats and complements the flavor of cheese.

Seasoned vinegars are the easiest condiments to prepare. Just add fresh herbs to a bottle or jar of vinegar. Store vinegars in the refrigerator or in a cool dark place for three weeks before they are opened to let flavors blend. Use only high-quality vinegars for the best flavor. Home-seasoned vinegars add fresh, subtle flavors to salad dressings. They also make attractive gifts.

Some of these recipes are similar to commercial products, but have a much richer flavor. However, you won't find anything similar to Spicy Tomato Mustard and Plum Barbeque Sauce—they are unique.

Tomato Sauce

Use this subtly flavored tomato sauce as a base for stews and casseroles.

10 lbs. firm ripe tomatoes
1 cup chopped onions
2 celery stalks with leaves, chopped
1 cup sliced carrots

2 bay leaves
5 tablespoons lemon juice
1 tablespoon salt

Wash tomatoes. Cut out cores; cut tomatoes into quarters. Cover bottom of a 6-quart pot with tomato pieces. Crush with a potato masher. Add remaining tomato pieces. Stirring occasionally, bring to a boil over medium heat. Add onions, celery and carrots. Bring back to a boil; reduce heat to low. Cover; simmer until vegetables are tender, about 45 minutes. Press through a food mill or sieve; discard seeds and pulp. For a smoother sauce, puree sieved mixture in blender. Return puree to pot. Add bay leaves, lemon juice and salt. Simmer, uncovered, until thickened. Wash twelve 1/2-pint or 6 pint jars in hot soapy water; rinse. Keep hot until needed. Prepare lids as manufacturer directs. Test doneness by plate test, page 58. Ladle hot sauce into 1 hot jar at a time, leaving 1/4 inch headspace. Wipe rim of jar with a clean damp cloth. Attach lid. Place in canner. Fill and close remaining jars. *Process in a boiling-water bath,* page 17.
    1/2-pints or pints: 45 minutes
Adjust time for altitude, page 20. Makes 5 to 6 pints or ten to twelve 1/2-pints.

Variation

Plain Tomato Sauce: Prepare tomatoes as above. Omit onion, celery, carrots and bay leaves. Add 2 teaspoons sugar with salt. Fill jars as above. *Process in a boiling-water bath,* page 17.
    1/2-pints or pints: 20 minutes
Adjust time for altitude, page 20. Makes 3 to 4 pints or six to eight 1/2-pints.

Marinara Sauce   Photo on pages 182-183.

An all-purpose Italian sauce for quick spaghetti, lasagna or pizza.

10 lbs. firm ripe tomatoes
1-1/2 cups chopped onions
4 garlic cloves, minced
1/4 cup chopped fresh parsley leaves
1/2 cup grated carrot
1 teaspoon dried leaf basil
2 teaspoons dried leaf oregano

1 teaspoon sugar
2 teaspoons salt
1/4 teaspoon pepper
1 cup red wine, or 3 tablespoons lemon juice
1 tablespoon lemon juice
3 tablespoons olive oil

Wash tomatoes. Cut out cores; cut tomatoes in half; set aside. In a 6- or 8-quart pot, combine tomato halves, onions, garlic, parsley, carrot, basil and oregano. Adjust heat until mixture simmers. Cover; simmer 1 hour. Press vegetables through a food mill or sieve. Discard seeds and skins. Return puree to pot. Stir in remaining ingredients. Cook over low heat until volume is reduced by half, about 2 hours. Wash 4 pint jars in hot soapy water; rinse. Keep hot until needed. Prepare lids as manufacturer directs. Ladle hot sauce into 1 hot jar at a time, leaving 1/4 inch headspace. Release trapped air. Wipe rim of jar with a clean damp cloth. Attach lid. Place in canner. Fill and close remaining jars. *Process in a boiling-water bath,* page 17.
    Pints: 45 minutes
Adjust time for altitude, page 20. Makes 3 to 4 pints.

Barbecue Sauce

Use this smoke-flavored, peppery sauce to baste roasts, chops or chicken or to dip meatballs.

8 lbs. firm ripe tomatoes
2 cups chopped onions
3 garlic cloves, minced
1 dried whole hot red pepper
1/2 cup molasses
1/4 cup packed brown sugar
2 tablespoons Worcestershire sauce

1 tablespoon dry mustard
1 teaspoon ground ginger
2 teaspoons salt
3/4 cup cider vinegar
2 tablespoons lemon juice
1 teaspoon liquid smoke, if desired

Wash, core and cut tomatoes into quarters. Cover bottom of a 6- or 8-quart pot with tomato pieces. Crush with a potato masher. Add remaining tomato pieces, onions, garlic and whole red pepper. Bring to a simmer. Cover; simmer over low heat until tomatoes are soft, about 45 minutes. Remove red pepper; discard. Press tomato mixture through a food mill or sieve; discard seeds and skins. Return puree to pot. Stir in molasses, brown sugar, Worcestershire sauce, dry mustard, ginger and salt. Bring back to a slow boil. Simmer, uncovered, until sauce is medium thick, about 2 hours. Wash 3 pint jars in hot soapy water; rinse. Keep hot until needed. Prepare lids as manufacturer directs. Puree 2 to 3 cups barbecue sauce at a time in a blender or food processor until smooth. Return to pot; add vinegar, lemon juice and liquid smoke, if desired. Stirring frequently, cook until thickened. Test doneness with plate test, page 58. Ladle into 1 hot jar at a time, leaving 1/4 inch headspace. Release trapped air. Wipe rim of jar with a clean damp cloth. Attach lid. Place in canner. Fill and close remaining jars. *Process in a boiling-water bath,* page 17.
   Pints: 15 minutes
Adjust time for altitude, page 20. Makes 2 to 3 pints.

Plum Barbecue Sauce

Rich and dark with a fruity, sweet taste—especially good on ribs.

4 lbs. red plums
4 cups red wine
2 cups chopped onions
4 garlic cloves, minced
1 medium lemon
2 cups tomato sauce
1 cup molasses

1 cup packed brown sugar
2 tablespoons Worcestershire sauce
2 tablespoons prepared mustard
1/2 cup red-wine vinegar
2 teaspoons salt
1 teaspoon coarsely ground black pepper

Wash and pit plums. In a 6-quart pot, combine plums, wine, onions and garlic. Scrub lemon under running water. Slice crosswise. Add to plum mixture. Stirring frequently, cook over medium-high heat until mixture is syrupy. Remove and discard lemon slices. Puree plum mixture in a blender or food processor. Return puree to pot. Add remaining ingredients. Bring back to a boil. Stirring frequently, simmer over low heat until thickened, about 1 hour. Wash six 1/2-pint jars in hot soapy water; rinse. Keep hot until needed. Prepare lids as manufacturer directs. Test doneness with plate test, page 58. Ladle into 1 hot jar at a time, leaving 1/4 inch headspace. Release trapped air. Wipe rim of jar with a clean damp cloth. Attach lid. Place in canner. Fill and close remaining jars. *Process in a boiling-water bath,* page 17.
   1/2-pints: 20 minutes
Adjust time for altitude, page 20. Makes five or six 1/2-pints.

Cornish Hens basted with Plum Barbecue Sauce.

Champagne Mustard

Champagne vinegar can be found in gourmet shops or ordered from kitchen specialty catalogues.

1-1/2 cups dry white champagne
3 cups champagne vinegar or
  white-wine vinegar
2 cups chopped onions
3 garlic cloves, minced

2 cups dry mustard, about 6 oz.
1/3 cup sugar
1 tablespoon cornstarch
1 tablespoon salt
4 eggs, well beaten

Combine champagne, vinegar, onions and garlic in a medium saucepan. Bring to a boil over medium-high heat; reduce heat to low. Cover; simmer 5 minutes. Set aside to cool completely, about 2 hours. Wash five 1/2-pint jars in hot soapy water; rinse. Keep hot until needed. Prepare lids as manufacturer directs. Strain champagne mixture through a fine sieve; discard onion and garlic. In top of a double boiler, combine dry mustard, sugar, cornstarch and salt. Gradually add cooled champagne mixture while beating with a whisk. Beat in eggs. Place mustard mixture over hot, but not boiling, water. Beat constantly with whisk until thickened, about 15 minutes. Ladle hot mustard into 1 hot jar at a time, leaving 1/4 inch headspace. Release trapped air. Wipe rim of jar with a clean damp cloth. Attach lid. Place in canner. Fill and close remaining jars. *Process in a boiling-water bath,* page 17.

   1/2-pints: 15 minutes
Adjust time for altitude, page 20. Makes five 1/2-pints.

Peach-Plum Chutney

Dark and spicy.

2 lbs. fresh peaches
Boiling water
2 cups packed brown sugar
1 cup light honey
2 cups cider vinegar
2 cups diced pitted prunes
1 cup chopped onions

4 small dried hot red peppers
2 teaspoons whole allspice
2 teaspoons whole cloves
2 teaspoons black peppercorns
2 teaspoons mustard seeds
2 lbs. tart red or prune plums, diced

Wash peaches. Immerse 4 or 5 peaches at a time in boiling water, 30 seconds. Plunge into cold water. Slip off skins. Slice peaches; discard pits. Set aside. In a 6-quart pot, combine brown sugar, honey, vinegar, prunes and onions. Tie red peppers, allspice, cloves, peppercorns and mustard seeds in a 6-inch square of cheesecloth. Add spice bag to sugar mixture. Bring to a boil over medium-high heat, stirring until sugar dissolves. Add sliced peaches and plums. Reduce heat to low; simmer until thickened, about 1 hour. Wash 6 pint jars in hot soapy water; rinse. Keep hot until needed. Prepare lids as manufacturer directs. Remove spice bag from chutney; discard. Ladle hot chutney into 1 hot jar at a time, leaving 1/4 inch headspace. Release trapped air. Wipe rim of jar with a clean damp cloth. Attach lid. Place in canner. Fill and close remaining jars. *Process in a boiling-water bath,* page 17.

   Pints: 20 minutes
Adjust time for altitude, page 20. Makes 6 pints.

Tomato Ketchup

Homemade ketchup has an incomparable flavor.

12 lbs. firm ripe tomatoes	4-1/2 teaspoons paprika
1-1/2 cups chopped onions	3/4 cup sugar
1/3 cup chopped red or green bell pepper	1-1/2 teaspoons mustard seeds
1/4 teaspoon red (cayenne) pepper	1-1/2 teaspoons black peppercorns
1-1/2 cups cider vinegar	3/4 teaspoon whole allspice
4 teaspoons salt	1 (2-inch) cinnamon stick

Wash tomatoes. Cut out cores; cut tomatoes into quarters. Cover bottom of a 6-quart pot with tomato pieces. Crush with a potato masher. Add remaining tomato pieces, onions, bell pepper and red pepper. Bring to a boil over medium-high heat; reduce heat to low. Cover; simmer until vegetables are soft, about 45 minutes. Press tomato mixture through a food mill or sieve. Discard seeds and skins. Return puree to pot. Stir in vinegar, salt, paprika and sugar. Tie mustard seeds, peppercorns, allspice and cinnamon in a 6-inch square of cheesecloth. Add to tomato mixture. Bring back to a boil; reduce heat to low. Stirring frequently, simmer, uncovered, until volume is reduced by half, about 1-1/2 hours. Wash 3 pint jars in hot soapy water; rinse. Keep hot until needed. Prepare lids as manufacturer directs. Remove spice bag from tomato mixture; discard. Puree tomato mixture, 2 or 3 cups at a time, in blender or food processor. Return to pot. Stirring occasionally, simmer until ketchup mounds slightly on a spoon. Test doneness with plate test, page 58. Ladle hot ketchup into 1 hot jar at a time, leaving 1/4 inch headspace. Release trapped air. Wipe rim of jar with a clean damp cloth. Attach lid. Place in canner. Fill and close remaining jars. *Process in a boiling-water bath,* page 17.

   Pints: 15 minutes

Adjust time for altitude, page 20. Makes 2 to 3 pints.

Calcutta-Style Chutney

Plan to make this chutney when mangoes and papayas are in greatest supply.

1 medium lemon	1/2 teaspoon hot red-pepper flakes or
1-1/2 cups cider vinegar	1 small dried whole red pepper
2 cups packed brown sugar	5 firm half-ripe mangoes
1 garlic clove, minced	1 large ripe papaya
1 teaspoon salt	1 cup golden raisins
3 tablespoons grated fresh gingerroot	1/2 cup coarsely chopped onion

Peel lemon, removing colored peel and white pith; discard. Slice lemon; chop coarsely. In a 4-quart pot, combine chopped lemon, vinegar, brown sugar, garlic, salt, gingerroot and red-pepper flakes or whole red pepper. Bring to a boil over medium-high heat, stirring until sugar is dissolved. Reduce heat to low. Cover; simmer 30 minutes. Peel mangoes; slice thinly. Peel papaya. Cut in half; discard seeds. Cut papaya into 1/2-inch cubes. Add mango slices, papaya cubes, raisins and onion to sugar syrup. Stirring occasionally, simmer until fruit is tender and mixture is thickened, about 30 minutes. Wash six 1/2-pint or 3 pint jars in hot soapy water; rinse. Keep hot until needed. Prepare lids as manufacturer directs. Ladle hot chutney into 1 hot jar at a time, leaving 1/4 inch headspace. Release trapped air. Wipe rim of jar with a clean damp cloth. Attach lid. Place in canner. Fill and close remaining jars. *Process in a boiling-water bath,* page 17.

   1/2-pints or pints: 10 minutes

Adjust time for altitude, page 20. Makes six 1/2-pints or 4 pints.

Western-Style Ketchup

This ketchup is for those who like spicy foods.

10 lbs. firm ripe tomatoes
2 garlic cloves, minced
2 cups chopped onions
2 dried whole hot red peppers
1 tablespoon salt
1/3 cup packed brown sugar
1/4 cup granulated sugar
1 tablespoon paprika

2 teaspoons dried leaf basil
1 bay leaf
1-1/2 teaspoons black peppercorns
1 tablespoon mustard seeds
1/4 teaspoon celery seeds
1 cup red-wine vinegar
1 teaspoon dry mustard

Wash tomatoes. Cut out cores; cut tomatoes in quarters. Cover bottom of an 8-quart pot with tomato pieces. Crush with a potato masher. Add remaining tomato pieces, garlic, onions and whole red peppers. Bring to a boil over medium-high heat; reduce heat to low. Cover; simmer until tomatoes are soft, about 45 minutes. Remove red peppers; discard. Press mixture through a food mill or sieve; discard seeds and skins. Return puree to pot. Stir in salt, brown sugar, granulated sugar and paprika. Tie basil, bay leaves, peppercorns, mustard seeds and celery seeds in a 6-inch square of cheesecloth. Add to puree. Bring to a boil over medium-high heat; reduce heat to low. Simmer, uncovered, until ketchup is medium thick, about 2 hours. Wash 3 pint jars in hot soapy water; rinse. Keep hot until needed. Prepare lids as manufacturer directs. Remove spice bag from ketchup; discard. Puree 2 to 3 cups ketchup at a time in a blender or food processor until smooth. Return to pot; add vinegar and mustard. Stirring frequently, continue cooking until thickened. Test doneness with plate test, page 58. Ladle hot ketchup into 1 hot jar at a time, leaving 1/4 inch headspace. Release trapped air. Wipe rim of jar with a clean damp cloth. Attach lid. Place in canner. Fill and close remaining jars. *Process in a boiling-water bath,* page 17.

   Pints: 15 minutes
Adjust time for altitude, page 20. Makes 2 to 3 pints.

Spicy Tomato Mustard

Flavorful but not too hot.

1 tablespoon vegetable oil
1 cup finely chopped onions
1 cup distilled white vinegar
1 cup tomato sauce
1 (4-oz.) can dry mustard

2 tablespoons molasses
2 teaspoons salt
1/4 teaspoon ground turmeric
1/4 teaspoon ground allspice
1/4 teaspoon ground cloves

Wash three 1/2-pint jars in hot soapy water; rinse. Keep hot until needed. Prepare lids as manufacturer directs. Heat oil in a small skillet over low heat. Add onions; sauté until soft. Set aside. In a small bowl, combine vinegar and tomato sauce. In a medium saucepan, gradually stir vinegar mixture into dry mustard; beat until smooth. Stir in sautéed onion with oil and remaining ingredients. Stirring constantly, cook over low heat until mustard thickens, about 30 minutes. Ladle hot mustard into 1 hot jar at a time, leaving 1/4 inch headspace. Release trapped air. Wipe rim of jar with a clean damp cloth. Attach lid. Place in canner. Fill and close remaining jars. *Process in a boiling-water bath,* page 17.

   1/2-pints: 15 minutes
Adjust time for altitude, page 20. Makes two or three 1/2-pints.

1/Press cooked tomato-onion mixture through a food mill or sieve to remove seeds and peel.

2/Puree thickened ketchup in a blender or food processor for a smoother texture.

Green-Chili Salsa

Mild, but flavorful. Use as a taco sauce, chip dip or seasoning sauce.

10 fresh hot green peppers or
   3 (4-oz.) cans chopped green chilies
8 lbs. firm ripe tomatoes
3 cups chopped onions
1 cup chopped green bell pepper

1/4 cup lemon juice
6 tablespoons distilled white vinegar
2 teaspoons dried leaf oregano
1 tablespoon salt

Wash 8 pint jars in hot soapy water; rinse. Keep hot until needed. Prepare lids as manufacturer directs. Peel fresh hot peppers if using, page 52. Discard seeds; chop peppers. Set aside. Wash tomatoes. Immerse in boiling water, 30 seconds. Plunge into cold water. Slip off skins. Cut out cores; coarsely chop tomatoes. In a 6-quart pot, combine chopped hot peppers, chopped tomatoes and remaining ingredients. Bring to a boil. Cover; simmer over low heat 5 minutes. Ladle hot salsa into 1 hot jar at a time, leaving 1/4 inch headspace. Wipe rim of jar with a clean damp cloth. Attach lid. Place in canner. Fill and close remaining jars. *Process in a boiling-water bath,* page 17.
   Pints: 45 minutes
Adjust time for altitude, page 20. Makes 8 pints.

Chunky Chili Sauce

Use as a seasoning sauce in meat dishes or as a condiment with meats.

10 lbs. tomatoes
1 medium onion, sliced
2 medium red bell peppers, cut in strips
1 (3-inch) piece celery, sliced
3 tablespoons canned chopped green chilies
1 cup packed brown sugar
1 tablespoon salt

1 teaspoon ground cinnamon
1/2 teaspoon ground ginger
1/2 teaspoon ground cloves
1 teaspoon dry mustard
1 dried whole hot red pepper
1-1/2 cups cider vinegar

Wash tomatoes. Immerse in boiling water, 30 seconds. Plunge into cold water; slip off peels. Core and cut tomatoes into quarters. Measure 16 cups tomatoes; set aside. Use remaining tomatoes for another purpose. In a blender or food processor, combine onion, bell peppers, celery and chilies. Add tomatoes until three-fourths full. Process at high speed a few seconds until uniformly chunky. Pour into a 6- or 8-quart pot. Process remaining tomatoes; add to pot. Bring to a slow boil. Cover; stirring occasionally, simmer over low heat, 45 minutes. Stir in remaining ingredients. Stirring frequently, cook, uncovered, until sauce mounds on a spoon and volume is reduced by half, about 2 hours. Wash 6 pint jars in hot soapy water; rinse. Keep hot. Prepare lids as manufacturer directs. Remove hot red pepper from sauce; discard. Ladle sauce into 1 hot jar at a time, leaving 1/4 inch headspace. Release trapped air. Wipe rim of jar with a clean damp cloth. Attach lid. Place in canner. Fill and close remaining jars. *Process in a boiling-water bath,* page 17.
   Pints: 15 minutes
Adjust time for altitude, page 20. Makes 5 to 6 pints.

Fruit Ketchup

Apples, pears and tomatoes give this interesting ketchup a spicy flavor.

5 lbs. firm ripe tomatoes
1 lb. pears
1 lb. tart apples
3/4 cup chopped onion
1/4 cup honey
1 teaspoon salt

1/4 teaspoon pepper
1 teaspoon dry mustard
1 teaspoon ground cinnamon
1/2 teaspoon ground cloves
1/4 teaspoon ground nutmeg
1/2 cup cider vinegar

Wash tomatoes and pears; core and cut in quarters; set aside. Wash apples; cut in quarters. Cover bottom of a 6-quart pot with tomato pieces. Crush with a potato masher. Add remaining tomato, apple and pear pieces and onion. Cover; simmer over low heat until apples and pears are soft, about 45 minutes. Press through a food mill or sieve. Discard seeds and skins. Return puree to pot. Stir in honey, salt, pepper, dry mustard, cinnamon, cloves and nutmeg. Stirring occasionally, simmer, uncovered, until medium thick. Wash 2 pint jars in hot soapy water; rinse. Keep hot until needed. Prepare lids as manufacturer directs. Process puree in a blender or food processor until smooth. Return to pot; stir in vinegar. Stirring frequently, simmer until ketchup is thickened. Test doneness with plate test, page 58. Ladle hot ketchup into 1 hot jar at a time, leaving 1/4 inch headspace. Release trapped air. Wipe rim of jar with a clean damp cloth. Attach lid. Place in canner. Fill and close remaining jars. *Process in a boiling-water bath,* page 17.
   Pints: 15 minutes
Adjust time for altitude, page 20. Makes 2 pints.

Mixed-Herb Vinegar   Photo on pages 182-183.

This vinegar is excellent in salad dressings.

2 qts. white-wine or red-wine vinegar
8 fresh bay leaves

12 (3-inch) fresh basil sprigs
12 (3-inch) fresh oregano sprigs

Wash 4 pint jars or bottles with caps or corks in hot soapy water; rinse. Prepare canning lids as manufacturer directs. Scald caps in boiling water. Dip corks in and out of boiling water 3 or 4 times. Heat vinegar over medium heat until it just comes to a boil. Place 2 bay leaves, 3 basil sprigs and 3 oregano sprigs in each jar or bottle. Pour hot vinegar over herbs, leaving 1/4 inch headspace. Wipe rims of jars with a clean damp cloth. Attach lids, caps or corks. Invert canning jars 5 to 10 seconds, then stand upright to cool. Seal bottles by dipping bottle top in melted paraffin, sealing wax or candle wax, if desired. Label; store in a cool dark place at least 3 weeks before using. Makes 4 pints.

Variations

Herb & Spice Vinegar: Place 3 (3-inch) fresh dill sprigs, 1/2 teaspoon mustard seeds, 1/4 teaspoon black peppercorns and 5 whole allspice in each pint jar or bottle. Fill with hot white-wine vinegar.

Lemon-Parsley Vinegar: Cut peel from 1 lemon in a single spiral; repeat with another lemon. Cut each peel spiral in half. Place 1 piece lemon peel in each pint jar or bottle. Add 1/2 cup fresh parsley sprigs to each. Fill with hot white-wine vinegar. Photo on cover.

Tarragon Vinegar: Place 3 (3-inch) fresh tarragon sprigs in each pint jar or bottle. Fill with hot white-wine vinegar.

Garlic-Wine Vinegar: Push 3 peeled garlic cloves on each of four 5-inch bamboo skewers. Place 1 skewer in each pint jar or bottle. Fill with hot red-wine vinegar.

Berry Vinegar

Add 1 or 2 tablespoons to stew or meat pie to give a piquant flavor.

5 cups fresh or frozen red raspberries,
   blueberries or strawberries

1 qt. white-wine vinegar
1/4 cup sugar

Wash berries. Reserve 1 cup berries. Place remaining berries in a large bowl or casserole with a lid. Crush with a potato masher. Add vinegar; stir well. Cover with plastic wrap or a lid; store in a refrigerator 2 days. Wash 3 pint jars or bottles with caps or corks in hot soapy water; rinse. Prepare canning lids as manufacturer directs. Scald caps in boiling water. Dip corks in and out of boiling water 3 or 4 times. Place a jelly bag or sieve lined with cheesecloth over a large bowl. Strain berry mixture through bag or sieve; do not squeeze. Discard pulp. In a large saucepan, over medium-high heat, bring juice just to a boil. Place 1/3 cup reserved berries in each hot jar or bottle. Add hot juice, leaving 1/4 inch headspace. Wipe rims of jars with a clean damp cloth. Attach lids, caps or corks. Invert canning jars 5 to 10 seconds, then stand upright to cool. Seal bottles by dipping bottle top in melted paraffin, sealing wax or candle wax, if desired. Label; store in a cool dark place at least 3 weeks before using. Makes 3 pints.

Using Canned Foods:

Recipes in the following chapters use home-canned foods. Their commercial counterparts are also listed. As a safety precaution, low-acid foods should be thoroughly heated before being served. Canned meats, poultry or fish and most vegetables should not be eaten directly from the can. Follow directions for heating and combining the canned foods *exactly* as given in the recipes.

Drinks & Snacks

Young and old will enjoy the frosty milkshakes you can make with canned fruits. Kids will beg for a Plum-Purple Frosty after school, and they can make it themselves. Eggnog fans will enjoy Apricot Nog served in a frosty mug. Place the mugs in the freezer for an hour before serving. Even breakfast-skippers can be persuaded to drink a Tutti-Frutti Smoothie or Peach-Yogurt Cooler for an instant breakfast. During the noon-time or early-evening slump, give the adults a pick-me-up with peppy Sangrita.

Snacks made with sauces and condiments, sweet spreads, fruits and vegetables appeal to everyone. Raspberry-Filled Cookies and Peachy Granola Bars will satisfy the small and big cookie monsters in your house.

Dips make a party, and they are simple to make from canned sauces and vegetables. Quick Salsa Dip combines cottage cheese and mild but flavorful Green-Chili Salsa. Serve tortilla chips or fresh vegetables for dippers.

Make Antipasto Platter using tangy Cocktail Vegetable Mix and Wine-Vinegar Pickles. Add some flavorful cheeses, salami, olives and tomatoes for a variety plate everyone will enjoy. Add some crisp breadsticks and your snack is complete.

For your next formal cocktail buffet, make Asparagus Dipping Fondue. Or, mix Curried Cheddar Spread several days ahead. Make hors d'oeuvres by spreading this cheese-and-chutney mixture on cocktail rye bread or crackers. Or, shape it into tiny cheese balls, roll them in nuts and serve with a platter of fresh fruits.

Quick Salsa Dip

Jícama is a crisp, mild-flavored Mexican vegetable.

2 cups small-curd cream-style cottage cheese
1 cup canned Green Chili Salsa, page 135,
   or 1 (8-oz.) can green chili salsa
Red (cayenne) pepper to taste
5 medium carrots, peeled, sliced crosswise

1/2 lb. jícama, peeled, cut in
   2-inch matchsticks
4 celery stalks, cut in 4-inch pieces
1 (9-oz.) pkg. tortilla chips

In a 4-cup container with a tight-fitting lid, combine cottage cheese and salsa. Stir in red pepper to desired peppery flavor. Cover; refrigerate until ready to serve. To serve, pour dip into a medium bowl; place in center of a platter. Surround with carrots, jícama, celery and tortilla chips. Makes about 3 cups dip.

Variation

Substitute zucchini or cucumber for jícama.

Curried-Cheddar Spread

Keeps well in the refrigerator to serve to unexpected guests.

1 cup shredded sharp Cheddar cheese (4 oz.)
3 tablespoons beer or apple cider
1 (3-oz.) pkg. cream cheese, softened
1 teaspoon curry powder

1/3 cup Calcutta-Style Chutney, page 133,
   or Peach-Plum Chutney, page 132
Cocktail rye bread, lightly toasted
Assorted crackers

Process Cheddar cheese, beer or apple cider, cream cheese and curry powder in blender or food processor until smooth and light. When using a blender, scrape sides and push spread down often. Spoon spread into a small bowl. Chop chutney; stir into spread. Cover tightly; refrigerate until ready to serve. Serve spread with toasted cocktail rye bread and crackers. Makes about 1 cup.

Variation

Cheddar Bites: Shape spoonfuls of cheese mixture into 1-inch balls. Roll in chopped nuts. Spear each with a 6-inch skewer. To each skewer, add a fresh strawberry, grape, pineapple cube and melon ball.

Peach-Yogurt Cooler

Good for an instant breakfast, too.

1 cup canned peaches, drained
1/2 cup milk
4 ice cubes

1 (8-oz.) carton lemon- or
   vanilla-flavored yogurt

Cut 2 thin slices from a peach, no more than 1/8 inch thick. Set aside for garnish. Combine remaining peaches, milk and ice cubes in blender. Puree until smooth. Add yogurt; blend until combined. Pour into 2 chilled drinking glasses. Float a peach slice in each glass. Makes 2 servings.

How to Make Raspberry-Filled Cookies

1/Cut half of rolled-out dough with a doughnut cutter. Remove center of cutter. Cut remaining dough in circles.

2/Spoon jam in center of round cookies. Top each with a doughnut-shaped cookie. Crimp edges with a fork.

Antipasto Platter

Serve as an appetizer or a salad.

8 oz. sliced provolone cheese
5 small tomatoes, thinly sliced
6 oz. hard salami, thinly sliced
10 pitted black olives
20 Wine-Vinegar Pickles, page 108, or
   French cornichons

1 qt. Cocktail Vegetable Mix, page 96, or
   1 (32-oz.) jar pickled mixed vegetables
1/2 cup grated Parmesan cheese (1-1/2 oz.)
Breadsticks

Cut provolone cheese slices in quarters. Overlap alternating slices of tomato, salami and cheese around edge of a platter. Placing 1 olive and 2 pickles together, arrange olives and pickles equidistant around platter over tomato, salami and cheese slices. Drain Cocktail Vegetable Mix; mound vegetables in center of platter. Sprinkle Parmesan cheese over platter. Serve with breadsticks. Makes 8 servings.

Raspberry-Filled Cookies

Serve with Peach-Yogurt Cooler, page 139, or a glass of cold milk.

1-1/2 cups sifted all-purpose flour	**2/3 cup packed brown sugar**
1/2 teaspoon baking soda	**1/2 cup granulated sugar**
1 teaspoon baking powder	**2 eggs**
1/2 teaspoon salt	**3 cups rolled oats**
1 teaspoon ground cinnamon	**1 to 1-1/2 cups raspberry jam**
3/4 cup shortening	

Into a medium bowl, sift together flour, baking soda, baking powder, salt and cinnamon. Set aside. In a large bowl, use electric mixer to cream shortening, brown sugar and granulated sugar until light and fluffy. Beat in eggs. Stir in flour mixture and oats. Preheat oven to 350F (175C). Grease a large baking sheet; set aside. On a lightly floured board, roll out one-third of dough at a time, 1/4 inch thick. Using a round doughnut cutter, cut half of dough into doughnut shapes. Remove small center from cutter. Cut remaining dough, making an equal number of round cookies and doughnut-shaped cookies. Arrange round cookies on prepared baking sheet. Spoon about 1 teaspoon jam onto center of each. Top with a doughnut-shaped cookie. Seal edges by pressing with tines of a fork. Bake in preheated oven until lightly browned, about 10 minutes. Makes 30 to 36 cookies.

Variations

Substitute apricot, peach, cherry or strawberry jam for raspberry jam.

Asparagus Dipping Fondue

This light-green fondue is also delicious in omelets.

2 tablespoons butter or margarine	**1 pint cut asparagus or**
1/2 cup chopped onion	**1 (15-oz.) can cut asparagus, drained**
4 oz. fresh mushrooms, sliced	**1 cup dairy sour cream**
1 (10-3/4-oz.) can cream of mushroom soup	**1 loaf French or Italian bread,**
1/2 teaspoon garlic salt	**cut in 1-inch cubes**
1 teaspoon Worcestershire sauce	

Heat butter or margarine in a large skillet over low heat until bubbly. Add onion and mushrooms. Sauté until onion is soft. Stir in mushroom soup, garlic salt, Worcestershire sauce and asparagus. Bring to a boil over medium heat; reduce heat to low. Cover; simmer 15 minutes. Stir in sour cream. Cover; simmer 5 minutes longer, but do not boil. Serve in a fondue pot. Use fondue forks to spear bread cubes for dipping. Makes about 3 cups.

Apricot Nog

A fruitful twist on an old-time favorite.

2 eggs, separated	1-1/2 cups milk
1 pint pitted apricots or	1 tablespoon sugar
1 (16-oz.) can pitted apricots	Ground nutmeg, if desired

In a medium bowl, beat egg yolks with whisk or electric mixer until lemon-colored and thick. Drain apricots; reserve juice for another use. Puree drained apricots in blender. Stir pureed apricots and milk into egg yolks. In another medium bowl, beat egg whites until foamy. Gradually beat in sugar, 1 teaspoon at a time. Continue to beat until soft peaks form. Add beaten egg-white mixture to apricot mixture; mix thoroughly. Pour into 2 chilled drinking glasses. Sprinkle tops with nutmeg, if desired. Makes 2 servings.

Sangrita

Great as a tangy Mexican drink by itself, or as a chaser for tequila.

1 qt. tomato juice, chilled	1-1/2 teaspoons chili powder
2 tablespoons chopped onion	1/2 teaspoon salt
2 cups orange juice, chilled	1 teaspoon sugar
1 tablespoon lemon juice	Tabasco sauce to taste
3 tablespoons lime juice	Tequila, if desired

In blender, puree 1 cup tomato juice and onion. Pour into a 2-quart pitcher. Stir in remaining tomato juice, orange, lemon and lime juices, chili powder, salt, sugar and Tabasco sauce to taste. Refrigerate until ready to serve. Serve in juice glasses or in small cocktail glasses. Serve with shot glasses of tequila, if desired. Makes 5-1/2 cups.

Plum-Purple Frosty

Keep this refreshing drink in the refrigerator and enjoy it for several days.

1 pint pitted plums or	1 (3-3/4-oz.) pkg. instant vanilla
1 (17-oz.) can pitted plums	pudding mix
3-1/2 cups milk	

Puree plums and juice in blender. In a medium bowl, combine puree, milk and pudding mix. Beat with a whisk until mixture thickens slightly, about 2 minutes. Serve in tall drinking glasses. Makes 6 servings.

Variations

Apricot Frosty: Substitute 1 pint pitted apricots or 1 (16-ounce) can pitted apricots for plums.
Peach Frosty: Substitute 1 pint peaches or 1 (16-ounce) can peaches for plums.

Peachy Granola Bars

Children love these as an after-school snack. Serve them warm from the oven.

2 cups raisin-nut granola
2 cups whole-wheat flour
1/2 cup packed brown sugar
1/2 cup honey

1/2 cup butter or margarine, melted
1 pint peaches or 1 (16-oz.) can peaches,
 drained

Preheat oven to 350F (175C). Grease a 9-inch square baking pan; set aside. In a large bowl, combine granola, flour and brown sugar. Stir in honey and melted butter or margarine until crumbly. Press half of crumb mixture into prepared baking pan. Thinly slice peaches; arrange on crumb mixture. Sprinkle top with remaining crumb mixture. Bake in preheated oven 30 minutes. Cool in pan. Cut into bars. Makes 12 bars.

Pear-Grape Pops

Even adults will enjoy these tangy frozen treats.

1 pint pears or 1 (16-oz.) can pears,
 drained

1 (6-oz.) can frozen grape-juice concentrate
1 (8-oz.) container plain yogurt

Process pears and grape-juice concentrate in blender until smooth. Add yogurt; blend. Pour into pop molds or 4-ounce paper cups until two-thirds full; insert a popsicle stick or plastic spoon in center of each. Freeze until firm, about 3 hours. Makes 10 to 12 pops.

Variation

Peach Pops: Substitute 1 pint peaches or 1 (16-ounce) can peaches for pears. Substitute 1 (6-ounce) can frozen lemonade concentrate for grape-juice concentrate.

Tutti-Frutti Smoothie

As thick and creamy as the perfect milkshake.

1 cup drained fruit cocktail or
 Tropical Fruit Cocktail, page 80
1 medium banana
1 cup milk
2 ice cubes

1 (8-oz.) carton pineapple-flavored yogurt
1 teaspoon rum extract, if desired
1 orange slice
2 maraschino cherries

Combine fruit cocktail, banana, milk and ice cubes in blender. Process until smooth. Add yogurt and rum extract, if desired. Blend until combined. Pour into 2 chilled drinking glasses. Cut orange slice in half. Press 1/2 orange slice and 1 cherry on a small wooden pick. Set 1 on edge of each glass. Makes 2 servings.

Salads & Side-Dishes

Side dishes are meal accompaniments that accent and complement the flavors, colors and textures of the main dish. Canned fruits and vegetables are an important part of these meal accompaniments.

Salads made with canned foods are best when combined with crisp, fresh vegetables or fruits, such as celery, lettuce, green onion or apple. Add Honey-Soy Dressing for a piquant flavor. Celery and crisp-fried bacon add crunch to Cheese & Peas Salad. Apples add freshness to Green-Bean Salad.

When adding drained, canned fruit to gelatin, use the juice or syrup in place of part of the water. Refrigerate the gelatin until it has the consistency of unbeaten egg white. This will keep the fruit from sinking to the bottom or floating on the top.

Gazpacho Mold contains the traditional tomatoes, green pepper, green chilies and avocado and is topped with Sour Cream & Chili Dressing. In Cherry-Cheese Layers, dark, sweet cherries shimmer through gelatin set on a whipped-cheese base. Use the ideas in this section to spark your own creativity with gelatin and canned fruits and vegetables.

Vegetable side dishes can be as simple as opening a jar of canned green beans. Add a new touch to the dish by tossing the hot beans with dill-seasoned butter or crushed, seasoned croutons. Creamy Succotash combines corn, tomatoes and beans in a soup-based sauce seasoned with mustard. Vegetables can also be combined with rice or pasta as in Vegetable Paella and Asparagus with Pasta.

Wild-Rice Pilaf

Serve with roast chicken or game hens and colorful Ruby Relish, page 115.

1 (5-oz.) pkg. brown and wild rice mix
2 tablespoons butter or margarine
1/2 cup chopped onion
1 (6-oz.) jar artichoke hearts

1/2 pint Marinated Button Mushrooms,
   page 93, or 1 (4-oz.) jar
   button mushrooms
1/2 teaspoon dried leaf thyme

Prepare brown and wild rice mix as directed on package. Heat butter or margarine in a large skillet over low heat. Add onion; sauté until soft. Add cooked rice and cooking liquid not absorbed. Drain artichoke hearts and mushrooms. Stir into rice mixture. Sprinkle thyme over top. Cover; simmer 15 minutes. Makes 4 to 6 servings.

Green-Bean Salad

Toasting almonds brings out their flavor.

Paprika Dressing, see below
1 pint cut green beans or
   1 (15-oz.) can cut green beans
1/2 cup slivered almonds

1 tablespoon butter or margarine
1/2 medium onion, sliced
2 medium, red apples

Paprika Dressing:
2 tablespoons distilled white vinegar
1 tablespoon lemon juice
1/3 cup vegetable oil
1/4 teaspoon dry mustard

1/2 teaspoon paprika
1/2 teaspoon salt
1/2 teaspoon sugar

Prepare Paprika Dressing; refrigerate. Pour home-canned beans with liquid into a medium saucepan. Bring to a gentle boil over medium heat. Cover; boil 15 minutes. Drain boiled or commercially canned beans. Chill in refrigerator. Toast almonds in a small heavy skillet over medium heat until lightly browned, stirring constantly to prevent burning. Cool on paper towels. Melt butter or margarine in small heavy skillet over low heat. Add onion; sauté until soft. In a medium bowl, combine chilled beans and sautéed onion. Core 1 apple but do not peel; dice. Add diced apple to bean mixture. Pour 1/4 cup Paprika Dressing over bean mixture; toss gently. Cover; refrigerate 1 hour or until chilled. Without peeling, cut reserved apple into 1/8-inch crosswise slices. Cut core from each slice with center of a doughnut cutter or a knife. Place cored apple slices in a shallow medium bowl. Pour several tablespoons Paprika Dressing over apple slices. Turn to coat slices. Refrigerate until ready to serve. To serve, sprinkle toasted almonds over bean mixture; toss gently. Arrange apple rings in a circle on a serving plate or round platter. Use a slotted spoon to lift bean salad out of bowl, draining off excess dressing. Spoon into center of ring made by sliced apple. Makes 4 servings.

Paprika Dressing:
Combine all ingredients in a small jar with a tight-fitting lid. Attach lid; shake vigorously, 1 minute. Makes about 1/2 cup.

Sweet Potatoes with Apricot Glaze

Bake in the oven along with a roast or chicken.

2 pints sweet potatoes or yams or
   2 (16-oz.) cans sweet potatoes or yams
1 pint apricot halves or
   1 (16-oz.) can apricot halves

2 tablespoons butter or margarine
1/3 cup packed brown sugar

Slice sweet potatoes or yams about 1/2 inch thick. Arrange slices in a shallow 2-quart casserole. Preheat oven to 375F (195C). Drain apricots, reserving juice. Arrange 1/2 cup drained apricots among sweet-potato or yam slices. In blender or food processor, puree remaining apricots and 1/2 cup reserved juice. Melt butter or margarine in a medium skillet over low heat. Stir in brown sugar until bubbly. Carefully stir in apricot puree; cook until syrup thickens slightly, 10 to 15 minutes. Pour syrup over sweet potatoes or yams. Bake in preheated oven, uncovered, 25 minutes. Makes 4 servings.

1/Sauté onion and garlic until tender. Add rice; cook over low heat until rice just begins to brown.

2/Stir in tomatoes and bouillon mixture. Bring to a boil. Cover and simmer 15 minutes.

Vegetable Paella

Excellent as a side dish with fish or seafood.

1 cup water
1 chicken bouillon cube
1/8 teaspoon crushed saffron threads
2 tablespoons olive oil or vegetable oil
1 garlic clove, minced
1 medium onion, chopped
1 cup uncooked long-grain rice

1 cup drained canned tomatoes, chopped
1/2 teaspoon salt
1 pint green peas or
   1 (17-oz.) can green peas
1/2 cup sliced black olives
2 oz. pepperoni, sliced

In a small saucepan, bring water to a boil. Add bouillon cube and saffron; set aside. Heat oil in a medium skillet over low heat. Add garlic and onion. Sauté until onion is soft. Add rice; cook and stir until rice is coated and lightly browned. Stir in tomatoes, salt and bouillon mixture. Bring mixture to a boil over high heat; reduce heat to low. Cover; simmer 15 minutes. Pour home-canned peas with liquid into a medium saucepan. Bring to a boil over medium-high heat. Cover; boil 15 minutes. Drain boiled or commercially canned beans. Stir into rice mixture. Arrange olives and pepperoni over top. Cover; simmer 10 minutes longer. Makes 6 servings.

Gazpacho Mold

Ole! Flavor, color and texture capture the Spanish spirit.

1 qt. canned tomatoes or	2 tablespoons olive oil
1 (28-oz.) can tomatoes	1/2 teaspoon salt
1 medium cucumber	2 tablespoons chopped canned green chilies
1 small green bell pepper	2 (1/4-oz.) envelopes unflavored gelatin
2 green onions, sliced	1 small avocado, diced
2 tablespoons red-wine vinegar	Sour Cream & Chili Dressing, see below

Sour Cream & Chili Dressing:

1/3 cup mayonnaise	1/2 teaspoon chili powder
1/3 cup dairy sour cream	Red (cayenne) pepper to taste

Place tomatoes with juice in blender or food processor; set aside. Cut cucumber crosswise into 3 equal pieces. Reserve 1 piece for garnish. Peel remaining pieces. Slice 1 peeled-cucumber piece; add to tomatoes. Chop remaining peeled-cucumber piece; set aside. Remove seeds and membranes from green pepper; cut in large pieces. Chop enough to make 1/3 cup; set aside. Add remaining green-pepper pieces to tomatoes. Reserve 2 tablespoons green onions. Add remaining green onion, vinegar, oil, salt and green chilies to tomato mixture. Blend until finely chopped. Pour 1 cup chopped tomato mixture into a small saucepan. Stir in gelatin. Stir constantly over medium heat until gelatin dissolves. In a medium bowl, combine gelatin mixture with remaining chopped tomato mixture. Refrigerate until mixture has consistency of unbeaten egg whites, 30 to 45 minutes. Stir in reserved chopped cucumber, chopped bell pepper, green onions and avocado. Pour into an 8-cup mold. Refrigerate until firm, 4 to 6 hours. Prepare Sour Cream & Chili Dressing. Invert mold onto a serving plate; remove mold. Thinly slice reserved, unpeeled cucumber. Cut slices in half; arrange around mold. Mound Sour Cream & Chili Dressing on top of salad. Makes 6 to 8 servings.

Sour Cream & Chili Dressing:
In a small bowl, combine all ingredients. Makes 2/3 cup.

Variation
For special occasions, add 1 (4-1/4-ounce) can small shrimp, drained.

Asparagus with Pasta

Canned asparagus is fragile—toss carefully.

1 pint cut asparagus or	1 garlic clove, minced
1 (14-1/2-oz.) can cut asparagus	1/2 cup chopped fresh parsley
1 (7-oz.) pkg. small pasta shells,	1/2 teaspoon dried leaf basil
bowknots or spirals	1/2 cup grated Parmesan cheese (1-1/2 oz.)
1/4 cup butter or margarine	

Pour home-canned asparagus with liquid into a medium saucepan. Bring to a gentle boil over medium heat. Cover; boil 15 minutes. Drain boiled or commercially canned asparagus; set aside. Cook pasta as package directs; drain. Melt butter or margarine in a large saucepan over low heat. Add garlic, parsley and basil; mix well. Stir in cooked pasta and drained asparagus. Sprinkle with cheese; toss lightly. Immediately turn into a serving dish. Makes 4 to 6 servings.

Creamy Succotash

You can purchase seasoned crumbs or crush seasoned croutons for the Crumb Topping.

1 tablespoon vegetable oil
1/2 cup coarsely chopped onion
2 tablespoons prepared mustard
1 (10-1/2-oz.) can cream of celery soup
1/3 cup milk
1 cup drained chopped canned tomatoes

1 pint whole-kernel corn or
   1 (17-oz.) can whole-kernel corn, drained
1 pint green lima beans, drained, or
   1 (16-oz.) can green lima beans, drained
Crumb Topping, if desired, see below

Crumb Topping:
1-1/2 teaspoons butter or margarine
1/2 cup seasoned breadcrumbs

3 tablespoons grated Parmesan cheese

Preheat oven to 350F (175C). Heat oil in a medium skillet over low heat. Add onion; sauté until soft. Stir in mustard, soup and milk. Combine tomatoes, corn and lima beans in a 2-quart casserole. Pour mustard sauce over vegetables. Stir gently to coat vegetables. If desired, prepare Crumb Topping. Sprinkle topping over casserole. Bake, uncovered, in preheated oven, 30 minutes. Makes 6 servings.

Crumb Topping:
Melt butter or margarine in a small skillet over low heat. Toast crumbs in skillet until golden, stirring constantly. In a small bowl, combine toasted crumbs and cheese.

Cheese & Pea Salad

Serve this delicious variation of wilted salad immediately after adding the hot dressing.

2 pints green peas or
   2 (17-oz.) cans green peas
1 (3-oz.) pkg. cream cheese
1/4 cup chopped pimiento
2 celery stalks, cut in
   1/4-inch diagonal slices
6 lettuce leaves
2 bacon slices

1/2 cup chopped onion
1/2 teaspoon sugar
1/4 cup cider vinegar
1/2 teaspoon salt
1/8 teaspoon pepper
1/2 cup Marinated Button Mushrooms,
   page 93, if desired

Pour home-canned peas with liquid into a medium saucepan. Bring to a gentle boil over medium heat. Cover; boil 15 minutes. Cool to room temperature. Drain boiled or commercially canned peas. Cut cream cheese into small cubes. In a medium bowl, combine drained peas, cream-cheese cubes, pimiento and celery; set aside. Arrange lettuce leaves on 6 salad plates; set aside. In a small skillet, fry bacon over medium heat until crisp. Drain on paper towels. Crumble cooked bacon over salad. Drain all but 3 tablespoons bacon drippings from skillet. Sauté onion in remaining drippings until soft. Stir in sugar, vinegar, salt and pepper. Bring to a boil over medium heat, stirring constantly. Pour hot dressing over salad; toss lightly. Spoon evenly onto lettuce leaves. Garnish with Marinated Button Mushrooms, if desired. Makes 6 servings.

Orange-Beet Salad

Beets are marinated several hours in a tangy orange-pineapple dressing.

1 pint sliced beets or
   1 (16-oz.) can sliced beets
2 medium oranges
4 canned pineapple slices with juice

1/4 cup vegetable oil
2 tablespoons distilled white vinegar
1/2 teaspoon salt
1/2 cup chopped red onion

Pour home-canned beets and liquid into a medium saucepan. Bring to a gentle boil over medium heat. Cover; boil 15 minutes. Drain boiled or commercially canned beets. Turn drained beets into a small bowl. Chill in refrigerator. Cut peel from oranges, removing all white pith. Slice peeled oranges, reserving juice in a 1-cup measure. Drain pineapple, reserving juice. Cut pineapple rings in half. Set orange slices and pineapple pieces aside. Add pineapple juice to orange juice to make 1/4 cup. Add oil, vinegar and salt. Pour into a jar with a tight-fitting lid. Attach lid; shake vigorously 1 minute. Pour marinade over chilled beets. Refrigerate at least 4 hours, stirring several times. To serve, use a slotted spoon to remove beets from marinade; reserve marinade. Alternately arrange 2 beet slices and 1 orange slice on a serving plate, slightly overlapping, until all are used. Garnish with halved pineapple rings. Sprinkle chopped onion over salad. Drizzle with reserved marinade. Makes 4 servings.

Cherry-Cheese Layers

Refreshing, even in the midst of winter!

1 pint dark sweet cherries or
   1 (17-oz.) can dark sweet cherries
Water
2 (3-oz.) pkgs. cherry-flavored gelatin
   powder

2-3/4 cup water
1 (3-oz.) pkg. cream cheese, softened
1/2 pint whipping cream or
   1 (8-oz.) pkg. frozen whipped topping,
   thawed

Drain cherries, reserving juice in a 1-cup measure. Add water to make 1 cup. Pour into a medium saucepan; bring to a boil. Stir in 1 package gelatin until dissolved. Stir in 1 cup water. Arrange drained cherries in an 8-inch square pan. Carefully pour gelatin mixture over cherries. Refrigerate until set, about 2 hours. After 1 hour, bring 1 cup water to a boil in a medium saucepan over medium-high heat. Stir in remaining package gelatin until dissolved; stir in remaining 3/4 cup water. Pour into a medium bowl; refrigerate until gelatin mounds when dropped from a spoon, 30 to 45 minutes. Beat partially set gelatin mixture with electric mixer until light and foamy. In a small bowl, beat cream cheese until light. Whip cream in a small deep bowl until soft peaks form. Stir cream cheese into whipped cream or topping; beat until smooth. Reserve 1/2 cup cheese mixture. Fold remaining cheese mixture into whipped gelatin. Spread over mixture containing cherries. Refrigerate until set, 2 to 4 hours. Invert onto a plate so layer containing cherries is on top. Cut into squares. Use a pastry tube or spoon to decorate top of each with reserved cheese mixture. Makes 6 to 8 servings.

Variation

Molded Cherry-Cheese Layers: Mold cherry and gelatin mixture in a 7- to 8-cup mold. Refrigerate until set. Spread cheese mixture over top. Refrigerate until set. Unmold onto a serving plate. Decorate top with reserved cheese mixture.

Light Meals & Brunches

Light meals are a boon to busy people. A single dish can be accompanied by a bread or salad to make a complete meal. Light meals offer enticing flavor combinations and colors. They are hunger-satisfying and can be served any time—not just for lunch.

Consider a light lunch of tomato soup with cheese popcorn sprinkled on top. Soups are popular for Sunday-evening suppers after a complete mid-day Sunday dinner. Harvest Vegetable Chowder is a meal in itself, containing potatoes, corn and beans.

When the day is rushed, Sloppy Sue's make a fast and easy sandwich supper. Ham & Swiss Puff is a cheese pie crust that puffs up in the oven. Filled with ham and vegetables, the puff is intriguing to look at and fun to eat. For a luncheon club, Blue-Cheese & Asparagus Salad is appropriately elegant.

You'll find several egg dishes suitable for company. Omelets are better suited to small gatherings or family brunches. Chutney-Cheese Omelet makes 4 individual omelets filled with cottage cheese and the piquant flavor of chutney.

Another exciting breakfast dish is French-Market Toast. The bread is soaked in egg and brandied fruit syrup. After baking, top the hot toast with brandied fruit.

Chutney-Cheese Omelets

Simple and elegant for a brunch or late supper.

1 pint small-curd cottage cheese	**8 eggs**
1/2 cup Peach-Plum Chutney, page 132,	**1/3 cup milk**
Calcutta-Style Chutney, page 133,	**1/2 teaspoon salt**
or other chutney	**1/4 cup butter or margarine**
1/2 cup chopped walnuts	**1 cup drained, canned peach slices**

In a small bowl, stir together cottage cheese, chutney and nuts. Set aside. In a medium bowl, beat eggs until just combined. Stir in milk and salt. Over medium-high heat, melt 1 tablespoon butter or margarine in an 8-inch omelet pan or skillet. Swirl pan to distribute. Pour 1/2 cup egg mixture into pan. Do not stir. As mixture cooks, lift edge and tilt pan to let uncooked mixture flow underneath. When omelet is set, but top is still moist, spread about 1/2 cup chutney mixture over half of omelet. Fold omelet over filling; turn out onto a plate. Top with a spoonful of chutney mixture and several peach slices. Serve immediately, or keep warm until ready to serve. Repeat with remaining egg mixture and filling. Makes 4 omelets.

Blue-Cheese & Asparagus Salad

Use your favorite pickled vegetables as a variation.

1/2 pint tuna or
  1 (6-3/4-oz.) can chunk tuna
Blue-Cheese Dressing, see below
Red-leaf lettuce
2 medium tomatoes, thinly sliced

3 hard-cooked eggs, sliced
1/2 pint Asparagus Spears with Tarragon,
  page 103
8 to 12 pimiento-stuffed olives

Blue-Cheese Dressing:
1/2 cup vegetable oil
2 tablespoons distilled white vinegar
1 egg yolk
1 tablespoon dry sherry

1/2 teaspoon salt
1/8 teaspoon pepper
1 teaspoon sugar
2 oz. blue cheese, crumbled

If using home-canned tuna, remove lid. Cover jar with foil. Preheat oven to 350F (175C). Bake tuna in jar 30 minutes. Or, place a thermometer in center of jar and heat in oven until fish in center of jar is heated to 185F (85C). Remove from oven; let stand 30 minutes. Drain home-canned or commercially canned tuna. Refrigerate until chilled. Prepare Blue-Cheese Dressing. Refrigerate until ready to serve. Arrange lettuce leaves on salad plates. Arrange tomato slices, egg slices and chunks of chilled tuna on lettuce leaves. Arrange asparagus spears over top. Spoon Blue-Cheese Dressing over salad. Garnish with olives. Makes 2 or 3 servings.

Blue-Cheese Dressing:

In blender, combine oil, vinegar, egg yolk, sherry, salt, pepper and sugar. Blend until smooth. Stir in blue cheese. Makes about 1 cup.

Variation

Substitute Pickled Sprouts & Cauliflower, page 93; or Dilly Beans, page 96, and Tiny Toms, page 91, for Asparagus Spears with Tarragon.

Plum Breakfast Pudding

Prepare the night before, then let it bake while you dress in the morning.

4 eggs
2 cups milk
1/4 cup sugar
1 teaspoon vanilla extract
1/2 teaspoon ground cinnamon

1/4 teaspoon salt
6 slices white bread
1 pint plums or 1 (17-oz.) can plums,
  drained

Beat eggs in a large bowl until well combined. Add milk, sugar, vanilla, cinnamon and salt. Stir to dissolve sugar. Trim crusts from bread; use crusts for another purpose. Cut trimmed bread into 1-inch cubes. Gently stir bread cubes and drained plums into egg mixture. Cover bowl; place in refrigerator overnight, or at least 4 hours. Preheat oven to 350F (175C). Spoon pudding mixture into 6 individual ovenproof casserole dishes or 10-ounce custard cups. Place dishes or cups in a baking pan. Pour hot water into pan around dishes. Bake in preheated oven until puffy and lightly browned, about 45 minutes. Serve warm. Makes 6 servings.

Mandarin Brunch Crepes

For an early brunch, make the crepes the day before and store them in the refrigerator.

8 Brunch Crepes, see below
1 pint pineapple chunks or
  2 (8-1/4-oz.) cans pineapple chunks
3 tablespoons cornstarch
1/4 cup water
2 tablespoons soy sauce
1/4 cup cider vinegar

1/2 cup sugar
1 medium, green bell pepper,
  cut in 1-inch squares
1 (11-oz.) can mardarin-orange sections,
  drained
16 fresh pork sausage links

Brunch Crepes:
1 egg
2/3 cup milk

2/3 cup all-purpose flour
1 tablespoon butter or margarine, melted

Prepare Brunch Crepes. Drain pineapple, reserving juice; set pineapple aside. Measure juice, adding water to make 1 cup, if necessary. In a medium saucepan, make a paste of cornstarch and 1/4 cup water. Stir in juice mixture, soy sauce, vinegar and sugar. Stirring constantly, bring to a boil over medium heat. Stir in drained pineapple, green pepper and orange sections. Cover; cook over very low heat, 10 minutes. In a medium skillet over medium heat, fry sausage until well browned on all sides. To serve, place 1 crepe on a flat surface. Place a generous spoonful of sauce, without including pepper squares and orange sections, on top of crepe; spread to cover crepe. Place 2 cooked sausage links side by side on center of crepe. Spoon sauce with pepper pieces and orange sections over sausage. Fold edges of crepe over sausage. Place filled crepe, seam-side down, in a chafing dish or on individual plates. Repeat with remaining crepes. Pour remaining fruit and sauce over crepes. Makes 4 servings.

Brunch Crepes:
Process egg and milk in blender until combined, 1 to 3 seconds. Add flour; blend until smooth, 3 to 5 seconds. Scrape down sides of container. Add butter or margarine; blend 1 second longer. Place a crepe pan or 8-inch skillet over medium-high heat; lightly butter. Lift pan from heat; pour about 2 tablespoons batter in pan. Quickly tilt and swirl pan so batter covers bottom of pan. Return pan to heat. Cook until bottom of crepe is lightly browned. Turn; cook 2 to 3 seconds longer. Remove from pan by inverting pan over plate. Repeat with remaining batter. Wrap crepes in foil; keep warm in a 250F (120C) oven. Makes 8 to 10 crepes.

Stuffed Peaches

Ruffled red-leaf or salad-bowl lettuce makes a pretty background.

12 canned peach halves
1 cup creamed cottage cheese
2 cups frozen whipped topping, thawed
1/4 cup lemon-flavored gelatin powder

1/2 cup chopped drained maraschino cherries
1/4 cup chopped pecans
Red-leaf or salad-bowl lettuce

Dry peach halves on paper towels. In a medium bowl, combine cottage cheese and whipped topping. Sprinkle gelatin over top; stir in. Stir in cherries and pecans. Arrange peach halves, cut-side up, in a 9-inch square pan. Mound cottage-cheese mixture on top of each. Refrigerate until ready to serve. Shape lettuce leaves into cups by overlapping base portions. Place folded leaves on salad plates. Sandwich 2 stuffed peach halves together with stuffing in center. Place in a lettuce cup. Repeat with remaining stuffed peach halves. Makes 6 servings.

Ham & Swiss Puff

This golden Swiss-cheese puff can be made ahead and served with hot ham filling.

1 cup water	1/2 cup shredded Swiss cheese (2 oz.)
1/3 cup butter or margarine	4 eggs
1 cup all-purpose flour	Ham-Amandine Filling, see below
1/8 teaspoon salt	1/2 cup sliced almonds

Ham-Amandine Filling:

1 (10-3/4-oz.) can cream of mushroom soup	1 (5-oz.) can water chestnuts, sliced
2 tablespoons soy sauce	1 pint green beans or
1/2 cup dairy sour cream	1 (15-oz.) can green beans, drained
1 (6-3/4-oz.) can chunk ham	

Preheat oven to 400F (205C). Grease a 9-inch pie plate; set aside. Over high heat, bring water to a boil in a medium saucepan. Stir in butter or margarine until melted. Remove from heat; add flour and salt, all at once. Stir vigorously until dough forms a ball. Stir in cheese. Add eggs, one at a time, beating after each addition until dough is smooth. Spread dough in prepared pie plate. Bake in preheated oven until puffed and browned, about 40 minutes. Center will rise, then fall. Remove from pie plate; cool on a rack. Prepare Ham-Amandine Filling; set aside. Toast almonds in a small skillet over medium heat, stirring constantly until lightly browned. Place cheese puff on a platter. Pour filling onto center of puff. Sprinkle almonds over filling. Cut in wedges to serve. Makes 6 to 8 servings.

Ham-Amandine Filling:
Combine cream of mushroom soup, soy sauce and sour cream in a medium saucepan; mix well. Stir in ham, water chestnuts and drained green beans. Cover; simmer over medium-low heat, 15 minutes. Do not boil.

Harvest Vegetable Chowder

Use mealy baking potatoes for a thick, smooth chowder.

4 medium potatoes, cooked	1 teaspoon salt
2 tablespoons butter or margarine	1 pint cream-style corn or
1/2 cup chopped onion	1 (17-oz.) can cream-style corn
1 (10-3/4-oz.) can chicken broth	1 pint lima beans or
2 cups milk	1 (16-oz.) can green lima beans, drained
1/2 teaspoon dried leaf basil	1 cup large-curd cottage cheese
1/4 teaspoon dried leaf thyme	

Reserve 1 potato; peel remaining potatoes. Cut into large pieces; set aside. Melt butter or margarine in a small skillet over low heat. Add onion; sauté until soft. In blender, combine potato pieces, sautéed onions, chicken broth and milk. Process until smooth. Pour potato mixture into a 3-quart saucepan. Stir in basil, thyme, salt, corn and drained lima beans. Cut reserved potato in 1/2-inch cubes; add to soup. Stirring occasionally, bring to a simmer over medium-low heat. Cover; simmer 10 minutes, stirring occasionally to prevent scorching. Stir in cottage cheese until cheese just begins to melt. Serve immediately. Makes 6 servings.

1/Beat flour, water and butter or margarine until dough pulls away from side of pan.

2/Add eggs, one at a time, beating until smooth after each addition.

French-Market Toast

Start birthday celebrations early in the day with this special breakfast dish.

1 pint Brandied Fruit Cocktail, page 86	1 teaspoon grated lemon peel
5 eggs	8 (1/2-inch) slices French or
1/4 cup milk	Italian-style bread
1/4 teaspoon salt	1 tablespoon cornstarch
2 tablespoons sugar	1/4 cup butter or margarine

Drain Brandied Fruit Cocktail, reserving syrup. Set fruit aside. In a large bowl, beat eggs until frothy. Beat in 1/4 cup reserved syrup, milk, salt, sugar and lemon peel. Dip bread slices in egg mixture, turning to coat them evenly. Place slices in a 13'' x 9'' baking pan. Pour any remaining egg mixture over slices. Set aside 1 hour. In a small saucepan, combine remaining reserved syrup and cornstarch. Stirring constantly, bring to a boil over medium heat. Stir in drained fruit. Set aside; keep warm. Melt 2 tablespoons butter or margarine in a large skillet over medium-high heat. Add 2 or 3 slices coated bread. Cook about 2 minutes on each side or until deeply browned. Remove from skillet; keep warm. Repeat with remaining butter or margarine and bread slices until all are cooked. For each serving, serve 2 slices toast topped with warm fruit mixture. Makes 4 servings.

Variation

Substitute 3 tablespoons brandy and 1 (16-ounce) can fruit cocktail for Brandied Fruit Cocktail.

Sloppy Sue's

Eat this easy supper sandwich with a fork or hold it in your hands.

1 pint Ground-Beef Mix, page 71	6 pita breads
1/2 cup Barbeque Sauce, page 130, or	1/2 cup cubed American cheese (2 oz.)
commercial barbeque sauce	Shoestring potatoes, if desired
1 tablespoon prepared mustard	Quick Dill Spears, page 107, if desired
1/3 cup sliced pimiento-stuffed olives	

In a medium saucepan, combine Ground-Beef Mix, Barbeque Sauce, mustard and olives. Bring to a boil over medium heat. Reduce heat to low; cover. Stirring occasionally, simmer 20 minutes: Preheat oven to 200F (95C). Cut a narrow slice off 1 side of each pita bread. Use narrow slice for another purpose. Wrap cut pita breads in foil. Heat in oven 10 minutes. Just before serving, gently open warmed pita breads to make pockets. Stir cheese cubes into meat sauce. Immediately spoon meat sauce into pita pockets. Serve with shoestring potatoes and Quick Dill Spears, if desired. Makes 6 servings.

Variation

Substitute large hamburger buns for pita breads. Open buns; toast under broiler until lightly browned. Place each bun on a plate. Spoon meat sauce generously over bottom of each bun. Top with remaining bun halves or place toasted-side up on plate.

Quick Ranchero Pie

Serve with an avocado-pear-orange salad topped with lemon yogurt.

1 tablespoon vegetable oil	1 teaspoon taco seasoning
1/4 cup chopped onion	1-1/2 cups milk
1 garlic clove, minced	3 eggs
1/2 medium, green bell pepper, chopped	2 tablespoons butter or margarine, melted
2 tablespoons chopped cooked green chilies	1/4 cup all-purpose flour
3 whole canned tomatoes, chopped	1/4 cup cornmeal
1 pint whole-kernel corn or	1 teaspoon salt
1 (15-oz.) can whole-kernel corn, drained	1 cup shredded Cheddar cheese (4 oz.)

Heat oil in a medium skillet over low heat. Sauté onion, garlic and green pepper in oil until onion is soft. Stir in green chilies, tomatoes, drained corn and taco seasoning. Cover; simmer 5 minutes. Preheat oven to 400F (205C). Grease a 9-inch pie plate; set aside. In blender, combine milk, eggs and melted butter or margarine. Blend 5 seconds. Add flour, cornmeal and salt; blend 10 seconds longer, or until smooth. Spread onion mixture in prepared pie plate. Sprinkle with cheese. Pour egg mixture evenly over top. Bake in preheated oven until top is golden brown and a knife inserted in center comes out clean, about 45 minutes. Let stand 5 minutes before serving. Cut into wedges; serve warm. Makes 6 to 8 servings.

Main Dishes

Use your own canned meats, fruits, vegetables, sauces and condiments for delightfully delicious main dishes and casseroles. Hungarian Goulash, Creamy Burgundy Beef or Spanish Chicken & Rice make quick meals a snap. Heat, add a salad and bread, and dinner is served.

Stew Beef is ready to eat in minutes while fresh beef cubes need at least an hour to simmer and become tender. If your supply of home-canned meats is depleted, substitute commercially canned meats. Freshly cooked or canned chicken can be substituted for home-canned Chunk Chicken or Chicken Pieces. Combine chicken, potatoes, peas and a rich sauce for a delicious chicken casserole. Top with baking-powder biscuits. Bake at 375F (190C) for 25 to 30 minutes.

Enrich the flavor of meats with tangy sauces. Plum Barbecue Sauce gives Oven-Barbecued Ribs a tart-sweet goodness that makes you come back for more. Lamb will be on your menu often after you taste the piquant spiciness of Chutney-Basted Lamb Kabobs.

Chicken in a Haystack

Serve green beans and almonds as a side dish and canned peaches, pears or apricots for dessert.

1 pint Chunk Chicken, page 71, or	6 tablespoons butter or margarine
2 cups diced cooked chicken	8 oz. linguine noodles, cooked
1 tablespoon vegetable oil	2 egg yolks
1 garlic clove, peeled, flattened	1 cup half and half
4 oz. fresh mushrooms, sliced	1/2 cup grated Parmesan cheese (1-1/2 oz.)

Pour home-canned chicken with broth into a medium saucepan. Bring to a boil over medium-high heat. Reduce heat until broth boils gently. Cover; boil 20 minutes. Drain, reserving broth for another purpose. Heat oil in a 4-quart pot over low heat; add garlic. Stirring constantly, sauté garlic 1 minute; remove and discard garlic. Add mushrooms; sauté 1 minute. Add butter or margarine; melt. Add linguine; toss to coat. Add chicken. In a small bowl, beat egg yolks; beat in half and half. Pour over linguine mixture. Gently stir over medium heat until heated through, 3 to 5 minutes. Sprinkle with cheese; toss. Serve immediately. Makes 6 servings.

Chutney-Basted Lamb Kabobs

Middle East spices in the marinade tenderize and flavor the lamb cubes.

2 lbs. boneless leg of lamb
1/2 cup olive oil or vegetable oil
1/4 cup red wine
1/4 cup distilled white vinegar
1 garlic clove, minced
1/2 teaspoon dried leaf rosemary
1/2 teaspoon dried mint leaves
1/2 teaspoon salt

Pinch coarsely ground pepper
2 cups fresh cherry tomatoes
2 medium, green bell peppers,
    cut in 1-1/2-inch pieces
8 oz. fresh mushrooms
1 cup Peach-Plum Chutney, page 132, or
    Calcutta-Style Chutney, page 133
3 cups hot cooked rice

Trim fat from lamb; cut meat into 1-inch cubes. Place in a 12" x 7" baking pan; set aside. In a small bowl, combine oil, wine, vinegar, garlic, rosemary, mint, salt and pepper. Pour marinade over lamb cubes. Cover; refrigerate overnight. Arrange lamb cubes, cherry tomatoes, green-pepper pieces and whole mushrooms on skewers. Reserve 1/2 cup chutney. Puree remaining chutney in blender. Baste kabobs with pureed chutney. Broil basted kabobs 4 inches from oven broiling element or from charcoal fire, about 5 minutes on each side. Brush frequently with pureed chutney. Spoon rice equally onto 4 serving dishes. To serve, lay each kabob over rice. Spoon some of reserved chutney over kabobs. Makes 4 servings.

Spaghetti Pie

Serve like a pie. Teenagers will like it as much as pizza!

Quick Italian Meat Sauce, see below
4 oz. thin spaghetti, cooked
1 tablespoon butter or margarine
1 tablespoon chopped fresh parsley
2 tablespoons grated Parmesan cheese

1 egg, beaten
1/2 cup grated Parmesan cheese (1-1/2 oz.)
1 (2-1/4-oz.) can sliced black olives

Quick Italian Meat Sauce:
1 pint Ground-Beef Mix, page 71
1/2 pint Tomato Sauce, page 129,
    or 1 (8-oz.) can tomato sauce
1 tablespoon olive oil
1 bay leaf

1/2 teaspoon dried leaf basil
1/4 teaspoon dried leaf oregano
1/8 teaspoon dried leaf thyme
Pinch sugar

Prepare Quick Italian Meat Sauce. Preheat oven to 350F (175C). Toss hot spaghetti with butter or margarine, chopped parsley and 2 tablespoons Parmesan cheese. Stir in beaten egg. Turn spaghetti mixture into a 9-inch pie pan. Press to form a crust. Bake 10 minutes. Pour Quick Italian Meat Sauce into spaghetti pie shell. Sprinkle 1/2 cup Parmesan cheese over top of filling. Arrange olives over cheese. Place pie under broiler until cheese bubbles. Let stand 10 minutes before cutting into wedges. Makes 4 to 6 servings.

Quick Italian Meat Sauce:
In a medium saucepan, combine Ground-Beef Mix, tomato sauce, olive oil and bay leaf. Crush basil, oregano and thyme together in palm of your hand. Add to sauce. Stir in sugar to taste. Place over low heat until mixture simmers. Cover; simmer 20 minutes. Remove and discard bay leaf.

Hungarian Goulash

If the family's not wild about sauerkraut, try the variation using noodles.

2 bacon slices, diced	1/2 cup beef broth
1 cup chopped onion	1 tablespoon tomato paste
1 garlic clove, minced	1 pint Sauerkraut, page 101, or
2 tablespoons paprika	1 (16-oz.) can sauerkraut
1 tablespoon all-purpose flour	Dairy sour cream
1-1/2 pints Stew Beef, page 69	1/4 teaspoon caraway seeds

In a large skillet over medium heat, fry bacon until crisp. Drain on paper towels. Crumble bacon; set aside. Sauté onion and garlic in bacon drippings until onion is soft. Stir in paprika and flour. Cook 1 minute, stirring constantly. Stir in Stew Beef with its broth, beef broth and tomato paste. Reduce heat to low. Cover; simmer 20 minutes. Drain sauerkraut, pressing out all liquid. Stir drained sauerkraut and crumbled bacon into beef mixture. Cover; simmer 15 minutes longer. Spoon goulash into a serving bowl. Top with a large dollop of sour cream; sprinkle with caraway seeds. Serve with additional sour cream. Makes 4 servings.

Variation

Hungarian Goulash with Noodles: Substitute 8 ounces fine noodles, cooked, for drained sauerkraut.

Creamy Burgundy Beef

Complete the meal with Orange-Beet Salad, page 151, and Cranberry-Yogurt Pie, page 181.

2 tablespoons vegetable oil	1/2 cup burgundy or dry red wine
1 carrot, sliced	1/4 teaspoon dried leaf thyme
1 medium onion, thinly sliced	1 bay leaf
1 garlic clove, minced	1 beef bouillon cube
4 oz. fresh mushrooms, sliced	1 cup dairy sour cream
2 tablespoons all-purpose flour	6 to 8 oz. wide egg noodles, cooked
1-1/2 pints Stew Beef, page 69	

Heat oil in a large skillet over low heat. Add carrot, onion, garlic and mushrooms. Sauté until onion is soft. Sprinkle flour over onion mixture; stir. Drain Stew Beef, reserving broth. Stir wine into reserved broth; stir into onion mixture. Stirring constantly, bring to a boil over medium-high heat. Stir in thyme, bay leaf, bouillon cube and beef cubes. Bring back to a boil; reduce heat to low. Cover; simmer 30 minutes. Remove and discard bay leaf. Stir sour cream into beef mixture. Keep hot but do not boil. To serve, spoon beef mixture over noodles. Makes 4 servings.

Chicken Chilaquilas

Serve with Gazpacho Mold, page 148, to continue the Mexican theme.

1 pint Chunk Chicken, page 71, or
  2 cups diced cooked chicken and
    1/2 cup chicken broth
2 tablespoons butter or margarine
1/2 cup chopped onion
2 tablespoons all-purpose flour
1/2 teaspoon salt

1 cup milk
6 corn tortillas
2 canned whole green chilies, chopped, or
  1 (4-oz.) can chopped green chilies
3/4 cup shredded Monterey Jack cheese
  (3 oz.)
3/4 cup shredded Cheddar cheese (3 oz.)

Pour home-canned chicken with broth into a medium saucepan. Bring to a boil over medium-high heat. Reduce heat until broth boils gently. Cover; boil 20 minutes. Drain, reserving broth. Melt butter or margarine in a medium saucepan over low heat; add onion. Sauté until soft. Stir in flour and salt until smooth. Gradually add reserved broth or 1/2 cup chicken broth and milk, stirring constantly. Cook and stir until sauce thickens. Tear tortillas into 2- to 3-inch pieces. Preheat oven to 375F (190C). Pour a thin layer of sauce in bottom of a shallow 2-quart casserole dish. Add one-third of each of the following: chicken, green chilies, tortilla pieces, Monterey Jack cheese, Cheddar cheese and sauce. Repeat layers until all ingredients are used, ending with sauce. Bake in preheated oven until bubbly, about 25 minutes. Makes 4 to 5 servings.

Spanish Chicken & Rice

A satisfying one-dish meal.

2 tablespoons vegetable oil
1 cup uncooked rice
1/2 cup chopped onion
1/2 cup chopped green bell pepper
1 garlic clove, minced
1 cup chopped canned tomatoes with juice

1 (10-3/4-oz.) can chicken broth
1/2 teaspoon salt
1/4 teaspoon pepper
1 teaspoon ground cumin
1-1/2 pints Chicken Pieces, page 72, or
  2 lbs. chicken pieces, cooked

Heat oil in a large skillet over low heat. Add rice, onion, green pepper and garlic. Stirring constantly, cook until rice is golden brown. Add tomatoes. Stir in chicken broth, salt, pepper and cumin. Remove skin from chicken pieces, if desired; add chicken to rice mixture. Spoon rice mixture over chicken pieces. Bring to a boil over medium-high heat. Reduce heat to low. Cover; simmer 30 minutes. To serve, spoon some of rice on individual plates. Arrange chicken on rice. Makes 4 servings.

How to Make Rolled Beef Loaf

1/Pat beef mixture into a rectangle. Make a 1/2-inch-high ridge along 1 long edge and both short edges.

2/Spread vegetable filling over beef. Carefully roll, starting from side with no ridge. Use waxed paper to help roll.

Oven-Barbecued Ribs

Country-style ribs are tender, tasty and easily prepared in the oven.

2 teaspoons salt
1/2 teaspoon pepper
1/2 teaspoon dried leaf oregano
2 tablespoons chili powder
4 lbs. country-style pork ribs or
  beef short ribs

3 tablespoons vegetable oil
1/2 cup red wine
1 medium onion, sliced
1 pint Plum Barbecue Sauce, page 130

Combine salt, pepper, oregano and chili powder in a small bowl. Rub mixed seasonings onto ribs. Heat 2 tablespoons oil in a large skillet over medium heat; add ribs. Brown ribs on all sides. Add wine; cover skillet. Reduce heat to low; simmer 30 minutes. Preheat oven to 400F (205C). In a medium skillet, heat remaining tablespoon oil. Add onion; sauté until soft. Stir in 1 cup Plum Barbecue Sauce. Spread onion mixture over bottom of a 13" x 9" baking pan. Arrange ribs on top. Spread remaining cup Plum Barbecue Sauce over ribs. Bake in preheated oven 15 minutes; reduce heat to 375F (190C). Bake 20 minutes longer, basting ribs every 10 minutes. Arrange baked ribs and onion slices on a platter. Spoon about 1/4 cup sauce from baking pan over ribs. Spoon remaining sauce into a small bowl; serve with ribs. Makes 6 servings.

Rolled Beef Loaf

Similar to an Argentinian rolled, stuffed steak called matambre.

2 lbs. lean ground beef
2 cups seasoned croutons, crushed
1/2 teaspoon salt
1/8 teaspoon pepper
1/2 teaspoon dried leaf basil
2 eggs, beaten

1 cup drained canned corn
1 cup drained green peas
4 canned tomatoes, chopped
1/2 cup finely chopped onion
1/2 cup grated Parmesan cheese (1-1/2 oz.)
Chili Sauce, see below

Chili Sauce:
1/2 cup Chunky Chili Sauce, page 136,
    or other chili sauce

1/2 cup tomato sauce
1/2 teaspoon garlic salt

Place ground beef in a large bowl. Reserve 1/2 cup crushed croutons. Add remaining croutons, salt, pepper and basil to beef; mix well. Stir in beaten eggs until combined. Preheat oven to 350F (175C). On a waxed paper square, pat beef mixture into a 12" x 8" rectangle. Make a raised ridge along 1 long side and both 8-inch sides, 1/2 inch thick. In a medium bowl, combine corn, peas, tomatoes and onion. Spread vegetable mixture over beef, leaving 1/2 inch uncovered on all sides. Sprinkle reserved 1/2 cup crushed croutons and Parmesan cheese over vegetables. Roll beef, jelly-roll fashion from the long side that does not have raised edge. Pinch to seal ends and long edge. Arrange seam-side down in a 13" x 9" baking pan. Bake in preheated oven 35 minutes. Prepare Chili Sauce. Cool beef loaf in pan 10 minutes. Place baked loaf on a platter. Spoon about 2 tablespoons Chili Sauce over top of loaf. Turn remaining sauce into a small bowl; serve with rolled loaf. Makes 4 to 6 servings.

Chili Sauce:
Combine all ingredients in a small saucepan. Bring to a boil over medium-high heat. Reduce heat to low. Keep hot until ready to serve.

Baked Fish Hawaiian

Serve with herb-seasoned rice and fresh steamed broccoli with lemon butter.

1 pint Tropical Fruit Cocktail, page 80,
    or 1 cup canned pineapple chunks,
    1 cup canned peaches and
    1/4 cup shredded coconut
2 tablespoons lemon juice
Salt

White pepper
1-1/2 lbs. sole, snapper or pike fillets
2 tablespoons butter or margarine
4 green onions, sliced
1/2 cup dry white wine

Preheat oven to 375F (190C). Drain fruit cocktail, reserving syrup. Sprinkle lemon juice, salt and pepper over fillets; set aside. Melt butter or margarine in a small saucepan. Add green onions, wine and 1/2 cup reserved syrup. Bring to a boil over medium-high heat. Stir in drained fruit; set aside. Arrange fish fillets in a 12" x 7" baking pan. Spoon fruit mixture over fillets. Pour remaining reserved syrup over fillets and fruit. Cover with foil or a lid. Bake in preheated oven until fish flakes when tested with a fork, 15 to 20 minutes. Use a large spatula to lift fish and fruit to a platter. Cover to keep warm. Pour liquid from baking pan into a small saucepan. Bring to a boil over high heat; boil until liquid is reduced to about 3/4 cup. Pour reduced liquid over fish. Serve immediately. Makes 4 servings.

Creamy-Corn Enchiladas

Beef in a tortilla topped with creamy corn sauce and shredded cheese.

1 pint cream-style corn or
  1 (17-oz.) can cream-style corn
1 tablespoon all-purpose flour
2 tablespoons cold water
1 tablespoon vegetable oil
1/2 cup chopped onion
1 garlic clove, minced
1/4 cup chopped canned green chilies
1/2 cup half and half
Salt to taste
1 lb. ground lean beef
1/2 teaspoon salt

1/8 teaspoon pepper
2 teaspoons chili powder
1/2 teaspoon dried leaf oregano
1 cup drained canned whole tomatoes,
  chopped
1/2 cup sliced pimiento-stuffed olives
8 (6-inch) flour tortillas
1 cup shredded Monterey Jack cheese (4 oz.)
1 cup shredded Cheddar cheese (4 oz.)
Green-Chili Salsa, page 135, or taco sauce,
  if desired

To thicken home-canned cream-style corn: In a small bowl, combine flour and water. Stir to make a smooth paste. In a small saucepan, stir flour mixture into home-canned corn. Stirring constantly, bring to a boil over medium heat. Cook and stir until thickened; set aside. Heat oil in a medium saucepan over low heat. Add onion and garlic. Sauté until onion is soft. Stir thickened corn or commercially canned corn, green chilies and half and half into onion mixture. Add salt to taste. Cover; simmer 15 minutes. In a 10-inch skillet, brown ground beef. Stir in 1/2 teaspoon salt, pepper, chili powder, oregano, tomatoes and olives. Preheat oven to 350F (175C). Spoon about 1/2 cup meat mixture in a strip across center of 1 tortilla. Sprinkle about 2 tablespoons Monterey Jack cheese over meat mixture. Roll up tightly, jelly-roll fashion. Place seam-side down in a 10" x 7" baking pan. Repeat with remaining tortillas and meat mixture. Pour corn sauce over center of rolled enchiladas in pan. Sprinkle Cheddar cheese evenly over sauce. Bake in preheated oven until cheese is melted and sauce is bubbly, 15 to 20 minutes. To serve, spoon Salsa or taco sauce over each serving, if desired. Makes 4 to 6 servings.

Bavarian Sauerkraut Bake

Cooking drained sauerkraut in beer makes it less tart and adds a distinctive taste.

2 tablespoons vegetable oil
1 cup chopped onion
2 tablespoons Dijon-style mustard
1 qt. Sauerkraut, page 101, or
  1 (29-oz.) can sauerkraut

1 cup beer
1 tablespoon caraway seeds, if desired
1 (12-oz.) can corned beef
1 lb. fully cooked smoked kielbasa,
  bratwurst or knockwurst sausage

Preheat oven to 375F (190C). Heat oil in a large skillet over low heat. Add onion. Sauté until onion is soft. Stir in mustard. Drain sauerkraut, pressing out all liquid. Add drained sauerkraut, beer and caraway seeds, if desired, to onion mixture. Mix well. Bring to a boil over medium-high heat. Spoon hot sauerkraut mixture into a 2-quart casserole dish with a lid. Cut corned beef into 1/2-inch cubes. Gently stir corned-beef cubes into sauerkraut mixture. Cut sausage into 3/4-inch pieces. Arrange over casserole. Press down into sauerkraut mixture until partially submerged. Cover; bake in preheated oven 30 minutes. Serve hot from casserole dish. Makes 4 to 6 servings.

Breads

Canned fruit in biscuits and muffins turns the ordinary into the extraordinary. Blueberry Drop Biscuits, served piping hot with butter, add pizazz to a bacon and egg breakfast. Chunky-Peach Muffins make a tomato and cottage-cheese lunch a bright spot in the day.

When canned fruit is added to breads, it makes them nutritious and delicious. Applesauce gives Apple-Yogurt Wheat Loaf the sweet taste of apple and a soft, moist texture.

Save some of your homemade sweet spreads for baking. Apricot-Cheese Lattice is homemade pastry topped with jam. Quick Bismarcks are refrigerator biscuits shaped into balls with jam or jelly tucked inside. What an easy way to have fresh, hot rolls for breakfast!

Fruit and nut breads are enticingly different. With home-canned cranberries in the pantry, you won't have to wait for cranberry season to make Cranberry-Nut Bread. Use Whole-Cranberry Sauce or Cranberry-Pineapple Sauce.

Dinner breads and rolls generally are not as sweet as breads and rolls served at other times of the day. Canned vegetables make breads unique while still complementing the rest of the meal. Spoonbread is the perfect companion for chili or barbecued meats. Double-Corn Fritters will complement meatloaf or minestrone soup.

Pear-Raisin Balls

Make the balls small so they will cook in the center.

1-1/2 cups sifted all-purpose flour	1 pint pears or 1 (15-oz.) can pears
1 tablespoon baking powder	About 1/4 cup milk
3 tablespoons sugar	1 egg, beaten
1/2 teaspoon salt	Oil for deep-frying
1/2 teaspoon ground ginger	Butter or margarine
1/2 cup raisins	Honey

Into a medium bowl, sift together flour, baking powder, sugar, salt and ginger. Stir in raisins; set aside. Drain pears, reserving juice in a 1-cup measure. Cut pears into 1/4-inch cubes. Add to flour mixture; toss until evenly coated. Add milk to reserved juice to make 3/4 cup. Stir in egg. Gently stir into flour mixture until dry ingredients are moistened. Pour oil 3 inches deep into a large heavy saucepan or deep-fryer. Heat oil to 350F (175C). Drop batter 1 tablespoonful at a time into hot oil. Fry 3 to 4 minutes until browned, turning once. Drain on paper towels. Serve warm with butter or margarine and honey. Makes about 20 small balls.

Apricot-Cheese Lattice

Makes three coffee cakes: one for a neighbor, one to enjoy fresh and one to freeze.

1 (1/4-oz.) pkg. active dry yeast (1 tablespoon)	1 egg, beaten
1/4 cup warm water	3-1/2 to 4 cups all-purpose flour
1 cup milk	1 (3-oz.) pkg. cream cheese, softened
1/3 cup butter or margarine	1/2 cup powdered sugar
1/4 cup granulated sugar	1/2 pint apricot jam
1 teaspoon salt	1 cup powdered sugar
	3 tablespoons milk

In a large bowl, stir yeast into warm water until dissolved. Set aside until foamy. Heat 1 cup milk in a small saucepan until small bubbles form at edge of pan. Stir in butter or margarine, granulated sugar and salt. Cool to lukewarm. Stir cooled milk mixture and egg into yeast. Stir in enough flour, 1 cup at a time, to make a soft dough. Turn dough out onto a lightly floured board. Knead until smooth, 8 to 10 minutes. Clean and grease bowl. Place dough in bowl, turning to grease all sides. Cover with a clean dry towel. Let rise in a warm place, free from drafts, until doubled in bulk, 1 to 1-1/2 hours. In a small bowl, beat cream cheese and 1/2 cup powdered sugar until smooth; set aside. Grease a large baking sheet; set aside. Punch down dough; turn out onto a lightly floured board. Divide dough into 3 equal portions. Roll 1 portion into a 12" x 7" rectangle. Using dull edge of a table knife, score dough crosswise in thirds. Spread one-third of Cheese Filling over center third of dough, leaving 1/2 inch uncovered at each outside edge of center third. Spread about 3 tablespoons jam over Cheese Filling. On a slight diagonal, cut uncovered dough in 1 inch strips from filling to outer edge, as pictured. Lightly dampen strips with water. Alternating from side to side, fold strips over filling. Lightly press strips together. Lightly pinch end strips to bottom dough. Place on prepared baking sheet. Repeat with remaining dough, filling and jam. Cover with towel; let rise 45 minutes. Preheat oven to 350F (175C). Bake until lightly browned, about 30 minutes. Place on a rack to cool. In a small bowl, beat 1 cup powdered sugar and 3 tablespoons milk until smooth. Drizzle over cooled coffee cakes. To freeze, do not frost. Wrap airtight in foil or freezer wrap. Label and store in freezer 3 to 4 weeks. To serve, remove from package. Thaw at room temperature, or while still frozen, warm in a preheated 300F (150C) oven, 15 minutes. Drizzle with frosting. Makes 3 coffee cakes.

Quick Bismarcks

Make the filling with Sunrise Marmalade, page 122, or Cherry-Berry Preserves, page 125.

1/4 cup finely chopped pecans, peanuts or almonds	1 (7-1/2-oz.) can refrigerator biscuits
1 tablespoon sugar	1/4 cup jam or jelly, any flavor
	2 tablespoons butter or margarine, melted

Preheat oven to 400F (205C). Combine chopped nuts and sugar in a small bowl; set aside. Separate biscuits; arrange on a lightly floured board. Make an indentation in center of each biscuit by pressing firmly with your thumb. Spoon about 1 teaspoon jam or jelly into each indentation. Pull edges of biscuits up over filling, pinching biscuit closed to make a ball. Dip each ball in melted butter or margarine, then roll in nut-sugar mixture. Arrange on an ungreased baking sheet, pinched-sides down. Flatten slightly by pressing with palm of your hand. Bake in preheated oven until golden brown, 8 to 10 minutes. Makes 10 rolls.

How to Make Apricot-Cheese Lattice

1/Spread filling and jam over center third of dough. On a slight diagonal, cut in 1-inch strips from filling to edge.

2/Starting at top, fold alternating strips over filling, overlapping ends. Lightly press strips together.

Cranberry-Nut Bread

Moist and tender melt-in-the-mouth bread with a hint of spice.

2 cups sifted all-purpose flour
1 tablespoon baking powder
1/2 teaspoon salt
1 teaspoon ground mace
1/3 cup shortening
2 eggs

1/2 cup sugar
1 pint Cranberry-Pineapple Sauce, page 83,
  1 pint Whole-Berry Sauce, page 30,
  or 1 (15-oz.) can whole-cranberry sauce
3/4 cup chopped pecans, walnuts or filberts

Preheat oven to 350F (175C). Grease a 9'' x 5'' loaf pan; set aside. Onto a sheet of waxed paper, sift together flour, baking powder, salt and mace. In a medium bowl, beat shortening until creamy. Beat in eggs and sugar until fluffy. Stir in Cranberry-Pineapple Sauce or cranberry sauce and nuts. Add flour mixture; fold in until flour is moistened. Pour into prepared loaf pan. Bake 50 minutes or until a pick inserted in center comes out clean. Cool in pan 10 minutes. Remove bread from pan; cool on a rack. Serve warm. Store unused portion in refrigerator up to 1 week. To freeze, wrap loaf airtight in foil or freezer wrap. Label and store in freezer 3 to 4 weeks. To serve, remove from package. Thaw at room temperature, or while still frozen, warm in a preheated 300F (150C) oven, 15 minutes. Makes 1 loaf.

Pumpkin Doughnuts

Keep a batch of these in the freezer for coffee breaks, snacks or breakfast.

2 eggs
1/4 cup packed brown sugar
3/4 cup Pumpkin Butter, page 119
2 tablespoons butter or margarine, melted
1/2 cup plain yogurt
3 cups sifted all-purpose flour

1/2 teaspoon salt
1 teaspoon baking powder
1 teaspoon baking soda
1 teaspoon ground allspice
Oil for deep-frying
Orange Glaze, see below

Orange Glaze:
1 cup sifted powdered sugar
1 teaspoon grated orange peel

1/4 cup orange juice

In a large bowl, beat eggs with electric mixer or whisk until pale and slightly thickened. Beat in brown sugar. Beat in Pumpkin Butter, butter or margarine and yogurt until smooth. On a sheet of waxed paper, sift together flour, salt, baking powder, baking soda and allspice. Stir into egg mixture until blended. Refrigerate at least 45 minutes. Turn chilled dough out onto a generously floured board. Dough will be quite sticky. Sprinkle flour from board over dough. Generously flour your hands. Gently pat and flatten dough. Use a floured rolling pin to roll out dough 1/2 inch thick. Cut with a floured doughnut cutter; set cut doughnuts aside. Gather remaining dough together; gently reroll. Cut remaining dough into doughnuts. Pour oil at least 3 inches deep into a deep-fryer or large heavy saucepan. Heat oil to 375F (190C). Use a spatula to lift doughnuts from board; carefully slide doughnuts into hot oil. Fry until golden on both sides, about 3 minutes. Bring oil back to 375F (190C) before adding more doughnuts. Prepare Orange Glaze. Drizzle glaze over warm doughnuts. Makes 24 doughnuts.

Orange Glaze:
In a small bowl, combine all ingredients. Beat with a whisk until blended.

Apple-Yogurt Wheat Loaf

Spread toasted slices of this delicious bread with soft cream cheese and honey or jam.

1-1/2 cups whole-wheat flour
3/4 cup all-purpose flour
1/2 cup packed brown sugar
3 teaspoons baking powder
1/2 teaspoon baking soda
1 teaspoon salt

1 teaspoon ground cinnamon
1 egg
1/3 cup vegetable oil
1 cup plain yogurt
1 cup applesauce
1/2 cup chopped pecans or walnuts

Preheat oven to 350F (175C). Grease a 9" x 5" loaf pan; set aside. In a medium bowl, stir together whole-wheat flour, all-purpose flour, brown sugar, baking powder, baking soda, salt and cinnamon. In another medium bowl, beat egg and oil until combined. Stir in yogurt, applesauce and nuts. Gently stir applesauce mixture into flour mixture until dry ingredients are moistened. Turn batter into prepared loaf pan. Bake in preheated oven 1 hour or until a wooden pick inserted in center comes out clean. Cool in pan 10 minutes. Remove from pan; cool on a rack. Makes 1 loaf.

Double-Corn Fritters

For a change of pace, serve fritters instead of potatoes.

1 cup sifted all-purpose flour
1/2 cup yellow cornmeal
3/4 teaspoon salt
2 teaspoons baking powder
1 egg, beaten
3/4 cup milk

1 tablespoon butter or margarine, melted
1 cup drained whole-kernel corn
Oil for deep-frying
Butter or margarine
Hot-Pepper Jelly, page 117

In a medium bowl, combine flour, cornmeal, salt and baking powder; set aside. In a small bowl, beat together egg, milk and 1 tablespoon butter or margarine. Stir corn into egg mixture. Add to flour mixture. Stir until flour is moistened. Pour oil 3 inches deep into a large heavy saucepan or deep-fryer. Heat oil to 375F (190C). Carefully drop batter by tablespoonfuls into hot oil. Fry until golden brown on all sides, 2 to 3 minutes. Fry no more than 4 fritters at a time so oil doesn't cool down. Drain on paper towels. Serve warm with butter or margarine and Hot-Pepper Jelly. Makes about 20 fritters.

Chunky-Peach Muffins

As light as cake. Serve with coffee or a salad lunch.

2 cups biscuit mix
1/3 cup sugar
1/4 teaspoon ground cinnamon
1/4 teaspoon ground mace
2 eggs
1/2 cup milk

2 tablespoons butter or margarine, melted
1 cup drained canned sliced peaches
1 tablespoon sugar
1 teaspoon ground cinnamon
Butter or margarine

Preheat oven to 375F (190C). Grease 12 muffin cups or line cups with paper liners. In a medium bowl, combine biscuit mix, 1/3 cup sugar, 1/4 teaspoon cinnamon and mace; set aside. In another medium bowl, beat eggs. Stir in milk and 2 tablespoons butter or margarine; set aside. Chop drained peaches; stir into egg mixture. Stir egg mixture into biscuit mix until dry ingredients are moistened. Fill prepared muffin cups two-thirds full with batter. In a small bowl, combine 1 tablespoon sugar and 1 teaspoon cinnamon. Sprinkle over muffin tops. Bake in preheated oven until golden brown, 20 to 25 minutes. Cool in muffin cups 5 minutes. Serve warm with butter or margarine. Makes 12 muffins.

Variations

Chunky-Apricot Muffins: Substitute 1 cup drained apricots for peaches.
Chunky-Plum Muffins: Substitute 1 cup drained plums for peaches. Omit mace; increase 1/4 teaspoon ground cinnamon to 1/2 teaspoon.
Chunky-Pear Muffins: Substitute 1 cup drained pears for peaches. Substitute 1/4 teaspoon ground ginger for mace.

Hawaiian Sweet Bread

A moist, tender pineapple bread that keeps well in the refrigerator.

3 to 3-1/2 cups all-purpose flour
1 (1/4-oz.) pkg. active dry yeast
  (1 tablespoon)
1 cup crushed pineapple or
  1 (8-1/4-oz.) can crushed pineapple
Water

1/4 cup sugar
1/2 teaspoon salt
1/4 cup butter or margarine
1 medium banana, mashed
1 egg, beaten
Coconut-Cheese Spread, see below

Coconut-Cheese Spread:
1 (3-oz.) pkg. cream cheese, softened
1 tablespoon honey

1/3 cup shredded coconut

In a large bowl, combine 1-1/2 cups flour and yeast; set aside. Drain pineapple in a sieve, pressing to remove as much juice as possible. Reserve juice in a 1-cup measure; add water to make 1/2 cup. Pour into a small saucepan. Add sugar, salt and butter or margarine. Stir constantly over medium-high heat until butter or margarine softens. Add juice mixture, banana and egg to flour mixture. Beat 1 minute with electric mixer on low speed. Scrape batter from side of bowl; beat 2 minutes longer at high speed. By hand, stir in enough remaining flour to make a soft dough. Stir in drained pineapple. Cover bowl with a clean dry towel. Let rise in a warm place, free from drafts, until doubled in bulk, 1 to 1-1/2 hours. Stir down dough. Grease a 2-quart casserole with high sides or a soufflé dish. Turn dough into dish. Cover with towel; let rise 45 minutes. Preheat oven to 375F (190C). Bake until golden brown, 30 to 40 minutes. Cool in dish 5 minutes; remove from dish. Prepare Coconut-Cheese Spread. Serve warm or at room temperature with Coconut-Cheese Spread. Makes 1 loaf.

Coconut-Cheese Spread:
In a small bowl, beat cream cheese and honey with electric mixer until light and fluffy. Stir in coconut. Makes about 1/2 cup.

Blueberry Drop Biscuits

The combination of blueberries and orange gives these biscuits a special flavor.

2 cups all-purpose flour
2 tablespoons baking powder
1/2 teaspoon baking soda
2 tablespoons sugar
1/2 teaspoon salt

1/3 cup butter or margarine
1 medium orange
1 pint blueberries or
  1 (15-1/2-oz.) can blueberries, drained
About 1/2 cup buttermilk

Preheat oven to 400F (205C). Lightly grease a large baking sheet; set aside. Into a large bowl, sift together flour, baking powder, baking soda, sugar and salt. Cut in butter or margarine with a pastry blender or 2 knives until mixture resembles cornmeal. Grate peel from orange. Add 1 tablespoon grated orange peel and drained blueberries to flour mixture. Gently toss to coat blueberries. Juice orange; add buttermilk to juice to make 1 cup. Add to flour mixture. Gently fold in until dry ingredients are moistened. Drop dough by tablespoonfuls onto prepared baking sheet. Bake 15 to 20 minutes until lightly browned. Serve warm with butter or margarine. Makes 24 biscuits.

Desserts

Serve canned fruit for a light dessert, but lift it out of the ordinary. Spoon it into wine glasses, parfaits or brandy snifters. Top it with sour cream or whipped topping and chopped nuts. Fruit canned in flavored syrup, such as Minty Pears, make light yet very special desserts.

For a more substantial dessert, bake a pie using a homemade pie filling. Or bake colorful Peachy Cherry Pie. This delightful fruit combination is baked in an almond crust. Cranberry-Yogurt Pie is simple to make with Whole-Cranberry Sauce.

Ginger-Pumpkin Cupcakes—deliciously light, tender gingerbread topped with a swirl of lemon buttercream—can also be baked as a cake.

Puddings made with canned fruits bring squeals of delight. Lemon-Blueberry Pudding Cake makes its own thick, blueberry-lemon pudding topped with lemon cake.

Desserts made with home-canned fruit can be elaborate or simple. They are elegant for entertaining. For your next dinner party, serve Cherry-Chocolate Meringue Cups—crisp, airy cups of chocolate meringue filled with vanilla cream and topped with a sauce of dark sweet cherries.

Lemon-Berry Pudding Cake

Separates to make a berry-lemon pudding topped with a thin layer of lemon cake.

**1 pint blueberries, blackberries or
    raspberries or 1 (15-1/2-oz.) can berries**
2 eggs, separated
1/4 cup lemon juice
2/3 cup milk

1 cup sugar
1/2 cup all-purpose flour
1/4 teaspoon salt
Whipped topping, if desired

Drain berries; reserve juice for another use. Set drained berries aside. Preheat oven to 350F (175C). Pour hot water 1 inch deep into a 13" x 9" baking pan. Place in preheating oven. Grease a 3-quart casserole dish; set aside. In a small bowl, beat egg whites with electric mixer until soft peaks form; set aside. In another small bowl, beat egg yolks until pale and thickened. Stir in lemon juice and milk. Add sugar, flour and salt; beat until smooth. Fold in drained berries. Fold beaten egg whites into berry mixture. Pour into prepared casserole. Place casserole in hot water in baking pan. Bake 45 to 50 minutes or until golden brown. Serve warm or at room temperature with whipped topping, if desired. Makes 4 servings.

Fruit Kugel

Noodle-custard pudding made extra special with fruit and spices.

1 pint Brandied Fruit Cocktail, page 86, or
  1 (16-oz.) can fruit cocktail
3 eggs
1/3 cup sugar
1 cup dairy sour cream

1/4 teaspoon ground cinnamon
6 to 8 lasagna noodles, cooked
1/4 teaspoon almond extract
1 cup whipped topping
1/3 cup slivered almonds

Drain fruit cocktail; reserve syrup for another use. Set drained fruit aside. Preheat oven to 350F (175C). Beat eggs in a medium bowl until foamy. Beat in sugar, sour cream and cinnamon. Stir in drained fruit cocktail; set aside. Generously butter an 8-inch square baking pan. Arrange 2 or 3 cooked noodles side-by-side in prepared pan. Spoon about one-third of egg mixture over noodles. Add another layer of noodles. Repeat layering, ending with fruit mixture. Bake in preheated oven until top is puffed and golden, about 60 minutes. Stir almond extract into whipped topping. Serve kugel warm. To serve, cut into 8 pieces. Place each piece on a dessert plate. Top each with a dollop of whipped topping. Sprinkle with almonds. Makes 8 servings.

Ginger-Pumpkin Cupcakes

Great for picnics, lunches and snacks.

2-1/2 cups sifted all-purpose flour
1-1/2 teaspoons baking soda
1/2 teaspoon ground ginger
1/2 teaspoon ground cinnamon
1/4 teaspoon ground cloves
3/4 teaspoon salt

1/2 cup shortening
1/2 cup sugar
1 egg
1 cup Pumpkin Butter, page 119
1/3 cup molasses
Lemon Buttercream, see below

Lemon Buttercream:
1 lemon
4 cups sifted powdered sugar

1/2 cup butter or margarine, softened
1 teaspoon lemon extract

Preheat oven to 350F (175C). Grease 24 muffin cups or line with paper liners. Into a medium bowl, sift together flour, baking soda, ginger, cinnamon, cloves and salt; set aside. In a large bowl, beat shortening and sugar with electric mixer until light and fluffy. Beat in egg until blended. Stir in Pumpkin Butter and molasses. Add flour mixture; stir until just combined. Spoon batter into muffin cups, filling two-thirds full. Bake 25 to 30 minutes until a pick inserted in center of cupcake comes out clean. Cool in muffin cups 5 minutes. Remove from muffin cups; cool on a rack. Prepare Lemon Buttercream. Frost cooled cupcakes with Lemon Buttercream. Makes 24 cupcakes.

Lemon Buttercream:

Grate 1/2 teaspoon lemon peel. Juice lemon; set grated peel and juice aside. In a medium bowl, combine 2 cups powdered sugar, butter or margarine and grated lemon peel. Add 3 tablespoons lemon juice. Beat until smooth. Gradually beat in remaining powdered sugar and lemon juice until frosting reaches spreading consistency. Stir in lemon extract.

Variation

Ginger-Pumpkin Cake: Grease and flour 2 round 8-inch cake pans. Pour batter into pans. Bake 30 to 40 minutes or until lightly browned. Turn out of pans; cool on a rack. Frost cooled cake.

Cherry-Chocolate Meringue Cups

Almost like eating crisp, airy, chocolate candy with a cream filling.

4 egg whites
1-1/2 cups sifted powdered sugar
1/3 cup unsweetened cocoa
1/4 teaspoon cream of tartar
1 pint pitted dark sweet cherries or
   1 (15-oz.) can pitted dark sweet cherries

Water
1/4 cup granulated sugar
2 tablespoons cornstarch
2 tablespoons cherry brandy or
   1/2 teaspoon almond extract
Creme Filling, see below

Creme Filling:
1 (3-5/8-oz.) pkg. vanilla-flavored
   pudding mix

3 cups milk
4 egg yolks

Let egg whites stand in a large bowl at room temperature 2 hours. Cover a baking sheet with brown paper. Draw 8 circles about 3 inches in diameter on brown paper; set aside. Preheat oven to 275F (135C). Into a large bowl, sift together powdered sugar and cocoa; set aside. Beat room-temperature egg whites and cream of tartar with electric mixer until foamy. Beat in half of cocoa mixture, sprinkling 1 teaspoon at a time over egg-white mixture. Beat in remaining cocoa mixture, sprinkling 1 tablespoon at a time over egg-white mixture. Continue beating until meringue is stiff and glossy. Spoon 1/2 cup meringue onto each circle on brown paper. Using back of a spoon, spread meringue into a cup shape, making bottom of meringue cup 1/2 inch thick and sides about 1-1/2 inches high. Or, use a pastry tube with a star tip to pipe sides of cups. Bake 1 hour in preheated oven. Do not remove from oven. Turn off oven heat. Let meringue cups dry at least 2 hours in oven. Drain cherries, reserving juice in a 1-cup measure. Add water to juice to make 1 cup; set aside. Combine granulated sugar and cornstarch in a medium saucepan. Gradually stir in juice mixture. Stirring constantly, bring to a boil over medium-high heat. Stir in drained cherries. Cool to room temperature. Stir in cherry brandy or almond extract. Prepare Creme Filling. Spoon about 1/3 cup Creme Filling into each meringue cup. Refrigerate until ready to serve. To serve, place 1 filled meringue cup on each plate. Top with cherry sauce. Makes 8 servings.

Creme Filling:
Combine pudding mix and milk in a medium saucepan. Stir constantly over medium heat until pudding comes to a full boil. Remove from heat. Beat egg yolks in a small bowl until blended. Stir 1/2 cup hot pudding into egg yolks, 1 tablespoonful at a time. Stir egg-yolk mixture into remaining pudding. To prevent a crust from forming, place plastic wrap or waxed paper on surface of Creme Filling. Cool to room temperature.

Peachy Cherry Pie

Serve warm with ice cream for a cheery, colorful winter treat.

Almond Pastry, see below

1-1/2 pints sliced peaches or
  1 (29-oz.) can peach slices

1-1/2 pints pitted sour cherries or
  2 (16-oz.) cans pitted sour cherries

Water

3/4 cup sugar

1/4 cup cornstarch

1 tablespoon lemon juice

1/2 teaspoon almond extract

Almond Pastry:

1/3 cup slivered almonds, toasted

1-1/2 cups sifted all-purpose flour

3/4 teaspoon salt

1/2 cup shortening

3 to 4 tablespoons cold water

Prepare Almond Pastry; set aside. Drain peaches and cherries, reserving juices in a 1-cup measure. Add water to make 1 cup. Combine sugar and cornstarch in a large saucepan. Stir in 1 cup reserved juice mixture. Stir constantly over medium heat until mixture thickens. Stir in lemon juice and almond extract. Gently stir in drained peaches and cherries. Preheat oven to 375F (190C). Pour peach mixture into pastry-lined pie pan. Top with rolled-out pastry round. Trim edges, turning top pastry under lower pastry edge. Flute edge. Cut vents in top pastry. Place pie on a baking sheet to catch spills. Bake until filling bubbles through vents, about 60 minutes. Remove from oven; cool. Serve warm or at room temperature. Makes 6 to 9 servings.

Almond Pastry:
Finely chop toasted almonds in blender or food processor. Combine chopped almonds, flour and salt in a medium bowl. Use a pastry blender to cut in 1/4 cup shortening until mixture resembles cornmeal. Coarsely cut in remaining shortening. Add water, 1 teaspoon at a time, tossing flour mixture with a fork until mixture forms a ball. Shape dough into 2 equal balls. On a lightly floured board, roll out 1 pastry ball to a 12-inch circle. Gently ease into a 9-inch pie pan. Trim edges, leaving a 1/2-inch overhang. Roll remaining pastry into a 10-inch circle.

Frozen Peach Yogurt

Your ice-cream maker will make this tangy frozen dessert extra smooth.

1 pint peaches or
  1 (16-oz.) can peaches, drained

1 (1/4-oz.) envelope unflavored gelatin

1/2 cup water

1/2 cup peach jam

3 cups plain yogurt

Finely chop enough drained peaches to make 1/2 cup. Puree remaining peaches in blender or food processor; set aside. Combine gelatin and water in a small saucepan. Stir over medium heat until gelatin dissolves. In a large bowl, combine peach puree, chopped peaches, gelatin mixture, peach jam and yogurt. Stir well. Refrigerate until set, at least 4 hours. Pour into ice-cream canister. Freeze in ice-cream maker as manufacturer directs. Makes 2 quarts.

Variations

Frozen Apricot Yogurt: Substitute 1 pint pitted apricots or 1 (16-ounce) can apricots for peaches. Substitute apricot jam for peach jam.

Frozen Pineapple Yogurt: Substitute 1 pint pineapple chunks or 1 (15-1/4-ounce) can pineapple chunks for peaches. Substitute apricot jam or apricot-pineapple jam for peach jam.

Cherry-Amaretto Squares

As rich and creamy as cheesecake—serve small portions.

1/2 cup sliced almonds	1 pint pitted sour cherries or
3/4 cup all-purpose flour	1 (16-oz.) can pitted sour cherries
1/2 cup rolled oats	1/2 cup sugar
1/4 cup packed brown sugar	2 tablespoons cornstarch
1/2 cup butter or margarine	Amaretto Cream, see below

Amaretto Cream:

1/2 pint whipping cream	3 tablespoons Amaretto liqueur or
2 (3-oz.) pkgs. cream cheese, softened	1 teaspoon almond extract
1/2 cup powdered sugar	

Toast almonds in a small heavy skillet over medium heat until lightly browned, stirring constantly to prevent burning. Cool on paper towels. Preheat oven to 400F (205C). In a medium bowl, combine flour, oats and brown sugar. Cut in butter or margarine with a pastry blender until mixture resembles cornmeal. Stir in toasted almonds. Press over bottom of a 8-inch square baking pan. Bake 15 minutes. Break up mixture to make crumbs; cool. Drain cherries, reserving juice. In a medium saucepan, combine sugar and cornstarch. Gradually stir in reserved cherry juice. Stirring constantly, bring to a boil over medium heat. Stir in drained cherries; cool to room temperature. Prepare Amaretto Cream. Sprinkle about two-thirds of crumb mixture into an 8-inch square baking pan. Spread Amaretto Cream over crumbs. Pour cooled cherry mixture over top. Sprinkle with remaining crumbs. Refrigerate at least 2 hours. Makes 8 or 9 servings.

Amaretto Cream:
In a small bowl, beat whipping cream with electric mixer until stiff peaks form; set aside. In another small bowl, beat cream cheese until fluffy. Gradually beat in powdered sugar. Stir in Amaretto liqueur or almond extract. Stir into whipped cream. Beat until combined.

Nutty Plum Crunch

A plum-good variation of apple crisp!

1 qt. pitted plums or	2/3 cup packed brown sugar
2 (17-oz.) cans pitted plums	1 teaspoon ground cinnamon
2 tablespoons cornstarch	1/4 teaspoon ground nutmeg
2 tablespoons cold water	1/2 cup finely chopped walnuts or pecans
1 teaspoon grated orange peel	1/2 cup butter or margarine, melted
1 cup whole-wheat flour	Lemon sherbet or vanilla ice cream,
1 cup rolled oats	if desired

Preheat oven to 350F (175C). Drain plums, reserving juice. Pour 1 cup juice into a medium saucepan. In a small bowl, make a paste of cornstarch and water. Stir into juice in saucepan. Add orange peel. Stir constantly over medium heat until slightly thickened. Arrange drained plums in a single layer in an 8-inch square baking pan. Pour thickened juice over plums. In a medium bowl, stir together flour, oats, brown sugar, cinnamon, nutmeg and nuts. Stir in butter or margarine until mixture is crumbly. Sprinkle crumbs over top of fruit. Bake in preheated oven 30 minutes or until bubbly. Cool slightly. Serve warm or at room temperature. Top each serving with sherbet or ice cream, if desired. Makes 6 servings.

Apricot Soufflé

No cooking—a foolproof, elegant souffle!

1 qt. pitted apricot halves or
  1 (28-oz.) can pitted apricot halves
Water
1 (6-oz.) pkg. apricot- or
  lemon-flavored gelatin

3 egg whites
1/2 pint whipping cream, whipped
1/2 cup apricot preserves

Drain apricots, reserving juice in a 2-cup measure. Add water to make 1-1/2 cups; set aside. Puree drained apricots in blender or food processor; set aside. In a medium saucepan, bring juice mixture to a boil over medium-high heat. Stir in gelatin until dissolved. Stir in apricot puree until blended. Refrigerate until mixture has consistency of unbeaten egg whites, about 1 hour. Cut a piece of waxed paper 4 inches longer than distance around a 1-1/2-quart soufflé dish or casserole with straight sides. Fold paper in half lengthwise to make a collar 6 inches wide. Wrap around outside of dish. Fasten ends together with tape. Attach to dish by tying string around waxed paper and dish, or placing a rubber band around paper and dish; set aside. In a medium bowl, beat egg whites with electric mixer until soft peaks form. Whip apricot mixture until fluffy. Fold beaten egg whites into apricot mixture. Fold in whipped cream. Spoon about one-third of apricot mixture into prepared dish. Swirl one-third of preserves through apricot mixture in dish. Repeat with remaining apricot mixture and preserves, using one-third at a time. Refrigerate until firm, at least 4 hours. Carefully remove waxed paper before serving. Makes 8 servings.

Spicy Fruit Cake

Enjoy warm cake with morning coffee.

Streusel Topping, see below
1 pint Brandied Fruit Cocktail, page 86,
  or 1 (16-oz.) can fruit cocktail and
  2 tablespoons brandy
1-1/2 cups all-purpose flour

3/4 cup sugar
1/2 teaspoon salt
2 teaspoons baking powder
1 egg
1/4 cup butter or margarine, melted

Streusel Topping:
1/3 cup all-purpose flour
2 tablespoons brown sugar
2 tablespoons granulated sugar

1/4 teaspoon ground cinnamon
2 tablespoons butter or margarine
1/4 cup chopped walnuts or pecans

Preheat oven to 350F (175C). Grease a round 8-inch baking pan; set aside. Prepare Streusel Topping; set aside. Drain Brandied Fruit Cocktail, reserving syrup. If using commercially canned fruit cocktail, drain; add brandy to syrup. In a medium bowl, stir together flour, sugar, salt and baking powder; set aside. In a small bowl, beat egg until foamy. Stir in butter or margarine, drained fruit cocktail and 1/2 cup reserved syrup. Stir egg mixture into flour mixture until dry ingredients are moistened. Batter will be lumpy. Pour into prepared baking pan. Sprinkle Streusel Topping over cake. Bake in preheated oven 40 to 50 minutes or until lightly browned and surface springs back when pressed with your fingers. Makes 8 servings.

Streusel Topping:
Combine flour, sugars and cinnamon in a small bowl. Cut in butter or margarine with a pastry blender until crumbs form. Stir in nuts.

How to Make Apricot Soufflé

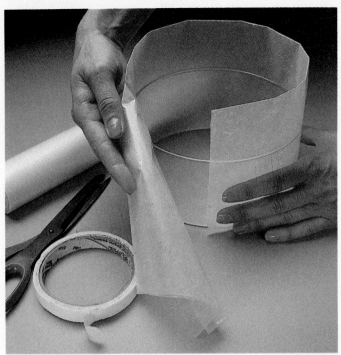

1/Tape ends of waxed paper collar around soufflé dish or casserole. Hold in place with string or an elastic band.

2/To serve, remove collar by cutting away string or elastic band and carefully peeling collar from around dish.

Cranberry-Yogurt Pie

Light and fluffy—ideal to serve after a Sunday dinner.

2 cups graham-cracker crumbs
1/4 cup sugar
1/2 cup butter or margarine, melted
1 (1/4-oz.) envelope unflavored gelatin
1 cup cold water
1 (6-oz.) can orange-juice concentrate, thawed

1 pint whole-cranberry sauce, 1 (16-oz.) can whole-cranberry sauce, or 1 pint Cranberry-Pineapple Sauce, page 83
1 (8-oz.) carton plain yogurt
1 (8-oz.) carton frozen whipped topping, thawed

Combine graham-cracker crumbs and sugar in a small bowl. Stir in butter or margarine until blended. Press crumbs into a 9-inch pie pan; set aside. Combine gelatin and water in a small saucepan. Stir over medium heat until gelatin dissolves. Stir in orange-juice concentrate and cranberry sauce. Refrigerate until mixture mounds when dropped from a spoon, 30 to 45 minutes. Beat with electric mixer until foamy. Stir in yogurt. Fold in whipped topping. Spoon cranberry filling into prepared graham-cracker crust. Refrigerate at least 3 hours. Makes 6 to 8 servings.

On following pages: Puffy Granny Caps, page 185, gift baskets containing needlepoint, cross-stitch and other lid decorations. Canned foods from top left: Sweet Cherries, page 30; Rhubarb Pie Filling, page 87; Green & Yellow Pickles, page 107; Marinara Sauce, page 129; Mixed-Herb Vinegar, page 137; Strawberry Jam, pages 62-63; Rum-Raisin Conserve, page 127; Cranberry-Claret Jelly, page 118; May-Day Jam, page 118; Lemon-Blueberry Marmalade, page 122.

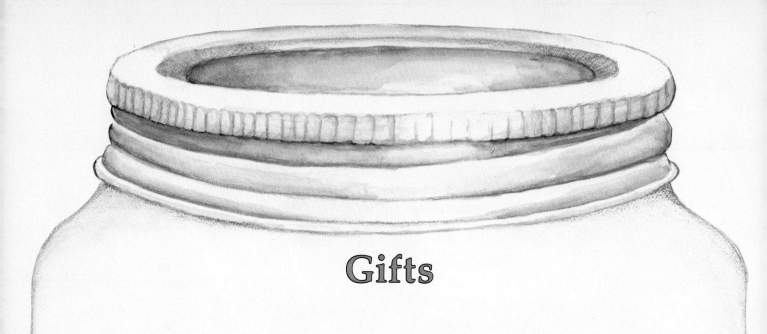

Gifts

Home-canned specialties make welcome gifts all year long. Take a jar of Barbecue Sauce to the neighbor's backyard barbecue. Say "thank you" to a hostess with Champagne Mustard or Kiwi Preserves. Combine several home-canned foods in a basket for a special picnic. Wrap a ceramic pie plate and several jars of pie filling for a bride-to-be. A special gift from your pantry is always the perfect gift to give.

For a larger gift, combine several home-canned foods with a cooking utensil, serving piece or basket. Tie them together as a gift set. Or, wrap several home-canned foods together in colored cellophane from an art-supply store. Other suggestions can be found on page 186.

To prepare jars from the pantry for gift-giving, wipe the jars with a clean damp cloth, then attach a clean screwband. Buy or make an attractive label that gives the name of the food and directions on how to store it. Include a recipe card telling how to use the canned food.

Decorate the jar simply or elaborately. A simple but lovely decoration is made by cutting a circle of gift-wrap paper 4 inches wider in diameter than the lid. Place the paper circle on the lid with a 2-inch extension on all sides. Press the extended paper down over the side. Tie with ribbon, colored yarn or twine, or rick rack. Or, in place of the paper, use fabric with a small fruit or vegetable print or a geometric design.

Lace is quick and easy to attach to the screwband and makes a jar look pretty. Cut the lace about 1 inch longer than needed to go around the screwband. Sew or glue the ends together so the lace fits tightly. Some lace has colored ribbon threaded through it. Choose one that is color coordinated with the contents of the jar. Tie the ribbon in a pretty bow. Stitch or glue a small embroidered fruit or vegetable to the lace at the side of the bow.

Colorful striped and patterned ribbons that are wide enough to cover the screwband are also pretty. Attach them as the lace is attached.

Needlepoint covers take time and some skill, but they make gifts to be treasured. Write a special message or do a decorative fruit in cross-stitch for the jar lid. After the jar is opened, suggest the top be framed in the decorated screwband, a small frame or a drapery hoop. Needlepoint patterns are available in craft-pattern books.

Puffy Granny Caps dress up canning jars with an old-fashioned look. The tops are easy to make with elastic thread, but require a sewing machine. After the jar has been emptied, fill the jar with candies, nuts or dried fruit. The granny cap lid makes a colorful decoration.

How to Decorate Jars for Gift-Giving

1/Cut circles of gift-wrap paper 4 inches wider in diameter than the lid to be covered. Center on lid. Tie with yarn, twine or rick rack.

2/Make Puffy Granny Caps as directed below. Needlepoint covers are extra special. Gather lace on a colorful ribbon for a ruffled edge.

Puffy Granny Caps

Barbara Sprick designed these easy-to-make caps.

1/2 yd. colorful cotton-blend fabric
7 yds. lace, rick-rack or
   1/4-inch bias binding, if desired

Elastic thread
Cotton-polyester thread
1 lb. fiber fill

Cut fabric in eight 9-inch circles for wide-mouth jars or twelve 7-inch circles for regular-mouth jars. If using trim, sew trim around edges of circles. If not using trim, turn edges of circles under and stitch by hand or machine. Wrap elastic thread around a bobbin by hand, stretching the thread slightly. Place bobbin in sewing machine. Thread top of sewing machine with cotton-polyester thread. Set machine for basting, 4 to 6 stitches per inch. Sew completely around circle 1-1/2 inches from edge with right side of fabric up. Do not backstitch. Gently pull both ends of elastic thread until cap fits snugly around jar top. Tie ends of elastic thread to secure. Stuff cap with fiber fill. Makes 8 caps for wide-mouth jars or 12 caps for regular jars.

Gift Sets

Package several home-canned foods together to make a gift set for a special occasion.

Country Picnic:
Place a checked cloth in a picnic basket. Fill with an assortment of pickled vegetables such as: Tiny Toms, page 91; Texas Spiced Okra, page 95; Pickled Sprouts & Cauliflower, page 93; Minty Cocktail Carrots, page 94; or Asparagus Spears with Tarragon, page 103. Add a jar of Wine-Vinegar Pickles, page 108; a loaf of French bread, a bottle of wine and an assortment of cheeses and cold cuts.

English-Breakfast Basket:
Tie 3 or 4 English muffin rings (tins) together with ribbon. Tie the ribbon in a bow. Arrange muffin rings, a jar of marmalade from pages 120 to 122 and a sunny napkin in a small basket.

Fruit Pie:
Wrap a wide ribbon or pretty towel around a ceramic or earthenware pie plate. Add several quart jars of pie filling: Pie Apples, page 85; Cherry Pie Filling or Peach Pie Filling, page 84; or Rhubarb Pie Filling, page 87. Include a recipe for using each of the pie fillings.

Homemade Bread:
Place a loaf of homemade bread and a jar of Apricot Honey, page 120, on a bread board. Wrap with a ribbon or colored cellophane.

Backyard Cookout:
In a long shallow basket, arrange a colorful chef's apron and long-handled grill tools with an assortment of pickles, relishes and condiments. These might include: Piccalilli, page 112; Spicy Sweet-Pepper Relish, page 114; Sandwich Pickle Slices, page 108; Spicy Tomato Mustard, page 134; Plum Barbeque Sauce, page 130; and Tomato Ketchup, page 133.

Snack Pack:
In a paper or cloth gift bag, place a box of crackers, a carton of whipped cream cheese and a jar of Hot-Pepper Jelly, page 117. Tie with a ribbon or colored twine.

Appetizers for Two:
On an appetizer platter, arrange 2 or 3 jars of pickled vegetables from pages 90 to 103. Add a cocktail fork, an herb-cheese spread and crackers. Cover it all with colored cellophane. Tie with ribbon. Add a split of champagne and glasses, if desired.

Salad Basket:
Crumple 2 to 4 sheets of spring-green color tissue paper. Arrange in a wire salad basket. Stand several jars of flavored vinegar in basket with parts of paper between jars. Include: Mixed-Herb Vinegar or Berry Vinegar, page 137.

Italian Spaghetti Supper:
Spread a colorful paper tablecloth in a basket with a handle. Add the following: For antipasto: 1 quart Cocktail Vegetable Mix, page 96, 1 pound provolone cheese, 1 pound dry salami, 1 (6-ounce) can black olives and breadsticks. For supper: 12 ounces long Italian spaghetti and 2 or 3 pints of Marinara Sauce, page 129. Include Lemon-Parsley Vinegar, page 137, to add to a salad dressing. Add a loaf of Italian bread.

Canning Index

Using Canned Foods Index

8.420862487714